Portal Administrator's Guide

Richard L. Sezov, Jr.

Liferay Administrator's Guide
by Richard L. Sezov, Jr.

ISBN 978-0-615-24733-5

Contributors:
Ray Auge, Jian Cao (Steven), Brian Chan, Alice Cheng, Bryan Cheung, Ivan Cheung, Shepherd Ching, Alexander Chow, Bruno Farache, Jorge Ferrer, JR Houn, Scott Lee, Wei Hong Ma (Sai), Charles May, James Min, Alberto Montero, Jerry Niu, Michael Saechang, Li Ji Shan (Dale), Ed Shin, Joseph Shum, Michael Young

Table of Contents

1. Introduction **15**
Created for the Enterprise 15
Personalization and easy customization 15
Workflow adaptable 16
Branding friendly 16
Flexible organization 16
Built With The End-User In Mind 16
Award-winning UI 16
One-Click Look and Feel Changes 16
Web OS 16
Technology to Help Developers 16
Standards Compliant 17
Ready Integration 17
Liferay Plugins Catalog 17
Supported Technologies 17
Languages 18
2. Initial Setup **19**
Obtaining Liferay 20
Installing a Bundle 20
Installing Liferay for a Developer 21
Standalone Liferay 22
Download the Tomcat Bundle 22
Uncompress the Bundle 23
Install a Lightweight SQL Database 23
Connect Liferay to the SQL Database 24
Launch Liferay! 25
Installing the Liferay Extension Environment 26
Install the Necessary Tools 26
Java Development Kit 27
Apache Ant 1.7.0 or Above 27
A Liferay-supported Database 28
Obtain the Liferay Source 30
Create Configuration Files 31
Create the Extension Environment 32
Install an Application Server 33
Deploy the Extension Environment 34
Installing Liferay for an Enterprise 34
Database Setup 35
Turning a Bundle into an Enterprise Portal 36
Further Configuration 37
Installing Liferay on an Existing Application Server 37
Geronimo 1.1 with Tomcat 5.0.28/5.5.17 38
Glassfish 2.x 39
Jetty 5.1.1 41
JBoss 4.03sp1/4.04/4.05 with Jetty 5.1.1 43
JBoss 4.03sp1/4.04/4.05/ 4.2 with Tomcat 46
Oracle Application Server (OC4J) 48

Resin 3.0.X / 3.1.X....56
Tomcat 5.0.X/5.5.X....57
WebLogic8 sp5....59
WebLogic 9 / 10....63
WebSphere 6.0.X.X....65
WebSphere 6.1....78
Making Liferay Coexist with Other Java EE Applications....88
3. Configuration....91
Liferay's User Interface....91
Navigating Liferay....92
Adding the Administrative Portlets....94
Portal Architecture....95
Users....96
User Groups....96
Roles....97
Organizations....97
Communities....97
Using Liferay's Administrative Portlets....98
Adding Users....98
User Management....100
Organizations....101
User Groups....103
User Groups and Page Templates....104
Roles....109
Defining Permissions on a Role....109
Global Server Settings....111
Password Policies....112
Settings....113
General....113
Authentication: General Settings....113
Authentication: LDAP....114
Single Sign-On....119
Authentication: Central Authentication Service (CAS)....119
Authentication: NTLM....121
Authentication: OpenID....121
Authentication: OpenSSO....122
Default User Associations....122
Reserved Screen Names....122
Mail Host Names....123
Email Notifications....123
The Admin Portlet....123
Resources....123
Log Levels....123
System Properties....124
Portal Properties....124
Shutdown....124
OpenOffice....124
Instances....125
Plugins....125
Summary....125
4. Advanced Liferay Configuration....127
The portal-ext.properties File....127

Properties Override....128
Portal Context....128
Resource Repositories Root....129
Technology Compatibility Kit....129
Schema....129
Upgrade....129
Verify....130
Auto Deploy....130
Hot Deploy....132
Hot Undeploy....132
Plugin....132
Portlet....133
Theme....133
Resource Actions....134
Model Hints....134
Spring....134
Hibernate....135
Custom SQL....136
Ehcache....137
Commons Pool....137
JavaScript....137
SQL Data....141
Company....141
Users....142
Groups and Roles....142
Organizations....144
Languages and Time Zones....144
Look and Feel....146
Request....146
Session....146
JAAS....148
LDAP....149
CAS....151
NTLM....151
OpenID....152
OpenSSO....152
Authentication Pipeline....152
Auto Login....155
SSO with MAC (Message Authentication Code)....156
Passwords....156
Permissions....157
Captcha....158
Startup Events....159
Shutdown Events....159
Portal Events....159
Login event....160
Logout event....160
Default Landing Page....160
Default Logout Page....161
Default Guest Public Layouts....161
Default User Private Layouts....162
Default User Public Layouts....163

Default Admin....163
Layouts....164
Default Settings Layouts....164
Portlet URL....168
Preferences....169
Struts....169
Images....169
Editors....169
Fields....170
Mime Types....170
Amazon License Keys....170
Instant Messenger....170
Lucene Search....171
SourceForge....173
Value Object....174
Last Modified....174
XSS (Cross Site Scripting)....174
Communication Link....175
Content Delivery Network....175
Counter....175
Lock....175
JBI....176
JCR....176
OpenOffice....176
POP....176
Quartz....177
Scheduler....177
Social Bookmarks....177
Velocity Engine....178
Virtual Hosts....178
HTTP....179
Servlet Filters....179
Upload Servlet Request....180
Web Server....180
WebDAV....181
Main Servlet....181
Axis Servlet....182
JSON Tunnel Servlet....182
Liferay Tunnel Servlet....182
Spring Remoting Servlet....182
WebDAV Servlet....182
Admin Portlet....182
Announcements Portlet....183
Blogs Portlet....183
Calendar Portlet....184
Communities Portlet....184
Document Library Portlet....184
Image Gallery Portlet....186
Invitation Portlet....186
Journal Portlet....186
Journal Articles Portlet....188
Mail Portlet....188

Message Boards Portlet....190
My Places Portlet....191
Navigation Portlet....191
Nested Portlets Portlet....191
Portlet CSS Portlet....191
Shopping Portlet....192
Software Catalog Portlet....192
Tags Compiler Portlet....193
Tags Portlet....193
Tasks Portlet....193
Translator Portlet....193
Web Form Portlet....193
Wiki Portlet....193
Plugin Management....195
Portlets....195
Themes....197
Layout Templates....197
Web Plugins....197
Installing Plugins from Liferay's Official and Community Repositories....198
Installing Plugins Manually....200
Plugin Troubleshooting....202
Liferay Configuration Issues....202
The Container Upon Which Liferay Is Running....204
Changing the Configuration Options in Multiple Places....204
How Liferay Is Being Launched....204
Creating Your Own Plugin Repository....205
The Software Catalog Portlet....206
Manually Creating A Software Catalog....212
Connecting to a Software Catalog....213
Liferay Services Oriented Architecture....213
Accessing Liferay's WSDL....215
5. Enterprise Configuration....217
Liferay Clustering....218
All Nodes Should Be Pointing to the Same Liferay Database....219
Jackrabbit Sharing....219
Search Configuration....220
Pluggable Enterprise Search....220
Lucene Configuration....222
Hot Deploy....223
Distributed Caching....223
Hibernate Cache Settings....225
Clustering Jackrabbit....226
Workflow....226
Installation and Test....227
Using Different Databases....228
Technical Explanations....228
Process Definitions....228
Integrating with Users, Communities, and Roles....228
Data Types and Error Checking....230
Sample Process Definitions....232
Warning Messages....233

Administration....234
Deploying Workflows....234
Managing Instances....236
Managing Tasks....237
Future Enhancements....238
Logging....238
Customizable Front-End....238
File Upload Data Type....239
Frequently Asked Questions....239
How do you write a new process definition?....239
Why are there "Duplicate File" exceptions when I change databases for jBPM?....239
Deploying A Customized Liferay....239
Deploying Directly on the Server....240
Deploying from a Client Machine....241
Performance Tuning....241
Memory....241
Properties File Changes....242
Servlet Filters....243
Portlets....243
6. Maintaining A Liferay Portal....245
Liferay Monitoring Using Google Analytics....245
Backing Up A Liferay Installation....246
Source Code....246
Liferay's File System....247
Database....247
Liferay's Logging System....247
Upgrading Liferay....249
Liferay Upgrade Procedure....249
Upgrade Steps....250
Upgrading Liferay 4.3 to Liferay 4.4....250
Prerequisite....250
If Your Developers Have Customized Liferay....250
Upgrading Liferay 4.4 to Liferay 5.0....251
Prerequisite....251
If Your Developers Have Customized Liferay....251
Converting wiki pages (optional)....251
Upgrade Troubleshooting....252
Upgrading Liferay 5.0 to Liferay 5.1....252
Changes in configuration properties....252
How to keep the old values....252
What has been changed?....252
If Your Developers Have Customized Liferay....252
Upgrading Themes....253
The Parent Element of the Dock May Change Positioning When Upgrading....254
The Class Names for Different UI Components Have Changed....254
Change in Theme CSS Fast Load....254
Change in Javascript Fast Load....255
Upgrading PHP Portlets....255
Javascript changes....255
7. Appendix: Documentation License....257

Creative Commons License........257
License........257
Creative Commons Notice........263
8. Colophon........265
Index........268

This page intentionally left blank.

PREFACE

Liferay Portal is the leading open source portal in the marketplace today. This is seen through having received awards from multiple leading industry publications, as well as its impressive download rate (over 40,000 downloads a month and over a million downloads total). Why is it so popular? Because Liferay Portal has *out of the box* all of the features you need to run a successful web site, whether that site is a public Internet site, a corporate Intranet, or anything in between.

This book was written with the server administrator in mind. It is a guide for anyone who wants to get a Liferay Portal server up and running, and will guide you step-by-step through the installation and configuration process. Use this book as a handbook to getting your Liferay Portal installation running smoothly.

The information contained herein has been organized in a way that hopefully makes it easy to locate information. We start at the beginning: downloading and configuring the Liferay bundles. From there, we work all the way through the multiple ways of installing Liferay manually on an application server, to portal administration. From there we go into advanced administration topics and enterprise configuration, including clustering and integrating Liferay with other services. We round things out by showing you how to optimize Liferay's performance, how to manage a Liferay installation, how to back it up, and how to upgrade Liferay if you are moving from a previous version.

What's New in the Second Edition

Certainly, Liferay Portal has not stood still since the last edition was written. This edition has been updated so that it covers Liferay Portal up to version 5.1. Chapter 4 (*Advanced Liferay Configuration*) has been completely revamped to that it covers all of the new portal properties, and the rest of the book has been exhaustively gone through and updated.

Additionally, a new chapter on Portal Administration (Chapter 3) has been written. This chapter goes over portal design, listing the things you might want to consider as you build your web site on Liferay Portal. It also covers Liferay's administrative portlets, leading the reader through Liferay's configuration using the **Enterprise Admin** and **Admin** portlets.

Other chapters have been expanded to include additional information. For example, Chapter 6 (*Maintaining a Liferay Portal*) now covers the upgrade process for Liferay, guiding the reader through the process for upgrading a Liferay installation all the way from version 4.3.0 (the version upon which the last edition of this book was based) to version 5.1.

Conventions

Sections are broken up into multiple levels of headings, and these are designed to make it easy to find information.

Tip: This is a tip. Tips are used to indicate a suggestion or a piece of information that affects whatever is being talked about in the surrounding text. They are always accompanied by this gray box and the icon to the left.

```
Source code and configuration file directives are presented like
this.
```

Italics are used to represent links or buttons to be clicked on in a user interface and to indicate a label or a name of a Java class.

Bold is used to describe field labels and portlets.

Page headers denote the chapters, and footers denote the particular section within the chapter.

Publisher Notes

It is our hope that this book will be valuable to you, and that it will be an indispensable resource as you begin to administer a Liferay portal server. If you need any assistance beyond what is covered in this book, Liferay, Inc. offers training, consulting, and support services to fill any need that you might have. Please see http://www.liferay.com/web/guest/services for further information about the services we can provide.

As always, we welcome any feedback. If there is any way you think we could make this book better, please feel free to mention it on our forums. You can also use any of the email addresses on our *Contact Us* page (http://www.liferay.com/web/guest/about_us/contact_us). We are here to serve you, our users and customers, and to help make your experience using Liferay Portal the best it can be.

Author Notes

The first edition of this book was outlined in a small notebook (paper, not a computer) on a plane flying from Philadelphia to Los Angeles. A couple of months later, it was rehashed electronically in outline form among a small group of Liferay employees until the final list of content was considered complete. This seemed like a big accomplishment at the time, but paled in comparison to the work of actually documenting all of the things we'd decided to include.

The writing and editing process for the first edition took a period of five months of mostly full time work. It would have taken much longer except for the fact that many fantastic contributions came unsolicited from many different people. I have endeavored to give credit to everyone who made a contribution (it's on the copyright page), but if I missed somebody—which would not be surprising—please let me know so your name is not left out of the next edition! I cannot express enough how wonderful it is to be surrounded by so many talented people who do everything they can to make this product the best it can be—even when a particular task is not their primary job.

The second edition was put together over the course of two and a half months of intensive work. Special thanks are due to Jorge Ferrer for his care and feeding of the Liferay wiki (http://wiki.liferay.com) as well as for his support of the writing process in general. The engineering team at Liferay is a fantastic group of people, and my job would be a lot more difficult were it not for their patience with me when I interrupt their work with some (pretty dumb, sometimes) questions. So special thanks are due to Ray Auge, Nate Cavanaugh, Brian Chan, Alex Chow, and Bruno Farache.

I'd also like to thank my daughter Julia for checking in on me from time to time and being satisfied with a "sticker" from my label maker instead of play time with Daddy during the day when I'm working. And of course, I want to thank my wife, Deborah, who continually has to put up with long hours as a computer widow, for her understanding and support. I couldn't do any of this without her.

Rich Sezov

http://www.liferay.com/web/rsezov/blog

1. INTRODUCTION

Liferay Portal is the world's leading open source enterprise portal solution using the latest in Java and Web 2.0 technologies.

1. Runs on all major application servers and servlet containers, databases, and operating systems, with over 700 deployment combinations
2. JSR-286 Compliant
3. Out-of-the-box usability with over 60 portlets pre-bundled.
4. Built in Content Management System (CMS) and Collaboration Suite
5. Personalized pages for all users
6. Benchmarked as among the most secure portal platforms using LogicLibrary's Logiscan suite

Created for the enterprise, Liferay Portal provides a virtual space where you can centralize, share and collaborate.

Built with the end user in mind, Liferay Portal's award winning user interface is easy enough to master by even the least technical of users.

Liferay Portal also remains one of the most popular portal technologies within the developer community with an ever-growing list of features that help your IT team deploy business solutions with minimal time and effort.

Created for the Enterprise

Personalization and easy customization

Give the right people the right access to the right applications and documents! A highly granular permissions system allows you to customize the user experience at the organizational and personal level.

Workflow adaptable

Liferay's technology is built to quickly adapt business and organizational changes, ensuring minimal downtime in today's fast-changing market.

Branding friendly

Liferay Portal is coded to easily adapt to your organization's desired branding and look and feel.

Flexible organization

Liferay Portal is highly scalable for large, growing user bases. It accommodates the functional needs of even the most complex of enterprises--For example, your sub organizations can each be given its own portal experience with unique URL, login, look and feel and security permissions!

Built With The End-User In Mind

Liferay Portal's award winning user interface offers dynamic, intuitive and time saving features that fosters user adoption across your entire organization.

Award-winning UI

Liferay Portal offers dynamic, intuitive and time saving features that foster user adoption across your entire organization. We were the first portal to introduce drag-and-drop portlet re-positioning and continue to deliver innovative usability features for even the least technical of users!

One-Click Look and Feel Changes

Deploy a new look and feel with one click without having to touch any code!

Web OS

Work with Liferay's Document Library like a network drive on your desktop with familiar folders. An optional free-floating portlet theme mimics the look and feel of your desktop environment.

Technology to Help Developers

Protect your development investment. Liferay Portal's active and mature community always keeps the developer experience in mind.

Standards Compliant

Liferay Portal complies with key industry standards, making it easy to work and integrate with.

Ready Integration

Partnerships with leading Open Source players such as Alfresco, ICEsoft, SpringSource, and Pentaho ensure unparalleled integration and support for these widely-used technologies.

Liferay Plugins Catalog

This exclusive feature of Liferay Portal keeps track of new versions of the software and instantly updates the technology without troublesome restarts.

- Application Servers

  Databases

  Operating Systems

Liferay supports ALL major app servers, databases, and operating systems with over 700 deployment configurations.

Please see our deployment matrix for more details.

Supported Technologies

Technologies Used:

- Apache ServiceMix
- ehcache
- Hibernate
- ICEfaces
- Java J2EE/JEE
- jBPM
- JGroups
- jQuery JavaScript Framework
- Lucene
- MuleSource ESB
- PHP
- Ruby
- Seam
- Spring & AOP
- Struts & Tiles
- Tapestry
- Velocity

Standards:

- AJAX
- iCalendar & Microformat
- JSR-168
- JSR-127
- JSR-170
- Seats on the JSR-286 (Portlet 2.0) and JSF-314 (JSF 2.0) committees
- OpenSearch
- Open platform with support for web services including:
  - JSON
  - Hessian
  - Burlap
  - REST
  - RMI
  - WSRP
- WebDAV

Languages

Liferay supports I18N for any language out-of-the-box and ships with default translations for 22 languages. Additional languages can be added very easily.

2. Initial Setup

You will find that because Liferay is extremely flexible in its deployment options, it is easy to install as well. If you already have an application server, you simply use the tools for deployment that came with your application server. If you do not have an application server, Liferay provides several application server bundles from which to choose. These are very easy to install and with a small amount of configuration can be made into production-ready systems.

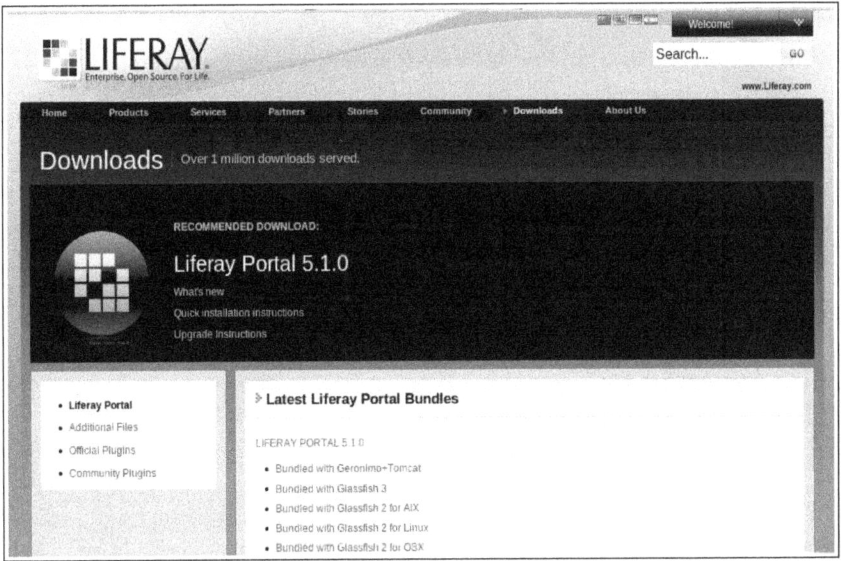

Illustration 1: Liferay's Download Page

Obtaining Liferay

Liferay is freely downloadable from our web site at http://www.liferay.com. Click on the *Downloads* link at the top of the page, and you will be presented with multiple options for getting a copy of Liferay.

If you want to install a bundle, there is a list of bundles available on the first download page, with a recommended bundle at the top. If you do not currently have an application server, it is best to download the bundle that Liferay recommends at the top of the page. If you have an application server preference, you can also choose the server you prefer from the available Liferay Portal bundles. Having a JDK (Java Development Kit) already installed is a prerequisite to running any of the bundles.

Please note that Liferay is not able to provide application server bundles for proprietary application servers such as WebLogic, WebSphere, or Oracle Application Server because the licenses for these servers do not allow for redistribution. Liferay Portal, however, runs just as well on these application servers as it does on open source application servers; it just needs to be installed manually.

If you wish to obtain a copy of Liferay Portal for a manual install, you can click on the *Additional Files* link on the left side of the *Downloads* page. Here you will find Liferay .war files as well as links to Liferay's dependency .jars that need to be on your application server's class path. Later in this chapter are instructions for installing Liferay on many of the major application servers available today.

Installing a Bundle

In most cases, installing a bundle is as easy as uncompressing the archive and then starting the application server. For example, if you were to install the recommended bundle (Liferay Portal on Tomcat), you would create a folder to store the uncompressed application server and then uncompress the archive into this folder.

What you wind up with after this is the following directory structure:

Now you would simply start Tomcat in the same way as you would if you had downloaded it manually. Tomcat is launched by way of a script which is found in the *bin* folder. If you drop to a command prompt and go to this folder, you can launch Tomcat via the following command on Windows:

```
startup
```

or the following command on Linux / Unix:

```
./startup.sh
```

The Liferay / Tomcat bundle will then launch. If you are on Windows, you will see another command prompt window appear with Tomcat's console in it. If you are on Linux, you can see the Tomcat console by issuing the following command:

```
tail -f ../logs/catalina.out
```

Once Tomcat has completed launching, you can then view your Liferay bundle in a web browser. Launch your web browser and then go to the following address: http://localhost:8080. The default Liferay home page will then appear in your web browser. It will be using an embedded database for its configuration, but it is fully functional. You can now begin exploring the various features of Liferay.

Installing a different bundle is done in exactly the same way: unzip the bundle into the folder of your choice, launch the application server, and then view the portal in your web browser. There is only one bundle that differs from this procedure. The Pramati bundle is currently the only bundle that is available from Liferay's web site that uses an installer. If you wish to use the Pramati bundle, you need to launch it via its installer.

The Pramati installer will have a file name such as liferay-portal-pramati-<version number>.jar. Download this file from Liferay's web site. Once it has been downloaded, you can launch the installer from the command prompt by issuing the following command:

```
java -jar <name of bundle file>
```

For example, if you downloaded liferay-portal-pramati-4.3.3.jar, you would issue the following command:

```
java -jar liferay-portal-pramati-4.3.3.jar
```

You will then see the Pramati installer appear on your screen.

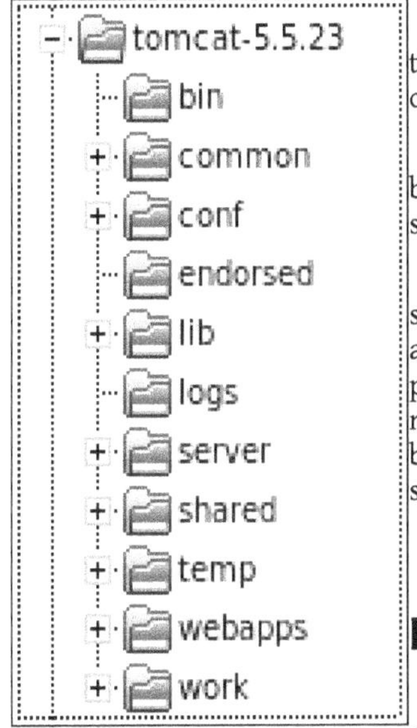

Illustration 2: Tomcat Directory Structure

Select the folder to which you wish to to install the bundle and click the *Next* button. There is only one other screen in the installer:

Click the *install* button and the bundle will then be installed. Please note that the Pramati bundle is supported on Windows operating systems only.

As you can see, bundles are the easiest way to get started with Liferay. They come pre-configured with a running Liferay that can be used immediately to explore all of the things that Liferay can do. And with minimal extra configuration (which we will see later), bundles can be converted into full production-ready systems.

Installing Liferay for a Developer

If you are beginning a Liferay-based project, chances are you will need to get your developers up and running before your production systems are ready. In order for a developer to do his or her work, an instance of Liferay needs to be running on his or her machine. Additionally, to prevent file-locking issues, a developer's version of Liferay should not use the embedded database, so a separate database will need to be installed.

Liferay Portal is an open source project, so it makes use of many open source tools for development. This has two benefits: 1) It removes any barriers to entry, as there are no expensive tools to purchase in order to make use of Liferay, and 2) It allows Liferay to remain as tool-agnostic as possible. If developers wish to use an IDE to work on Liferay, great. If developers want to use a text editor and the command line, that's great too. Developers can choose the tools they are most comfortable with to write code on Liferay's platform.

There are, however, some tools that are required in order to develop with Liferay. These are at a minimum:

- Apache Ant 1.7.0 or above
- A Java Development Kit
- A Liferay-supported database (MySQL recommended for a developer machine)
- The IDE or development environment of your choice

If you will be customizing Liferay via the Extension Environment (please see the *Liferay Developer's Guide* for further details), you may need:

- A Subversion client (optional: you can also download the Liferay source from the web site)

Standalone Liferay

Installing a standalone Liferay for a developer is a straightforward process:

1. Download the Tomcat bundle from the Liferay web site
2. Uncompress the bundle to a suitable location on the developer's local machine
3. Install a lightweight SQL database that Liferay supports (MySQL recommended)
4. Connect the local Liferay to the SQL database
5. Launch Liferay!

Download the Tomcat Bundle

We recommend using the Tomcat bundle from the Liferay web site for several reasons:

1. Tomcat is small and fast. Because it is a servlet container only and not a full Java EE container, it requires less resources than a full application server, yet it provides all of the resources Liferay needs to run.
2. Tomcat is open source, and so is easy to bundle with Liferay, as the licenses are compatible.
3. Liferay will have to share resources on the developer machine with an SQL database as well as with other tools. Running it in Tomcat ensures that it has as lightweight a footprint as possible.

With that said, if your developers have sufficient resources on their machines to run a different application server (such as Glassfish or JBoss), there is no reason besides the performance reasons mentioned above why they could not do that. Simply substitute the instructions below that reference the Liferay-Tomcat bundle with the bundle that more closely resembles the application server your developers want to use.

Uncompress the Bundle

Uncompress the Tomcat bundle to a suitable location on the developer's machine. It is best to use a local directory, and not a networked drive for performance reasons. Liferay will run from a networked drive, but I/O issues may cause it to perform poorly.

Install a Lightweight SQL Database

Liferay is database-agnostic, but it needs a database in order to run. The embedded database is fine for demoing Liferay, but for development a real SQL database server should be used. We recommend that you use MySQL for this purpose, as it is small, free, and very fast. If your developers use Linux, it generally comes with their Linux distribution of choice. If your developers use Windows, there is an easy graphical installer that automatically configures it.

Again, if your organization has standardized on a different database, there is no reason not to use that database on your developers' machines as long as those machines have the resources to run it. Liferay supports any database that your application server can provide access to via a JDBC data source.

To install MySQL for a developer, you will need four components: *MySQL Server, MySQL Query Browser, MySQL Administrator, and MySQL Connector/J*, which is the JDBC driver for MySQL. The first component is the server itself, which on Windows will get installed as a service. The second component is a database browsing and querying tool, and the third is an administration utility that enables the end user to create databases and user IDs graphically. If your developer is running Windows or Mac, download these three components from MySQL's web site (http://www.mysql.com). Run through the graphical installers for each, accepting the defaults. If your developer is running Linux, have him / her install these tools via the package management tool in his / her distribution.

Once you have a running MySQL database server, drop to a command line and launch the MySQL command line utility. You can find this in the *bin* directory where MySQL is installed, or in the case of Linux, it will be on your system's *path*. Launch it via the following command:

```
mysql -u root
```

By default, MySQL does not have an administrative (root) password set, and this is fine for a developer's machine. If you have set an administrative password, issue the following command instead:

```
mysql -u root -p
```

Once you launch it, it will display some messages and then a MySQL prompt:

```
Welcome to the MySQL monitor.  Commands end with ; or \g.
Your MySQL connection id is 47
Server version: 5.0.51a-3ubuntu5.1 (Ubuntu)

Type 'help;' or '\h' for help. Type '\c' to clear the buffer.

mysql>
```

At the command prompt, type the following command:

```
create database lportal character set utf8;
```

MySQL should return the following message:

```
Query OK, 1 row affected (0.12 sec)
```

You will be back at the MySQL prompt. You can type *quit* and press enter, and you will return to your operating system's command prompt.

Note that on some Linux distributions MySQL is configured so that it will not listen on the network for connections. This is done for security reasons, but it prevents Java from being able to connect to MySQL via the JDBC driver. To fix this, search for your *my.cnf* file (it is probably in */etc* or */etc/sysconfig*). There are two ways in which this may be disabled. If you find a directive called *skip-networking*, comment it by putting a hash mark (#) in front of it. If you find a directive called *bind-address* and it is configured to bind only to localhost (127.0.0.1), comment it out by putting a hash mark (#) in front of it. Save the file and then restart MySQL.

By default, Liferay 4.4 and higher include the MySQL JDBC driver in the bundles. If you are using an earlier version, you will need to copy the MySQL JDBC driver—a .jar file—to the proper location in the Tomcat server, so that the Tomcat server can find it.

Connect Liferay to the SQL Database

Next, if you are using a version of Liferay prior to 4.4, you will need to copy the MySQL JDBC driver—a .jar file—to the proper location in the Tomcat server, so that the Tomcat server can find it. If you're using a newer version of Liferay, skip to the next paragraph. The file should be copied to the common/lib/ext folder of your Tomcat installation. This makes it available on Tomcat's global class path. If you are using a different application server, copy the driver to a location on the server's global class path.

Once this file is copied, you will need to change a configuration file in Tomcat to point it to your new database. Navigate to the following folder in Tomcat:

```
<Tomcat Home>/conf/Catalina/localhost
```

In this folder is a file called *ROOT.xml*. Open this file in a text editor. You should see a lot of commented out Resource tags in this file; one out of all of them is uncommented—it's the reference to the HSQL database. Comment the HSQL Resource out and then uncomment the MySQL reference, which looks like this:

```
<Resource
        name="jdbc/LiferayPool"
```

```
        auth="Container"
        type="javax.sql.DataSource"
        driverClassName="com.mysql.jdbc.Driver"
        url="jdbc:mysql://localhost/lportal?useUnicode=true&amp;charac-
terEncoding=UTF-8"
        username="root"
        password=""
        maxActive="20"
/>
```

Make sure you enter the user name and password to access the database. Save and close the file.

Again, if you are using a different application server, modify the LiferayPool data source so that it uses the MySQL driver and points to your MySQL database.

Launch Liferay!

You are now ready to launch Liferay. Navigate to your <Tomcat Home>/bin folder in your command prompt. On Windows, type:

```
startup
```

On Linux, type:

```
./startup.sh
```

Press Enter. On Windows, another command prompt window should appear with the Tomcat console in it. On Linux, you will need to issue another command to see the console:

```
tail -f ../logs/catalina.out
```

Liferay will start as usual. Because this is the first time Liferay will be launched against your new MySQL database, it will take some extra time creating all of the tables it needs in the database. Once the messages have stopped scrolling, navigate to the following URL in your web browser:

```
http://localhost:8080
```

The default Liferay home page will be displayed.

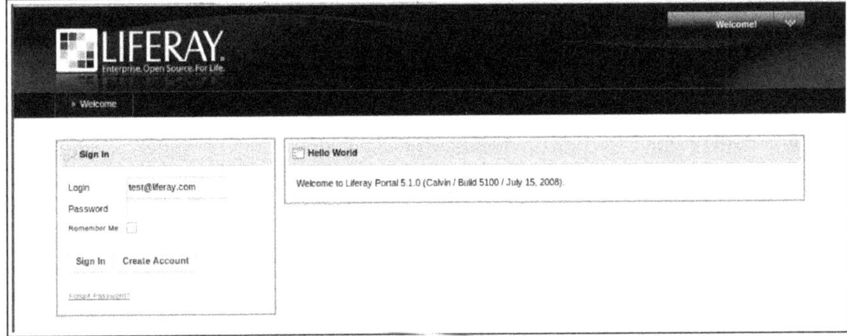

Illustration 3: Default Liferay Page

To log in to your new portal, use the default administrative credentials:

```
Login: test@liferay.com
Password: test
```

Your developer now has a standalone version of Liferay installed on his / her machine, and can use the tools of his / her choice to launch a completely local Liferay instance in order to test code. Additionally, he / she is free to point whatever development tool (IDE, text editor, etc.) at this Tomcat instance in order to start it in debug mode. This Liferay instance can be used to develop, deploy, and test portal plugins (portlet .war files and Liferay themes).

Installing the Liferay Extension Environment

Because Liferay Portal is an open source project, all of its source code is available for developers to view and modify if they wish. Because many of Liferay's customers wish to extend the functionality of the portal, Liferay has provided a means of customization which enables clear separation of customized code from the Liferay core source. This provides several benefits:

- The upgrade path is kept clear, as customizations are kept separate from the Liferay source
- Organization or environment specific customizations don't need to be contributed back to the Liferay project
- One, separate project for all customizations can be checked in to an organization's source code repository and applied to multiple instances of Liferay, or the reverse: an organization can have several instances of Liferay with different customizations

Just like installing a standalone Liferay, the extension environment is tool-agnostic. Developers can use whatever tools they are most comfortable with. This allows them to be as productive as possible, right out of the gate.

The procedure for installing a Liferay extension environment is as follows:

- Install the necessary tools
- Obtain the Liferay source
- Create configuration files
- Create the extension environment
- Install an application server in which to debug
- Deploy the extension environment

Install the Necessary Tools

You will need the full list of development tools (all open source and freely available) to customize Liferay in the extension environment:

- A Java Development Kit

- Apache Ant 1.7.0 or above
- A Liferay-supported database (MySQL recommended for a developer machine)
- A Subversion client (optional: you can also download the Liferay source from the web site)
- The IDE or development environment of your choice

Java Development Kit

Download and install JDK 1.5 or above. It is generally best to install this in a folder that does not have spaces in its name. Once the install has completed, set an environment variable called JAVA_HOME which points to your JDK directory. Each operating system differs in how to do this. On Windows operating systems, you would do this through the Control Panel -> System -> Advanced -> Environment Variables. On Unix-like operating systems, your distribution usually handles this for you, or you can set it manually by modifying your .bash_profile file in your user directory.

Apache Ant 1.7.0 or Above

Download the latest version of Ant from http://ant.apache.org. This is the build tool that is used extensively by both the Liferay source and the extension environment. Uncompress the archive into an appropriate folder of your choosing.

Next, set an environment variable called ANT_HOME which points to the folder to which you installed Ant. Use this variable to add the binaries for Ant to your PATH by adding ANT_HOME/bin to your PATH environment variable.

To do this on a Windows platform, go to Start -> Control Panel, and double-click the System icon. Go to Advanced, and then click the Environment Variables button. Under System Variables, select *New*. Make the **Variable Name** *ANT_HOME* and the **Variable Value** *<Path To>\apache-ant-1.7.0* (e.g., *C:\Java\apache-ant-1.7.0*), and click *OK*.

Select *New* again. This time name the **Variable Name** *ANT_OPTS* and the **Variable Value** *-Xms256M -Xmx512M*

Scroll down until you find the PATH environment variable. Select it and select *Edit*. Add %ANT_HOME%\bin to the end or beginning of the Path. Select *OK*, and then select *OK* again. Open a command prompt and type *ant* and press Enter. If you get a build file not found error, you have correctly installed Ant. If not, check your environment variable settings and make sure they are pointing to the directory to which you unzipped Ant.

To do this on a Linux or Mac system, navigate to your home folder and edit the file called *.bash_profile*. It is a hidden file that resides in the root of your home folder. Add the following lines to it, substituting the path to which you installed Ant:

```
ANT_HOME=/java/apache-ant-1.7.0
ANT_OPTS="-Xms256M -Xmx512M"
PATH=$PATH:$HOME/bin:$ANT_HOME/bin
export ANT_HOME ANT_OPTS PATH
```

Save the file and then open a new terminal window and type *ant* and press Enter. If you get a build file not found error, you have correctly installed Ant. If not, check your environment variable settings and make sure they are pointing to the directory to which you unzipped Ant.

A Liferay-supported Database

We recommend that if your organization doesn't have a standard for local development databases, you should use MySQL for this, as it is small, free, and very fast. If your developers use Linux, it generally comes with their Linux distribution of choice. If your developers use Windows, there is an easy graphical installer that automatically configures it.

To install MySQL for a developer, you will need four components: *MySQL Server, MySQL Query Browser, MySQL Administrator, and MySQL Connector/J*, which is the JDBC driver for MySQL. The first component is the server itself, which on Windows will get installed as a service. The second component is a database browsing and querying tool, and the third is an administration utility that enables the end user to create databases and user IDs graphically. If your developer is running Windows, download these three components from MySQL's web site (http://www.mysql.com). Run through the graphical installers for each, accepting the defaults. If your developer is running Linux, have him / her install these tools via the package management tool in his / her distribution.

Once you have a running MySQL database server, drop to a command line and launch the MySQL command line utility. You can find this in the *bin* directory where MySQL is installed, or in the case of Linux, it will be on your system's *path*. Launch it via the following command:

```
mysql -u root
```

By default, MySQL does not have an administrative (root) password set, and this is fine for a developer's machine. If you have set an administrative password, issue the following command instead:

```
mysql -u root -p
```

Once you launch it, it will display some messages and then a MySQL prompt:

```
Welcome to the MySQL monitor.  Commands end with ; or \g.
Your MySQL connection id is 47
Server version: 5.0.51a-3ubuntu5.1 (Ubuntu)

Type 'help;' or '\h' for help. Type '\c' to clear the buffer.

mysql>
```

At the command prompt, type the following command:

```
create database lportal character set utf8;
```

MySQL should return the following message:

```
Query OK, 1 row affected (0.12 sec)
```

You will be back at the MySQL prompt. You can type *quit* and press enter, and you will return to your operating system's command prompt.

Note that on some Linux distributions MySQL is configured so that it will not listen on the network for connections. This is done for security reasons, but it prevents Java from being able to connect to MySQL via the JDBC driver. To fix this, search for your *my.cnf* file (it is probably in */etc* or */etc/sysconfig*). There are two ways in which this may be disabled. If you find a directive called *skip-networking*, comment it by putting a hash mark (#) in front of it. If you find a directive called *bind-address* and it is configured to bind only to localhost (127.0.0.1), comment it out by putting a hash mark (#) in front of it. Save the file and then restart MySQL.

By default, Liferay 4.4 and higher include the MySQL JDBC driver in the bundles. If you are using an earlier version, you will need to copy the MySQL JDBC driver—a .jar file—to the proper location in the Tomcat server, so that the Tomcat server can find it, but we will need to perform several other steps first. If you are using an older version, you will need to copy it into the *lib/global* folder of the extension environment once you build it. This will become clear as you follow the next steps.

A Subversion Client (optional)

In order to work in the extension environment, you will need to obtain a copy of the Liferay source code. You can do this in two ways: you can download a particular release from Liferay's web site, or you can check out the source from the Subversion repository at Sourceforge. One benefit of using a Subversion client is that you can switch easily to newer versions of the Portal source when they become available. Or, if you wish to keep up with a particular branch of code, you can connect to the latest branch to obtain bug fixes as quickly as possible. If you are really adventurous, you can connect to the trunk and run the latest bleeding-edge code.

If you don't want to use a Subversion client, then getting the source code is easy: download the latest source release from Liferay's web site and unzip it to where you are going to store your Liferay development projects.

If you would like to use a Subversion client, GUI clients and command line clients are available for just about every operating system, such as TortoiseSVN (for Windows), KDESVN (for Linux), or RapidSVN (for Mac). Select the one you think is most appropriate and then install it.

The IDE or Development Environment of Your Choice

Liferay is IDE-agnostic. Developers can use anything from a simple text editor and command line tools to a full-blown IDE such as Eclipse or Netbeans. Your developer should decide what environment he / she is most productive in once the Liferay source and extension environment have been installed on his / her machine. If your developer(s) do not have a particular tool of choice, we recommend starting with Eclipse or Netbeans. Both of them are open-source IDEs with lots of functionality to help streamline development. Additionally, both of them have plugins for Subversion (Netbeans has it built-in, the one for Eclipse is called *Subclipse* and needs to be installed separately) which allows developers to connect to Liferay's code repository directly from within the IDE. Please see the *Liferay Developer's Guide* for further information.

Obtain the Liferay Source

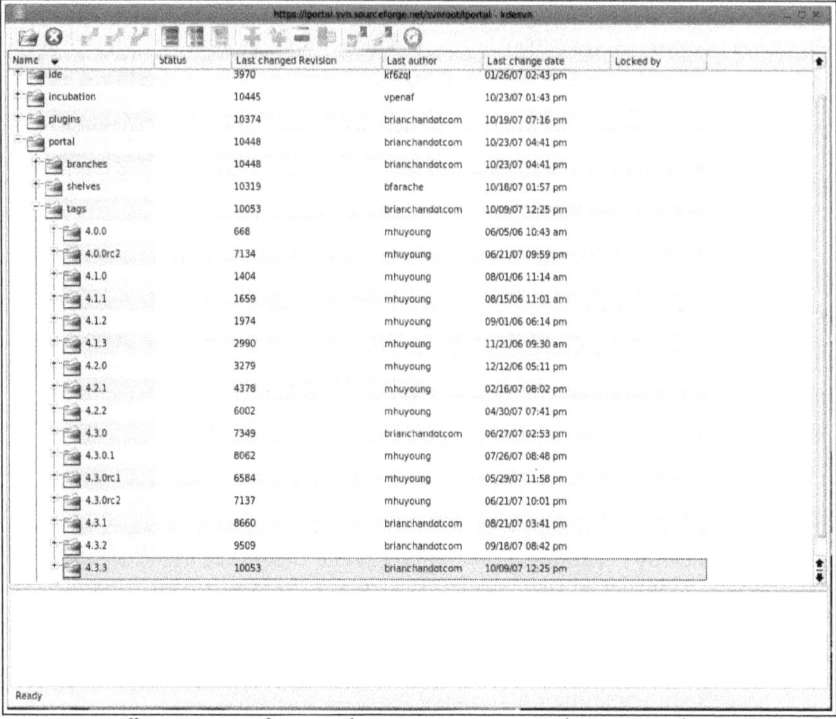

Illustration 4: Liferay's Subversion Repository, in the KDESVN client

If you are not using a Subversion client, you will need to download the Liferay source from Liferay's download page. Unzip the source code into a folder called *portal.*

If you are using a Subversion client, point your client to the following repository:

```
https://lportal.svn.sourceforge.net/svnroot/lportal
```

From there, you should be able to browse to the version of the source you want. Open the top level project called *portal.* If you want to download a particular release of the portal, you'll then want to open the folder called *tags.* From there, you can see the various versions of the software that have been tagged.

If you would rather work from a branch, open the *branches* folder. Here you will see the development branches for the various releases, such as 4.3.x, 4.4.x, and 5.0.x, and 5.1.x. Bug fixes are back ported to these branches when they become available, and so it is likely that if a support ticket for a particular bug has been closed, but the fix has not yet been part of a release of the software, you will find the fix in the branch. Once a good number of bug fixes have been checked into a branch, the development team creates another release, which you'll then see in the *tags* folder.

If you want to work from the bleeding-edge development version of the code, go to the *trunk* folder. There are no sub folders here; this is the latest version of the code. Note that this code (likely) has bugs and unimplemented features, and you will probably want to update from the repository regularly. Also note that any extensions that are developed against this version of the code will likely need refactoring as the Liferay code itself is refactored. For this reason, unless your developers really know the Liferay source well, it is best to stick with a tagged version of the code or a branch.

Check out the code using the Subversion client of your choice into a folder on your developer's local machine called *portal*. This could take a while, as the Liferay code base has become rather large. You may want to have it run in the background while you perform other tasks.

Create Configuration Files

The Liferay source project consists of a number of top level folders (some with sub folders), some properties files, and a number of Ant build scripts. Rather than modify the properties files directly (and thus potentially lose their default values), Liferay allows the developer to *override* these defaults by creating new properties files based on the developer's user name. This is generally the name one would use to log in to his / her machine (e.g., jsmith).

Navigate to the folder in which you have now stored the Liferay source code. Inside this folder you will find several properties files (they have the extension *.properties*). There are two of them that will need to be customized, but you won't have to edit them. Instead, you will create new versions of the files that have your user name in them.

The two files that need to be customized are *release.properties* and *app.server.properties*. You will create new versions of these files with the user name inserted in a dot-delimited fashion. For example, if your user name is *jsmith*, you will create *release.jsmith.properties* and *app.server.jsmith.properties.*

We'll start with the customized version of *release.properties.* Open your custom version (the one with your user name in the file name) and the default version at the same time. There are at least three properties that we may need to customize:

```
##
## Release Source
##

    lp.source.dir=${project.dir}/../source

##
## Extension Environment
##

    lp.ext.dir=${project.dir}/../ext

##
## Plugins Environment
##

    lp.plugins.dir=${project.dir}/../../plugins/build
```

Copy this from the original file into your new file. The first property defines where you are storing the Liferay Portal source on your local machine. If you are storing it in a directory called something other than *source*, you will want to change it to match If your developers are using the extension environment (see the *Liferay Developer's Guide* for further information), do the same thing for the folder where the extension environment is stored. Again, do the same thing for the Plugins SDK.

The slashes on a Windows box are changed from backslashes to forward slashes because backslashes are generally used to escape out another character. Since Java knows what operating system it is running on, it can transparently convert the forward slashes in the properties file to backslashes.

Once you have changed the *release.<username>.properties* file to define where you have placed the portal project, the Plugins SDK, and the extension environment project, save it and close it.

Next, you will do the same for the *app.server.properties* file. Open that file and your custom version (the one with your user name in the file name). The original file allows for the extension environment to be deployed to many different kinds of application servers. The default value is fine: we will be installing Tomcat as part of the extension environment, but we will paste it into our customized file anyway to enable us to switch application servers later if we wish:

```
app.server.type=tomcat
```

The default folder name where Tomcat is installed is defined as follows:

```
app.server.tomcat.dir=${app.server.parent.dir}/tomcat-5.5.26
```

This will not match the folder name that is in the Liferay bundle, so you will need to do one of two things: 1) Change this property so that it refers to the folder name of the bundle, or 2) change the folder name of the bundle (once you unzip it) to what is referenced here.

The other property to note is the folder where we want to store our application server(s). This is called the Server Directory. The default is this:

```
##
## Server Directory
##

    app.server.parent.dir=${project.dir}/../bundles
```

You can leave the default if you like (and this is the recommended practice). This is the folder where you will unzip your Liferay bundle(s).

Create the Extension Environment

You are now ready to create your extension environment. Open up a command window in your operating system and navigate to your *portal* project folder. This is the folder into which you just put the customized properties files. Issue the following command:

```
ant clean start build-ext
```

Ant will use the build script in this folder (called *build.xml*) to compile Liferay and create a clean extension environment in the folder you specified in the properties files. When it finishes, you should have a new folder called *ext* in the same location as your *portal* folder.

Copy your customized properties files from your *portal* folder into your new *ext* folder. The same properties apply to the extension environment that apply to the portal source project.

Install an Application Server

Your final step is to install an application server in which to run and debug the extension environment code. You can do this by downloading one of the bundles and unzipping it into a *bundles* folder that is on the same level as the Liferay source and extension environment project folders.

You can install any application server for which Liferay provides a bundle in this way. If you open the original *app.server.properties* file, you will see a number of different application servers defined. They all have properties which look like *app.server.<server name>*. If you want to install and use a different application server, simply modify the *app.server.type* property in your customized *app.server.username.properties* file to reference one of the other application servers that are supported, such as *glassfish* or *jboss-tomcat*.

Once this is done, all of your extension environment deploys will now go to the application server you chose. You can have as many of the application servers installed at one time as you like. When you want to deploy your extension environment to a particular application server that you have installed, all you need to do is modify the *app.server.type* property to reference the application server you have chosen. This provides an easy way to test your code on a multitude of application servers.

You now need to modify the data source in your Tomcat instance to point to the MySQL database you created earlier. Navigate to the new Tomcat folder that is inside your *ext/servers* folder. Inside this folder are a number of sub folders. Navigate to the *conf/Catalina/localhost* folder. In this folder is a file called *ROOT.xml*. Open this file in a text editor. You should see a lot of commented out Resource tags in this file; one out of all of them is uncommented—it's the reference to the HSQL database. Comment the HSQL Resource out and then uncomment the MySQL reference, which looks like this:

```
<Resource
        name="jdbc/LiferayPool"
        auth="Container"
        type="javax.sql.DataSource"
        driverClassName="com.mysql.jdbc.Driver"
        url="jdbc:mysql://localhost/lportal?useUnicode=true&amp;charac-
terEncoding=UTF-8"
        username="root"
        password=""
        maxActive="20"
/>
```

Make sure you enter the user name and password to access the database. Save and close the file.

Deploy the Extension Environment

You are now ready to deploy the extension environment to your Tomcat instance for the first time. Open a command window and navigate to your *ext* folder. While in this folder, issue the following command:

```
ant clean deploy
```

The contents of the *portal* project will be merged with the contents of the *ext* project and the result will be deployed to your new Tomcat instance. Since you don't currently have any customizations in the extension environment, the end result will be that you will have deployed the version of Liferay whose source you downloaded, plus the sample Reports portlet that is in the extension environment by default.

You can start Tomcat by navigating to the directory in *bundles* to which Tomcat was installed. Inside this directory is another directory called *bin.* Navigate to this directory. To start Tomcat on Windows, type:

```
startup
```

On Linux, type:

```
./startup.sh
```

Press Enter. On Windows, another command prompt window should appear with the Tomcat console in it. On Linux, you will need to issue another command to see the console:

```
tail -f ../logs/catalina.out
```

Liferay will start as usual. Because this is the first time Liferay will be launched against your new MySQL database, it will take some extra time creating all of the tables it needs in the database. Once the messages have stopped scrolling, navigate to the following URL in your web browser:

```
http://localhost:8080
```

The default Liferay home page will be displayed.

To log in to your new portal, use the default administrative credentials:

```
Login: test@liferay.com
Password: test
```

Please see the *Liferay Developer's Guide* for further information on how to customize Liferay by use of the extension environment.

Installing Liferay for an Enterprise

Eventually, you will want to install Liferay onto a real server, rather than on a developer's machine. It is easiest to do this by starting with a bundle and then reconfiguring that bundle so that it is enterprise-ready. Because this is by far the quickest and easiest method to get a production Liferay system running, we will look at this first. Often, however, enterprises will have an established Java EE infrastructure upon which they would like to install Liferay. In this situation, a bundle will not suffice. Most of this section, therefore, will focus on installing Liferay onto an already-established application server.

Database Setup

Regardless of which method is used to install Liferay, you will need to configure the Liferay database first. Even though Liferay can now create its database automatically, many enterprises prefer *not* to allow the user ID configured in an application server to have that many permissions over the database. For security reasons, Select, Insert, Update, and Delete are generally all the permissions that most DBAs will grant, and so we will go over how to set up the database manually. If your organization's DBAs *are* willing to grant the Liferay user ID permissions to create and drop tables in the database—and this is the recommended configuration—you can skip this section.

Illustration 5: SQL Scripts Folder Structure

One other caveat is this: Liferay has an automatic database upgrade function which runs when the version of Liferay is upgraded to a new release. If the user ID that accesses the database does not have enough rights to create / modify / drop tables in the database, you will need to grant those rights to the ID before you start your upgraded Liferay for the first time. Once the upgrade is complete, you can remove those rights until the next upgrade.

Liferay provides an SQL script archive download on the web site. It is in the *Additional Files* section of the Downloads page. Download this file and unzip it. You will find that it contains a folder structure that is broken down by the type of script (full, minimal, or upgrade), and then further by database vendor type.

It is best to use the *create-minimal* script if you are installing a fresh version of Liferay on development, QA, or production server. This script creates the necessary Liferay tables in the database, with a minimum configuration. This is most appropriate for a new installation of Liferay.

The *create* script, by contrast, configures a Liferay database with a portion of the content from http://www.liferay.com embedded in it. This can be useful from a development perspective, as it contains working examples of the use of many of Liferay's features, including the Journal Content Management System.

Inside the *create* or *create-minimal* folders are scripts for every database that Liferay supports. A DBA can use the script provided to create the Liferay database, complete with the indexes necessary for optimal performance. Once this is done, be sure that the ID that the portal will use to connect to the database has at least Select, Insert, Update, and Delete permissions. Preferably, however, the ID should also have rights to create, modify, and drop tables and indexes, as this makes upgrading easier. This, however, is not necessary for the daily operation of Liferay.

Once your DBA has created the database and provided the credentials for accessing it, you are ready to begin 1) making a bundle enterprise-ready or 2) manually installing Liferay on your application server.

Turning a Bundle into an Enterprise Portal

Liferay Portal is distributed with the following bundle options for servlet containers and full Java EE application servers:

- Geronimo+Tomcat
- Glassfish
- JBoss+Jetty 4.0
- JBoss+Tomcat 4.0
- JBoss+Tomcat 4.2
- Jetty
- JOnAS+Jetty
- JOnAS+Tomcat
- Pramati
- Resin
- Tomcat 5.5 for JDK 1.4
- Tomcat 5.5 for JDK 5.0
- Tomcat 6.0

Choose your preferred bundle and download it from the downloads page on Liferay's web site. A prerequisite for running any of the bundles is that you have the proper version of Java (1.4 or 1.5) installed on the machine to which you are installing Liferay. Make sure that you have also created the JAVA_HOME variable and have pointed it to your Java installation.

Unzip the bundle to the location from which you are going to run it. For example, you might use c:\apps in Windows or /usr/local/ in Linux or UNIX variants. The default bundle installation of Liferay Portal uses an embedded database. While this is a good method to have it up and running fast for reviewing or developing, it has several drawbacks:

- Only one user can access it at a time. This is because the data is stored on a file on disk and HSQL locks it when doing changes.
- The data is stored inside the application server and might be lost on redeployment.
- This configuration does not scale well and will have performance problems when multiple users are accessing the system.

Obviously, you do not want to be running Liferay against the embedded database. Fortunately, Liferay has great support for a good number of production-ready databases, and it is easy to configure Liferay to use them. The exact instructions will depend on the application server and database, but can be summarized as:

1. Create the database in your DBMS of choice (see the above section labeled *Database Setup* for further information).
2. Reconfigure the Data Source named LiferayPool in your Application Server or servlet container to point to the recently created database. The bundles by default have this configured to go to the embedded database.
3. Reconfigure the Mail resource to point to the mail server Liferay will use to send notifications.
4. Start Liferay. If your DBAs have given the Create Table permissions to the user ID Liferay will be using to connect to the database, Liferay will create the tables automatically and start. Otherwise, you will have had to prepare the database first by running the appropriate *create* script.

Refer to the manual installation instructions below for further details on configuring the various application servers. There is no difference between the Liferay bundles and the regular distribution archives of the application servers as they are available from their own sites, with the exception that Liferay is pre-installed in them.

Further Configuration

The configuration in the bundle is set to connect to a mail server installed on the same machine as the application server (referred to as localhost in the configuration). It also assumes that certain paths are present in the system. You will likely need to customize these settings for your particular environment. We will go over these settings in Chapter Two.

Installing Liferay on an Existing Application Server

This section contains detailed instructions for installing Liferay Portal using its WAR distribution. This allows system administrators to deploy Liferay in existing application server installations. It is recommended that you have a good understanding of how to deploy Java EE applications in your application server of choice.

Please note that while Liferay Portal supports a wide rage of databases, for brevity this section assumes MySQL as the database and that the database has already been created. To use other databases, substitute the JDBC driver and URL construct for your database in place of the MySQL ones shown here. We also assume your application server is already installed and running successfully. If you still need to install your application server, please follow your vendor's instructions first.

The following instructions assume an installation on a local machine. When installing to a remote server, substitute *localhost* with the host name or IP of the server.

> **Tip:** Note that Liferay 5.x *requires* JDK 1.5 or greater. Do not attempt to install Liferay 5.x on an application server that runs under Java 1.4 or lower; it will not work. If you are running an application server that ships with a JDK and that JDK is 1.4 or lower, you will need to upgrade your application server in order to user Liferay 5.x. Liferay 4.x, however, will run fine on these application servers.

Geronimo 1.1 with Tomcat 5.0.28/5.5.17

1. Download and install Geronimo/Tomcat into your preferred directory. From now on, the directory where you installed Geronimo will be referred to as GERONIMO_HOME.
2. Download and install JDK 5. Set an environment variable called JAVA_HOME to point to your JDK directory.
3. Download the WAR for the latest available version of Liferay Portal.
4. Edit *GERONIMO_HOME\bin\geronimo.bat* (Windows) or *geronimo.sh* (Linux). Insert at approximately line 219:

```
set JAVA_OPTS=-Xms128m -Xmx512m -Dfile.encoding=UTF8 -Duser.-
timezone=GMT
```

5. Download the Portal Dependencies.
6. Point browser to *http://localhost:8080/console* to enter Administration Console. Login in as **User:** system and **Password:** manager.
7. Click Common Libs under Services. Click Browse, find portal-kernel.jar and add

   Group: Liferay

   Artifact: Portal-kernel

   Version: enter version number of jar

   Type: Jar

   Click *Install*
8. Repeat the last step for each of the libraries in the dependencies ZIP file.
9. Click *Database Pools* under *Services*. Click *Using the Geronimo database pool* wizard.

   Name of Database Pool: LiferayPool

   Database Type: MySQL

   Click *Next*

   Driver Jar: click Download a Driver and select MySQL Connector/J

   Click *Next*

DB User Name: <none>

DB Password: <none>

Port: 3306 (default)

Host: localhost

Database: lportal

Click *Next*

Click *Test Connection*

Click *Deploy*

10. Click *Deploy New* under *Applications.*

    Archive: Browse for liferay-portal-x.x.x.war (substitute x with the version you've downloaded)

    Click *Install*

11. Click *Web App WARs.*

    Uninstall geronimo/welcome-tomcat/1.1/car

    Start -default/liferayportal/xxxxxxx.../war

12. Open your browser to http://localhost:8080. You should see the default Liferay home page.

Glassfish 2.x

1. Download the latest liferay-portal-x.x.x.war and dependencies.
2. Copy the dependencies .jars into *$GLASSFISH_HOME/domains/domain1/lib*, where *$GLASSFISH_HOME* is the directory where Glassfish is installed.
3. Copy *xercesImpl.jar* and JDBC driver into the same place.
4. Start Glassfish if it hasn't already been started. Go to the Glassfish Administration Console at http://localhost:4848.
5. Default login credentials are **user name:** *admin*; **password:** *adminadmin.*

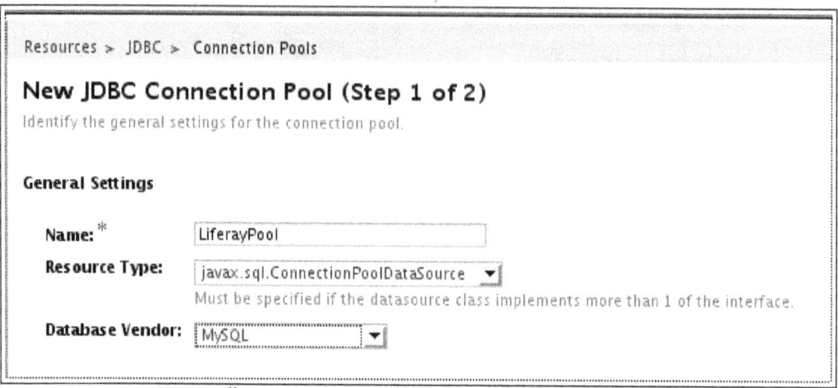

Illustration 6: Glassfish JDBC Connection Pool

6. Under *Other Tasks*, select *Create New JDBC Connection Pool.*

7. In the first screen, give it a name of *LiferayPool*, a Resource Type of *javax.sql.-ConnectionPoolDataSource*, and select *MySQL* as the Database Vendor. Click *Next.*

8. On the next page, scroll down to the *Additional Properties* section. Find the property called *URL*, and set its value to:

```
jdbc:mysql://localhost/lportal?useUnicode=true&amp;characterEncod-
ing=UTF-8&amp;emulateLocators=true
```

   If your database is not on the same server as Glassfish, substitute your database server's host name for *localhost* above.

9. Click *Add Property*, and add a property called *user* with a value of the user name to connect to the database.

10. Click *Add Property* again, and add a property called *password* with a value of the password to connect to the database.

11. Click *Finish.*

12. You will now see a list of Connection Pools. To test your connection, click the *LiferayPool* and click the *Ping* button. If you get a **Ping Succeeded** message, everything has been set up correctly.

13. Click *JDBC Resources*. You will see a list of JDBC Resources by JNDI Name.

14. Click *New.*

15. Make the JNDI Name *jdbc/LiferayPool* and select the LiferayPool you created earlier.

16. Click *OK.*

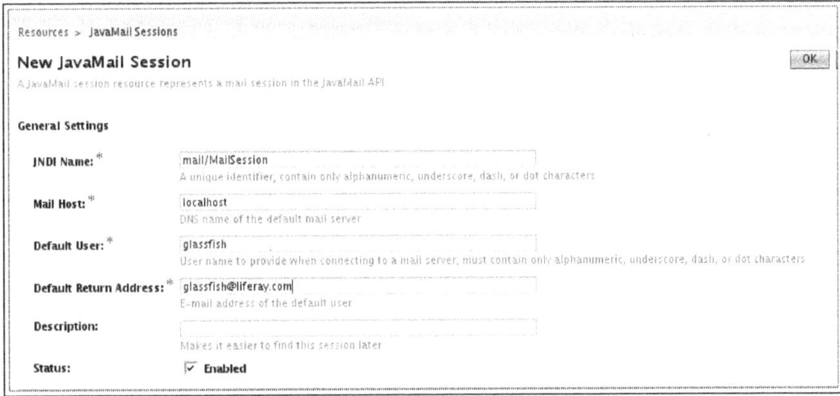

Illustration 7: Glassfish Mail Session

17. Under *Resources*, click *JavaMail Sessions.*
18. Click *New.*
19. Give the JavaMail Session a JNDI name of *mail/MailSession*, and fill out the rest of the form with the appropriate information for your mail server.
20. Click *OK.*
21. Click *Application Server* at the top of the tree hierarchy on the left.
22. Click *JVM Settings -> JVM Options.*
23. Click *Add JVM Option*, and enter the following:

```
-Dcom.sun.enterprise.server.ss.ASQuickStartup=false
```

24. Click *Save.*
25. Log out of the Administration Console and stop Glassfish.
26. Deploy Liferay by copying the liferay-portal-x.x.x.war file you downloaded in step 1 into the *$GLASSFISH_HOME/domains/domain1/autodeploy* directory.
27. Start Glassfish. When Liferay finishes starting, open http://localhost:8080 in your browser. You should see the default Liferay home page.

Jetty 5.1.1

1. Download and install Jetty 5.1.10-all.zip.

   Note: Only this version of Jetty is supported by Liferay. Others may work but will not be covered in this documentation. From now on the home directory where you installed Jetty will be called $JETTY_HOME.

2. Download liferay-portal-x.x.x.war.
3. Download Liferay Portal Dependencies.
4. Create a *$JETTY_HOME/lib/ext* directory and copy unzip the dependencies in it.

5. Edit *$JETTY_HOME/extra/etc/start-plus.config*.

```
$(jetty.home)/lib/ext/
$(jetty.home)/lib/ext/*
```

6. Create a data source bound to *jdbc/LiferayPool* by editing *$JETTY_HOME/etc/jetty.xml*.

```
<Call name="addService">
        <Arg>
                <New  class="org.mortbay.jetty.plus.JotmService">
                        <Set  name="Name">TransactionMgr</Set>
                        <Call  name="addDataSource">
                                <Arg>jdbc/LiferayPool</Arg>
                                <Arg>
                                        <New  class="org.enhydra.jd-
bc.standard.StandardXADataSource">
                                                <Set  name="Driver-
Name">com.mysql.jdbc.Driver</Set>
<Set name="Url">jdbc:mysql://localhost/lportal?
useUnicode=true&amp;characterEncoding=UTF-8</Set>
                                                <Set  name="User"></
Set>
                                                <Set  name="Pass-
word"></Set>
                                        </New>
                                </Arg>
                                <Arg>
                                        <New  class="org.enhydra.jd-
bc.pool.StandardXAPoolDataSource">
                                                <Arg
type="Integer">4</Arg>
                                                <Set
name="MinSize">4</Set>
                                                <Set
name="MaxSize">15</Set>
                                        </New>
                                </Arg>
                        </Call>
                </New>
        </Arg>
</Call>
```

7. Download *mysql-connector-java-{$version}-bin.jar* and copy to to *$JETTY_HOME/lib/ext*. This is the JDBC driver for MySQL. If you are using a different database, copy the appropriate driver.

8. Create a mail session bound to *mail/MailSession* by editing *$JETTY_HOME/etc/jetty.xml*:

```
<Call name="addService">
<Arg>
<New  class="org.mortbay.jetty.plus.MailService">
<Set  name="Name">MailService</Set>
```

```
<Set namc="JNDI">mail/MailSession</Set>
<Put name="mail.smtp.host">localhost</Put>
</New>
</Arg>
</Call>
```

9. Create *$JETTY_HOME/etc/jaas.config.*

```
PortalRealm {
com.liferay.portal.kernel.security.jaas.PortalLoginModule required;
};
```

10. Create directory *$JETTY_HOME/webapps/root* and unpack *liferay-portal-4.3.x.war* into it.

11. Go to *$JETTY_HOME/webapps/root/WEB-INF/lib* and delete *xercesImpl.jar* and *xml-apis.jar*.

15. Copy *$JETTY_HOME/webapps/root/WEB-INF/lib/commons-logging.jar* to *$JETTY_HOME/ext* (overwriting existing one).

16. Create batch file.

    1. Create a directory *$JETTY_HOME/bin.*

    2. Create *run.bat* (Note, this is for Windows platform. For other platforms, configure accordingly).

```
@echo off

if "" == "%JAVA_HOME%" goto errorJavaHome

%JAVA_HOME%/bin/java -Xmx512m -Dfile.encoding=UTF8 -Duser.timezone=GMT -
Djava.security.auth.login.config=../etc/jaas.config
-DSTART=../extra/etc/start-plus.config -jar ../start.jar ../etc/jetty.xml

goto end

:errorJavaHome
echo JAVA_HOME not defined.

goto end

:end
```

Note: If you get a java.lang.OutOfMemoryError exception while starting up Jetty, give your JVM more memory by setting *-Xmx512m*.

Start Liferay by running *run.bat*. Open your browser to http://localhost:8080. You should see the default Liferay home page.

JBoss 4.03sp1/4.04/4.05 with Jetty 5.1.1

1. Download and install Jboss AS into your preferred directory. This directory will be referred to below as *$JBOSS_HOME*.

2. Download the latest version of the liferay-portal-x.x.x.war.
3. Create file $JBOSS_HOME/server/default/deploy/liferay-ds.xml with following content:

```
<?xml version="1.0"?>
<datasources>
      <local-tx-datasource>
          <jndi-name>jdbc/LiferayPool</jndi-name>
          <connection-url>
                  jdbc:mysql://localhost/lportal?
useUnicode=true&amp;characterEncoding=UTF-8
          </connection-url>
          <driver-class>com.mysql.jdbc.Driver</driver-class>
          <user-name></user-name>
          <password></password>
          <min-pool-size>0</min-pool-size>
      </local-tx-datasource>
</datasources>
```

4. Go to *$JBOSS_HOME/server/default/lib/*. Download mysql-connector-java-{$version}-bin.jar and copy to this directory. (This is the JDBC connector for MySQL, for other databases, go to appropriate website to download.)
5. Create a database for Liferay. For example:

```
create database lportal character set utf8;
```

   Liferay will automatically create the tables and populate it the first time it starts.

6. Download Liferay's Portal Dependencies. Unzip to *$JBOSS_HOME/server/default/lib*.
7. Set mail properties by replacing the contents of *$JBOSS_HOME/server/default/deploy/mail-service.xml* with:

```
<?xml version="1.0"?>
<server>
<mbean code="org.jboss.mail.MailService" name="jboss:service=MailSession">
<attribute name="JNDIName">mail/MailSession</attribute>
<attribute name="User">nobody</attribute>
<attribute name="Password">password</attribute>
<attribute name="Configuration">
<configuration>
<property name="mail.store.protocol" value="imap" />
<property name="mail.transport.protocol" value="smtp" />
<property name="mail.imap.host" value="localhost" />
<property name="mail.pop3.host" value="localhost" />
<property name="mail.smtp.host" value="localhost" />
</configuration>
</attribute>
</mbean>
```

```
</server>
```

8. Configure JAAS. Edit *$JBOSS_HOME/server/default/conf/login-config.xml* and comment out the entire XML for policy *other* in lines 140-156.

```
<!--<application-policy name = "other">-->
        ...
              <!--<authentication>
                    <login-module  code  =  "org.jboss.securi-
ty.auth.spi.UsersRolesLoginModule"
                          flag  =  "required"  />
              </authentication>
        </application-policy>-->
```

9. Deploy liferay-portal-x.x.x.war.

   1. Create directory *$JBOSS_HOME/server/default/deploy/liferay-portal.war.*

   2. Unzip liferay-portal-x.x.x.war to directory.

   3. Go to *$JBOSS_HOME/server/default/deploy/liferay-portal.war/lib.*

   4. Move dom4j.jar, jaxen.jar to *$JBOSS_HOME/lib.*

   5. Move commons-collections.jar to *$JBOSS_HOME/server/default/lib.*

   6. Remove hibernate3.jar,jboss-hibernate.jar from *$JBOSS_HOME/server/default/lib.*

10. Edit *$JBOSS_HOME/server/default/deploy/jbossjca-service.xml.* Change Debug attribute in line 63 from true to false:

```
<attribute  name="Debug">false</attribute>
```

11. In *$JBOSS/server/default/deploy/jbossws14.sar/META-INF/jboss-service.xml*, comment out the deployer service for JSE and EJB2.1 endpoints (lines 36-40 and lines 45-49).

```
<!--<mbean name="jboss.ws:service=WebServiceDeployerEJB21"
code="org.jboss.ws.server.WebServiceDeployerEJB21">
           <depends-list  optional-attribute-name="Interceptables">
                 <depends-list-element>jboss.ejb:service=EJBDeploy-
er</depends-list-element>
           </depends-list>
     </mbean>-->
```

lines 72-75

```
<!--<mbean name="jboss.ws:service=WebServiceDeployerNestedJSE"
code="org.jboss.ws.server.WebServiceDeployerNestedJSE">
           <depends  optional-attribute-name="MainDeployer"  proxy-
type="attribute">jboss.system:service=MainDeployer</depends>
           <depends>jboss.ws:service=WebServiceDeployerJSE</de-
pends>
     </mbean>-->
```

12. Edit *$JBOSS_HOME/server/default/deploy/jms/jbossmq-destinations-service.xml.* Clear out text between server tags:

```
<?xml version="1.0"?>
<server>
</server>
```

13. Start JBoss. Open your browser to http://localhost:8080. You should see the default Liferay home page.

JBoss 4.03sp1/4.04/4.05/ 4.2 with Tomcat

1. Download and install JBoss AS into your preferred directory. From now on, the directory where you installed JBoss will be referred to as $JBOSS_HOME.
2. Download liferay-portal-x.x.x.war.
3. Edit *$JBOSS_HOME/server/default/deploy/jbossweb-tomcat55.sar/conf/web.xml*. Replace the default servlet (lines 79-91) :

```
<servlet>
            <servlet-name>default</servlet-name>
            <servlet-class>org.apache.catalina.servlets.Default-
Servlet</servlet-class>
            <init-param>
                  <param-name>debug</param-name>
                  <param-value>0</param-value>
            </init-param>
            <init-param>
                  <param-name>listings</param-name>
                  <param-value>true</param-value>
            </init-param>
            <load-on-startup>1</load-on-startup>
      </servlet>
```

with:

```
<servlet>
            <servlet-name>default</servlet-name>
            <servlet-class>org.apache.catalina.servlets.Default-
Servlet</servlet-class>
            <init-param>
                  <param-name>debug</param-name>
                  <param-value>0</param-value>
            </init-param>
            <init-param>
                  <param-name>listings</param-name>
                  <param-value>false</param-value>
            </init-param>
            <init-param>
                  <param-name>input</param-name>
                  <param-value>4096</param-value>
            </init-param>
            <init-param>
                  <param-name>output</param-name>
```

```
                <param-value>4096</param-value>
        </init-param>
        <load-on-startup>1</load-on-startup>
</servlet>
```

4. Create *$JBOSS_HOME/server/default/deploy/liferay-ds.xml* with following content:

```
<datasources>
        <local-tx-datasource>
            <jndi-name>jdbc/LiferayPool</jndi-name>
            <connection-url>
                    jdbc:mysql://localhost/lportal?
useUnicode=true&amp;characterEncoding=UTF-8
            </connection-url>
            <driver-class>com.mysql.jdbc.Driver</driver-class>
            <user-name></user-name>
            <password></password>
            <min-pool-size>0</min-pool-size>
        </local-tx-datasource>
</datasources>
```

5. Go to *$JBOSS_HOME/server/default/lib/*, download mysql-connector-java-{$version}-bin.jar and copy to this directory. This is the JDBC driver for MySQL. If you are using a different database, copy the appropriate driver.

6. Download Liferay's Portal Dependencies. Unzip the downloaded archive into *$JBOSS_HOME/server/default/lib*.

7. Set mail properties by replacing the contents of *$JBOSS_HOME/server/default/deploy/mail-service.xml* with:

```
<?xml version="1.0"?>
<server>
<mbean code="org.jboss.mail.MailService" name="jboss:ser-
vice=MailSession">
<attribute name="JNDIName">mail/MailSession</attribute>
<attribute name="User">nobody</attribute>
<attribute name="Password">password</attribute>
<attribute name="Configuration">
<configuration>
<property name="mail.store.protocol" value="imap" />
<property name="mail.transport.protocol" value="smtp" />
<property name="mail.imap.host" value="localhost" />
<property name="mail.pop3.host" value="localhost" />
<property name="mail.smtp.host" value="localhost" />
</configuration>
</attribute>
</mbean>
</server>
```

8. Configure JAAS. Edit *$JBOSS_HOME/server/default/conf/login-config.xml* and comment out the entire XML for policy other in lines 140-156.

```
<!--<application-policy name = "other">-->
        ...
            <!--<authentication>
                <login-module code = "org.jboss.securi-
ty.auth.spi.UsersRolesLoginModule"
                    flag = "required" />
            </authentication>
        </application-policy>-->
```

9. Deploy liferay-portal-x.x.x.war.
    - Create new directory *$JBOSS_HOME/server/default/deploy/liferay-portal.war.*
    - Unzip liferay-portal-x.x.x.war to directory.
    - Go into *$JBOSS_HOME/server/default/deploy/liferay-portal.war/lib.*
        - Move dom4j.jar, jaxen.jar to *$JBOSS_HOME/lib.*
        - Move commons-collections.jar goes to *$JBOSS_HOME/server/default/lib.*
        - remove hibernate3.jar, jboss-hibernate.jar from *$JBOSS_HOME/server/default/lib.*
10. Edit *$JBOSS_HOME/server/default/deploy/jbossjca-service.xml*. Change the Debug attribute in line 63 from true to false:

```
<attribute name="Debug">false</attribute>
```

11. Edit *$JBOSS_HOME/server/default/deploy/jms/jbossmq-destinations-service.xml.* Clear out text between server tags:

```
<?xml version="1.0"?>
<server>
</server>
```

12. Start JBoss. Open your browser to http://localhost:8080. You should see the default Liferay home page.

Oracle Application Server (OC4J)

These instructions assume you have an installed OC4J container in a folder that will be referred to as *$OC4J_HOME.*

Unzip the dependencies archive (which is downloadable from Liferay's web site) into *$OC4J_HOME/j2ee/home/applib*. If you're using a database other than Oracle, put your JDBC driver here as well.

Shared Libraries

You will first need to create a Shared Library within OC4J that includes Apache's XML parser, which Liferay requires. You may either download this from http://xerces.apache.org or you can retrieve the files *xercesImpl.jar and xml-apis.jar* from the Liferay .war file.

1. Start OC4J. Go to http://<server>:8888/em.
2. Login in with the administrative credentials you used when you installed OC4J (user ID: oc4jadmin, password of your choosing).
3. Click *Administration -> Shared Libraries*.

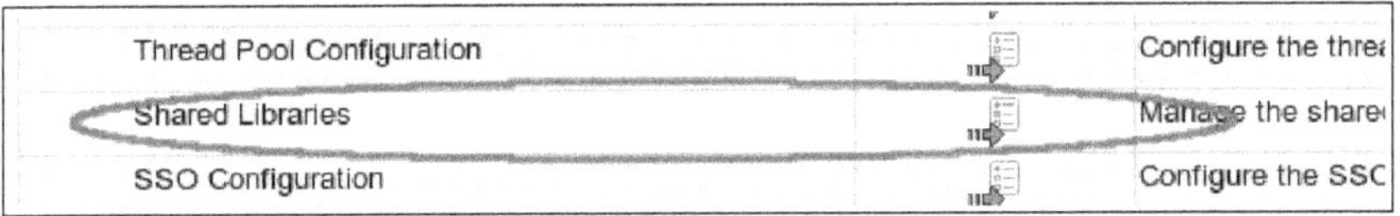

Illustration 8: OC4J Shared Libraries

4. Click the *Create* button. For Shared Library Name, enter *apache.xml* and for Shared Library Version, enter the version number of Xerces that you downloaded. Click *Next*.
5. You will add two archives to this Shared Library: *xercesImpl.jar* and *xml-apis.-jar*. Click the *Add* button and browse to where you expanded your download of Xerces. First, add *xercesImpl.jar*, then click the *Add* button again and add *xml-apis.jar*. Click *Next*.

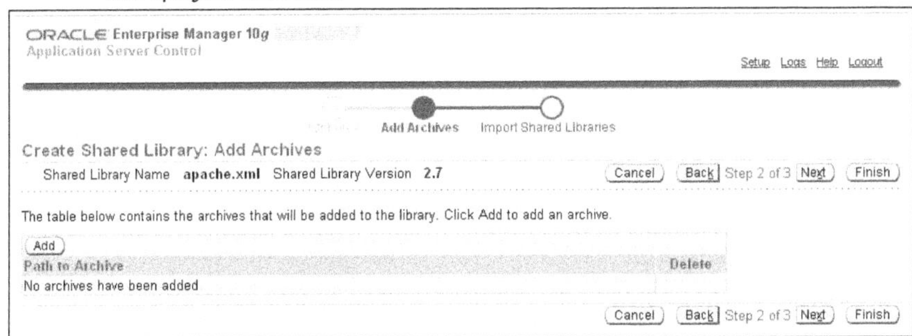

Illustration 9: OC4J: Adding Archives to a Shared Library

6. Click *Finish*. You'll be brought back to the Shared Library page.
7. Next, click the *OC4J: home* link in the top left of the page. This will bring you back to the home page of the OC4J console.

Database and Connection Pool

1. Click *Administration -> JDBC Resources*.

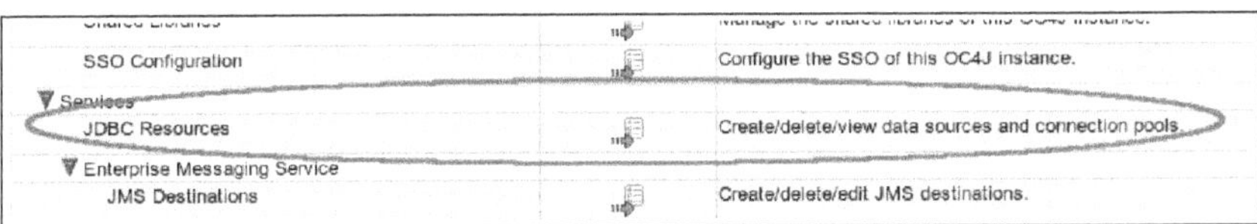

Illustration 10: OC4J: JDBC Resources

2. Under *Connection Pools*, click *Create.*
3. Select *New Connection Pool* and click *Continue.*
4. Give it a name, such as *LiferayPool*. If you are not using an Oracle database,

you will have to specify the connection factory class manually. For example, the connection factory class for MySQL is *com.mysql.jdbc.jdbc2.optional.MysqlConnectionPoolDataSource*.

5. Fill out the JDBC URL to your database. You should have already configured your database and optionally run the Liferay create script.

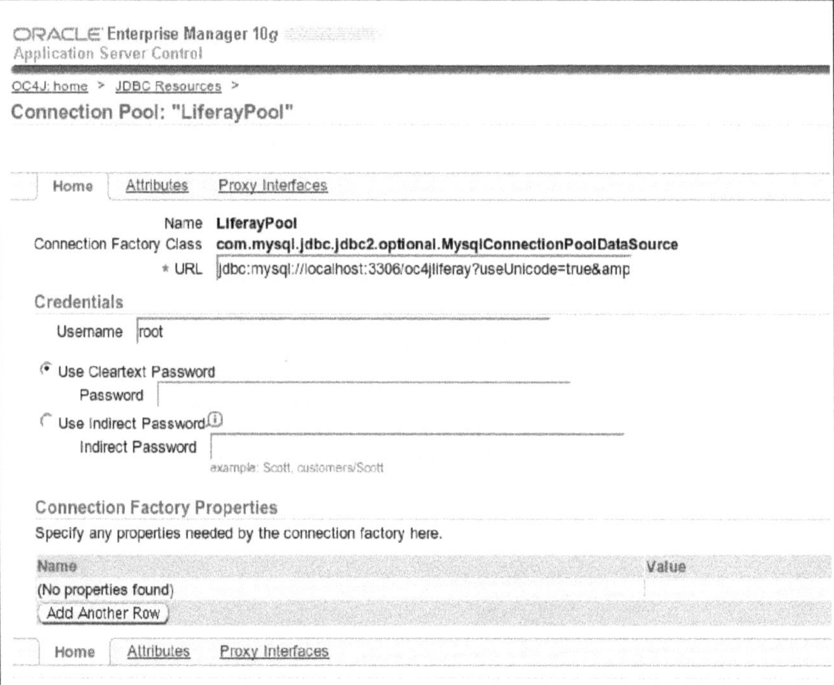

Illustration 11: OC4J: Connection Pool

6. Click *Finish*. Under *Data Sources*, click *Create*. Select *Managed Data Source* (default) and click *Continue*.

7. Give it a name (*LiferayDataSource*) and a JNDI location of *jdbc/LiferayPool*.

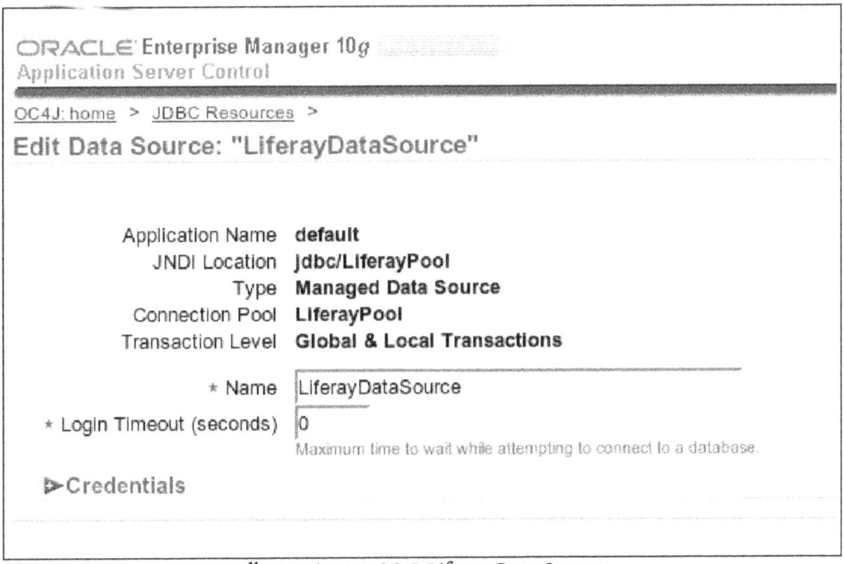

ORACLE Enterprise Manager 10g
Application Server Control

OC4J: home > JDBC Resources >

Edit Data Source: "LiferayDataSource"

Application Name	**default**
JNDI Location	**jdbc/LiferayPool**
Type	**Managed Data Source**
Connection Pool	**LiferayPool**
Transaction Level	**Global & Local Transactions**
* Name	LiferayDataSource
* Login Timeout (seconds)	0 Maximum time to wait while attempting to connect to a database.

▶Credentials

Illustration 12: OC4J: Liferay Data Source

8. Select the Connection Pool you created in the previous step and then click *Finish*.

9. Click the *Test Connection* icon. If you are not using an Oracle database, change the test SQL to something like *SELECT * from User_*, and then click Test. You should get a message saying *Connection to "LiferayDataSource" established successfully*. If not, go back and check your settings.

10. Click the *OC4J: home* link in the top left of the page.

Installing Liferay

1. Click *Applications*.

2. Click *Deploy*. Leave the default selected under Archive, and click the *Browse* button. Browse to where your Liferay .war file is.

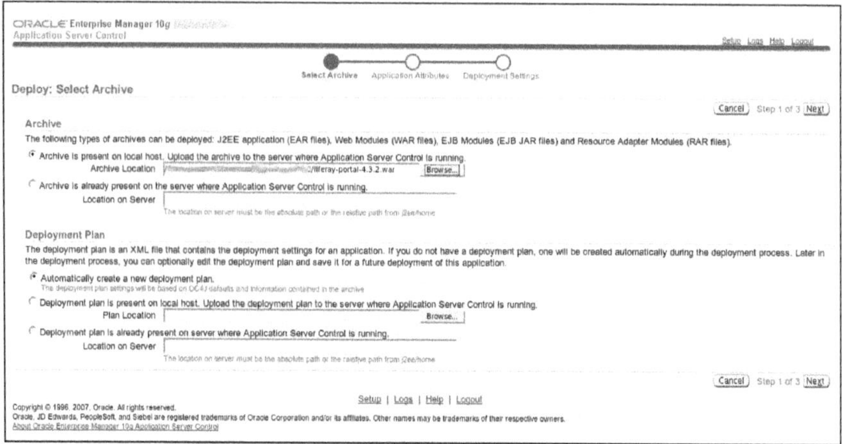

Illustration 13: OC4J: Uploading the Liferay .war file

3. With the location of the Liferay .war file in the Archive Location field, click *Next*. Wait a while while OC4J uploads the Liferay .war file.

4. The next screen allows you to give the application a name and set its context root. Use *Liferay* for the name and */portal* as the context root. Click *Next*.

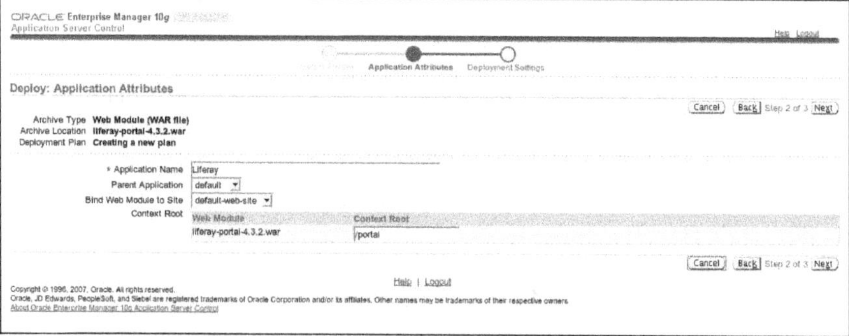

Illustration 14: OC4J: Setting the Context Root

5. On the next screen, click the *Configure Class Loading* Link. You will see a list of all the Shared Libraries currently defined in the server. On this first page, click the *apache.xml* Shared Library that you created previously.

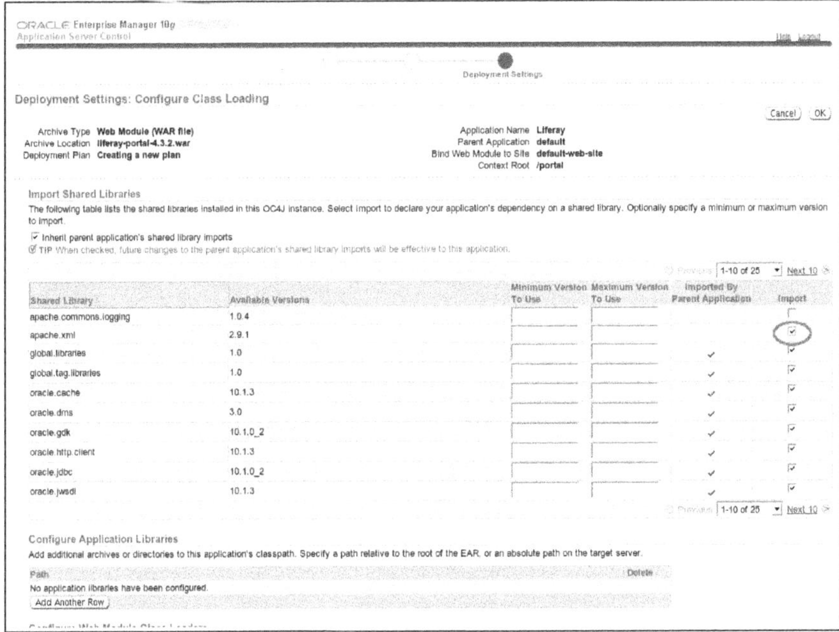

Illustration 15: OC4J: Configure Class Loading

6. Click the *Next 10* link at the bottom right of the page.

7. At the bottom of the next page, there may be an *oracle.xml* Shared Library. It also may appear on another page. If you don't see it, keep clicking the *Next 10* link until you find it. When you do find it, uncheck it.

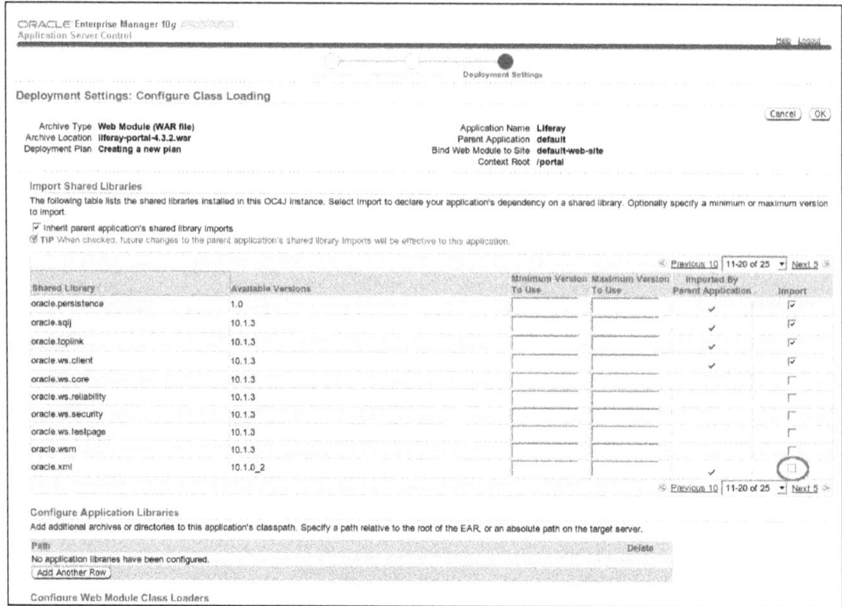

Illustration 16: OC4J: Selecting XML class loading

8. Click the *OK* button at the top of this page. You will be brought back to the previous screen. Click the *Deploy* button at the top right of the screen. OC4J will then deploy Liferay.

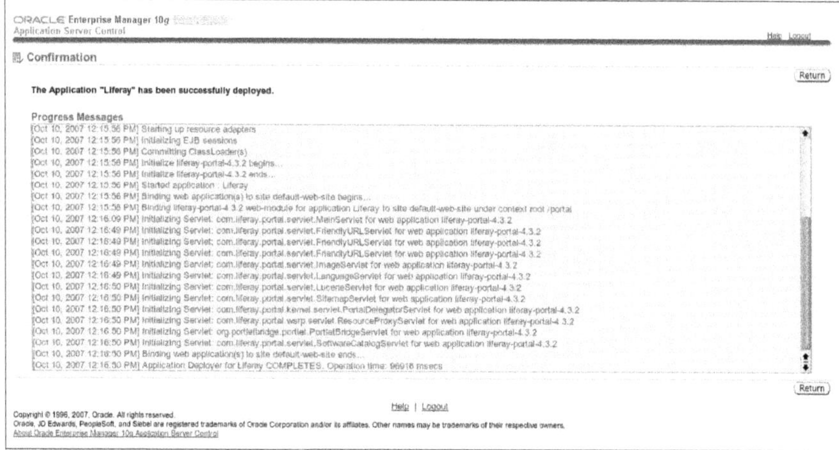

Illustration 17: OC4J: Deploying Liferay

9. Click the *Return* button at the top of the page.

10. Next, navigate to *$OC4J_HOME/j2ee/home/applications/Liferay/liferay-portal-x.x.x/WEB-INF/classes*. In this folder should be a file called *portal-ext.properties*. Open this file in a text editor. Add a directive for Portal Context, and give it a value of /portal, like so:

```
portal.ctx=/portal
```

11. Save this file.

12. Next, stop the OC4J instance to which you just installed Liferay. After it comes down, restart it. You should see Liferay start when the OC4J container starts.

13. You may see some messages stating that there are already some shared libraries on the class path, and that OC4J is going to use the ones it has rather than the ones that came with Liferay. You can remove these message either one of two ways:

    1. Go to *$OC4J_HOME/j2ee/home/applications/Liferay/liferay-portal-x.x.x/WEB-INF/lib* and remove the .jar files that are listed in the messages. Then shut down and restart OC4J.

    2. Create Shared Libraries for each one of the .jar files listed in the messages as you did above for the apache.xml .jars. Once you have done that, you will have to undeploy Liferay and then redeploy Liferay and select the Shared Libraries you have created for it during the deployment.

14. Once you have done one of the two steps above, OC4J should start normally without any messages other than the standard Liferay ones:

```
Starting OC4J from /usr/local/java/oc4j/j2ee/home ...
07/10/10 12:32:39 Loading code-source:/usr/local/java/oc4j/j2ee/home/appli-
cations/Liferay/liferay-portal-4.3.2/WEB-INF/lib/portal-impl.jar!/sys-
tem.properties
07/10/10 12:32:40 Loading code-source:/usr/local/java/oc4j/j2ee/home/appli-
cations/Liferay/liferay-portal-4.3.2/WEB-INF/lib/portal-impl.jar!/por-
tal.properties
07/10/10 12:32:40 Loading file:/usr/local/java/oc4j/j2ee/home/applica-
tions/Liferay/liferay-portal-4.3.2/WEB-INF/classes/portal-ext.properties
07/10/10 12:32:49 Starting Liferay Enterprise Portal 4.3.2 (Owen / Build
4302 / September 18, 2007)
12:32:53,180 INFO  [com.liferay.portal.spring.hibernate.DynamicDialect] De-
termining dialect for MySQL 5
12:32:53,191 INFO  [com.liferay.portal.spring.hibernate.DynamicDialect] Us-
ing dialect org.hibernate.dialect.MySQLDialect
12:32:58,248 INFO  [com.liferay.portal.deploy.hot.PluginPackageHotDeployLis-
tener] Reading plugin package for the root context
12:32:58,941 INFO  [com.liferay.portal.kernel.deploy.hot.HotDeployUtil] Ini-
tializing hot deploy manager 11099528
12:32:59,322 INFO  [com.liferay.portal.kernel.util.ServerDetector] Detected
server oc4j
12:32:59,616 INFO  [com.liferay.portal.kernel.deploy.auto.AutoDeployDir]
Auto deploy scanner started for /home/sezovr/liferay/deploy
07/10/10 12:33:02 Loading code-source:/usr/local/java/oc4j/j2ee/home/appli-
cations/Liferay/liferay-portal-4.3.2/WEB-INF/lib/portal-impl.jar!/por-
tal.properties for 10092
07/10/10 12:33:02 Loading file:/usr/local/java/oc4j/j2ee/home/applica-
tions/Liferay/liferay-portal-4.3.2/WEB-INF/classes/portal-ext.properties for
10092
07/10/10 12:33:03 Oracle Containers for J2EE 10g (10.1.3.3.0)  initialized
```

Resin 3.0.X / 3.1.X

1. Download and install Resin into your preferred directory. From now on, the directory where you installed Resin will be referred to as *$RESIN_HOME*.
2. Edit *$RESIN_HOME/conf/resin.conf*. Replace lines 60-64 with:

```
<class-loader>
            <tree-loader path="${resin.home}/lib"/>
            <tree-loader path="${server.root}/lib"/>
            <compiling-loader path="${server.rootDir}/common/class-
es"/>
            <library-loader path="${server.rootDir}/common/lib"/>
        </class-loader>
```

And add the following:

```
<database>
<jndi-name>jdbc/LiferayPool</jndi-name>
<driver type="com.mysql.jdbc.Driver">
<url>jdbc:mysql://localhost/lportal?useUnicode=true&amp;characterEn-
coding=UTF-8</url>
<user></user>
<password></password>
</driver>
<prepared-statement-cache-size>8</prepared-statement-cache-size>
<max-connections>20</max-connections>
<max-idle-time>30s</max-idle-time>
</database>
<resource jndi-name="mail/MailSession" type="javax.mail.Session">
<init>
<mail.store.protocol>imap</mail.store.protocol>
<mail.transport.protocol>smtp</mail.transport.protocol>
<mail.imap.host>localhost</mail.imap.host>
<mail.pop3.host>localhost</mail.pop3.host>
<mail.smtp.host>localhost</mail.smtp.host>
</init>
</resource>
<system-property
 javax.xml.parsers.DocumentBuilderFactory="org.apache.xerces.jaxp.-
DocumentBuilderFactoryImpl"
 />
<system-property javax.xml.parsers.SAXParserFactory="org.apache.x-
erces.jaxp.SAXParserFactoryImpl" />
<system-property javax.xml.transform.TransformerFactory="org.a-
pache.xalan.processor.TransformerFactoryImpl" />
<system-property org.xml.sax.driver="org.apache.xerces.parsers.SAX-
Parser" />
```

3. Go to *$RESIN_HOME* and create new directory *common/lib*. Download *mysql-connector-java-{$version}-bin .jar* and copy to this directory. (This is the JDBC connector for MySQL, for other databases, go to appropriate website to download.)

4. Create a database for Liferay. For example:

```
create database lportal character set utf8;
```

   Liferay will automatically create the tables and populate it the first time it starts.

5. Download the Liferay Portal Dependencies and unzip into *$RESIN_HOME/common/lib*.

6. Delete contents of *$RESIN_HOME/webapps/ROOT*.

7. Unzip liferay-portal-x.x.x.war to *$RESIN_HOME/webapps/ROOT*.

8. Download the sources of Liferay Portal and unzip them to a temporary directory:

   1. Go to *$LIFERAY_SOURCE/lib/development/* and copy activation.jar and mail.jar to *$RESIN_HOME/common/lib*. Copy saxpath.jar and xalan.jar to *$RESIN_HOME/lib*.

   2. Go to *$LIFERAY_SOURCE/lib/portal* and copy xercesImpl.jar and xml-apis.-jar to *$RESIN_HOME/lib*.

9. To start the server, open a command prompt, navigate to the $RESIN_HOME and type:

```
java -jar lib/resin.jar start
```

10. Open your browser to http://localhost:8080. You should see the default Liferay home page.

Tomcat 5.0.X/5.5.X

1. Download and install Tomcat 5.5.X into your preferred directory. From now on, the directory where you installed Tomcat will be referred to as $TOMCAT_HOME.

   Note: For JDK 5 users: move *$TOMCAT_HOME/webapps/ROOT/WEB-INF/lib/xercesImpl.jar* to *$TOMCAT_HOME/common/endorsed*. JDK 1.4 is no longer supported in Liferay 5.x and above.

2. Create and edit *$TOMCAT_HOME/conf/Catalina/localhost/ROOT.xml* to set up the portal web application.

```
<Context path="">
</Context>
```

3. Download liferay-portal-x.x.x.war.

4. Download Liferay's Portal Dependencies. Create a *$TOMCAT_HOME/common/lib/ext* directory and unzip the dependencies ZIP in there. If the files do not extract to this directory, make sure they are in the correct directory by moving them there.

5. Edit $TOMCAT_HOME/conf/catalina.properties:

```
common.loader=
```

```
        ${catalina.home}/common/classes,\
        ...\
        ${catalina.home}/common/lib/ext/*.jar
```

6. Make sure your database server is installed and is working. If it's installed in a different machine, make sure that it's accessible from the one where Liferay is being installed.

7. Configure data sources for your database. Make sure the JDBC driver for your database is accessible by Tomcat. Obtain the JDBC driver for your version of the database server. In the case of MySQL use *mysql-connector-java-{$version}-bin.jar*. Next, copy the JAR file to *$TOMCAT_HOME/common/lib/ext*.

8. Edit *$TOMCAT_HOME/conf/Catalina/localhost/ROOT.xml*.

```
<Context...>
        <Resource
                name="jdbc/LiferayPool"
                auth="Container"
                type="javax.sql.DataSource"
                driverClassName="com.mysql.jdbc.Driver"
                url="jdbc:mysql://localhost/lportal?
useUnicode=true&amp;characterEncoding=UTF-8"
                username=""
                password=""
                maxActive="100"
                maxIdle="30"
                maxWait="10000"
        />
</Context>
```

9. Be sure to enter the user name and password to your database in the appropriate fields above.

10. Create a mail session bound to *mail/MailSession*. Edit *$TOMCAT_HOME/conf/Catalina/localhost/ROOT.xml* and configure a mail session.

```
<Context...>
<Resource
name="mail/MailSession"
auth="Container"
type="javax.mail.Session"
mail.transport.protocol="smtp"
mail.smtp.host="localhost"
mail.store.protocol="imap"
mail.imap.host="localhost"
/>
</Context>
```

11. Configure JAAS. Edit *$TOMCAT_HOME/conf/Catalina/localhost/ROOT.xml* and configure a security realm.

```
<Context...>
```

```
<Realm
className="org.apache.catalina.realm.JAASRealm"
appName="PortalRealm"
userClassNames="com.liferay.portal.security.jaas.PortalPrincipal"
roleClassNames="com.liferay.portal.security.jaas.PortalRole"
debug="99"
useContextClassLoader="false"
/>
</Context>
```

14. Create *$TOMCAT_HOME/conf/jaas.config.*

```
PortalRealm {
com.liferay.portal.kernel.security.jaas.PortalLoginModule  required;
};
```

15. Edit *$TOMCAT_HOME/bin/catalina.bat* (on Windows) or *$TOMCAT_HOME/bin/catalina.sh* (on Linux / Mac / Unix) so that Tomcat can reference the login module.

```
rem ----- Execute...
set  JAVA_OPTS=-Xms128m  -Xmx512m  -Dfile.encoding=UTF8  -Duser.-
timezone=GMT  -Djava.security.auth.login.config=%CATALINA_HOME
%/conf/jaas.config
```

16. Delete contents *$TOMCAT_HOME/webapps/ROOT* directory. This undeploys the default Tomcat home page.

17. Unpack liferay-portal-x.x.x.war to *$TOMCAT_HOME/webapps/ROOT.*

18. For supporting UTF-8 URI Encoding, edit *$TOMCAT_HOME/conf/server.xml*:

```
<!-- Define a non-SSL HTTP/1.1 Connector on port 8080 -->
      <Connector  port="8080"  maxHttpHeaderSize="8192"
                               maxThreads="150"  minSpareThreads="25"
maxSpareThreads="75"
                               enableLookups="false"
redirectPort="8443"  acceptCount="100"
                               connectionTimeout="20000"  disableU-
ploadTimeout="true"
                               URIEncoding="UTF-8"
      />
```

19. Run Tomcat, point browser to http://localhost:8080. You should see the default Liferay home page.

WebLogic8 sp5

Tip: WebLogic 8 does not support JDK 1.5. You will not be able to install Liferay 5.x and above on WebLogic 8. Liferay 4.x can be installed on WebLogic 8.

Installation

1. Put the necessary global .jars on the server class path. You can do this by creating a lib folder in your domain folder (i.e., *bea/user_projects/domains/mydomain/lib*) and then copying the following .jars into this directory:
    - portal-kernel.jar
    - portal-service.jar
    - portlet.jar
    - database driver (i.e., MySQL) .jar
    - xml-apis.jar and xercesImpl.jar (downloadable from http://xml.apache.org)
2. Inside your domain folder is a *startWebLogic.sh* (Unix) or *startWebLogic.cmd* (Windows) script. Open it and add the following (follow the syntax for your operating system):

```
# Set Liferay classpath
LIFERAY_WL_HOME="/<path to>/bea/user_projects/domains/mydomain/lib"
CLASSPATH="${WEBLOGIC_CLASSPATH}:${POINTBASE_CLASSPATH}:$
{JAVA_HOME}/jre/lib/rt.jar:${WL_HOME}/server/lib/webservices.jar:$
{LIFERAY_WL_HOME}/xercesImpl.jar:${LIFERAY_WL_HOME}/xml-apis.jar:$
{LIFERAY_WL_HOME}/portlet.jar:${LIFERAY_WL_HOME}/portal-kernel.jar:$
{LIFERAY_WL_HOME}/portal-service.jar:${LIFERAY_WL_HOME}/mysql-con-
nector-java-5.0.5-bin.jar"
```

3. Start WebLogic.
4. Open the WebLogic Server Administration Console.
5. Under JDBC, click Connection Pools.
6. Click *Configure a New Connection Pool.*

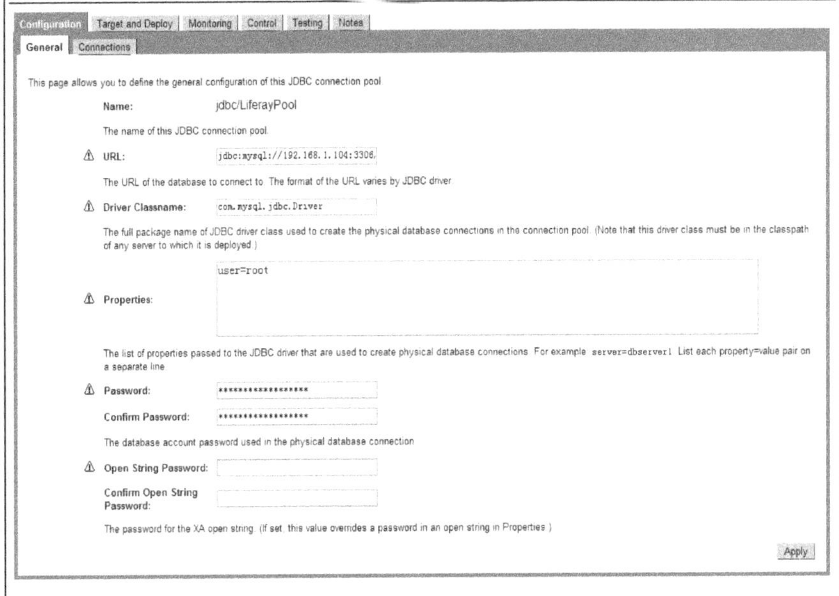

Illustration 18: Connecting to a database in WebLogic 8

7. Select MySQL from the list. Select Other for Driver Type.
8. For the driver class name, use *com.mysql.jdbc.jdbc2.optional.MysqlConnectionPoolDataSource.*
9. For the database URL, use:

```
jdbc:mysql://<your server>/<your db name>?useUnicode=true&amp;char-
acterEncoding=UTF-8
```

10. Use the user name and password you have set up for your database.
11. Click *Test Connection*, and after the connection is successful, click *Create and Deploy*.
12. Under JDBC, click Data Sources.
13. Click Configure a New JDBC Data Source.
14. Enter the name of the data source. The JNDI name should be *jdbc/LiferayPool.*
15. You will be presented with the Connect to Connection Pool screen. Select the Connection Pool you created earlier from the drop down, and click Continue.
16. Select the server to which you want to target this data source, and then click the Create button.
17. Under Deployments, click Web Application Modules.

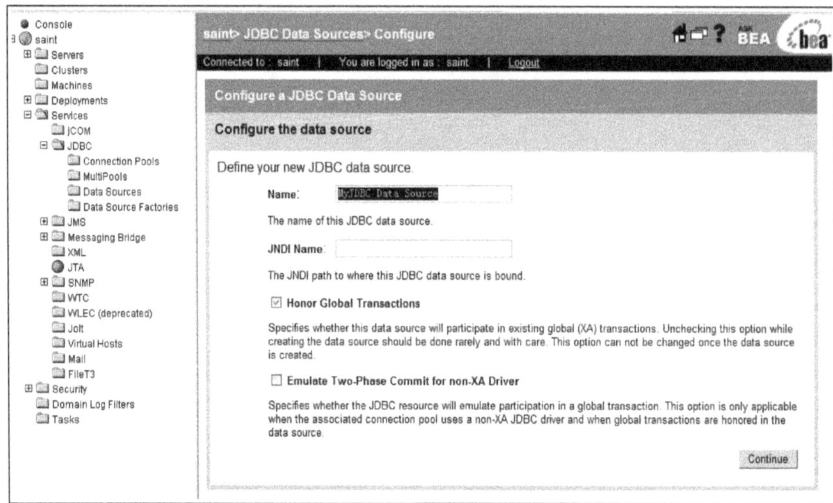

Illustration 19: WebLogic 8 Data Source

18. Click Deploy a New Web Application Module.

19. Select the *Upload Your File(s)* link.

20. Browse to where your Liferay .war file (for WebLogic 8.1, use the Servlet 2.3 .war) is and click the *Upload* button.

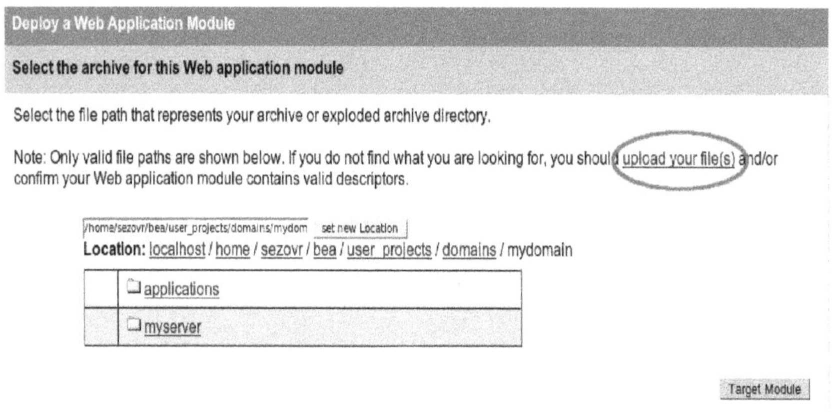

Illustration 20: Uploading the Liferay .war to WebLogic 8

21. Select the Liferay .war you just uploaded and click the Target Module button.

22. Click Deploy.

23. Stop WebLogic and restart it. Point your browser to http://localhost:7001. You should see the default Liferay home page.

Troubleshooting

Weblogic 8 doesn't support JDK1.5 and servlet2.4. Make sure you have deployed the servlet 2.3 version of Liferay.

If a SocialBookmarkTag exception is thrown, add *util-taglib.jar* in your liferay-portal-4.x.x war to your domain's *lib* folder and reference it in the startup script you edited above.

If you can't see the home page, check your *weblogic.xml* for Liferay and make sure the following is set:

```
<context-root>/</context-root>
```

WebLogic 9 / 10

These instructions assume that you have already configured a domain and server, and that you have access to the WebLogic console.

Dependency Jars

1. Navigate to the folder which corresponds to the domain to which you will be installing Liferay. Inside this folder is a *lib* folder. Unzip the Liferay dependencies archive to this folder.
2. Copy the JDBC driver for your database to this folder as well.
3. You will also need the *xercesImpl.jar* or you will get SAX parsing errors after you deploy Liferay. You may download this from http://xerces.apache.org. Copy the *xercesImpl.jar* file into this directory.

Installing Liferay

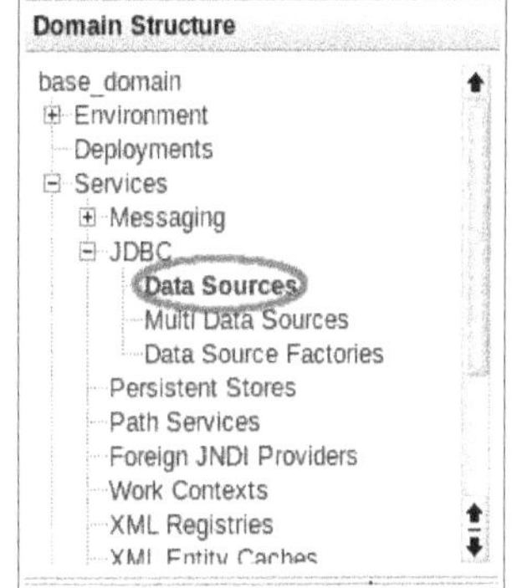

Illustration 21: WebLogic: Data Sources

1. Browse to your WebLogic Console. Click the *Lock & Edit* button above the Domain Structure tree on the left side of the page.
2. From the Domain Structure tree on the left, select Data Sources. Then click the *New* button on the right side of the screen.
3. Give the Data Source a name, such as LiferayDataSource.
4. Define the JNDI name as jdbc/LiferayPool.
5. Select your Database Type and the Driver class, and then click the *Next* button.
6. Accept the defaults on the next screen by clicking *Next*.
7. On the next screen, put in your *Database Name, Host Name, Database User Name,* and *Password.* If you have been following the defaults we have been using so far, you would use *lportal, localhost, root,* and no password as the val-

ues. Click Next.

8. The next screen allows you to test your database configuration. Click the *Test Connection* button. If the test succeeds, you have configured your database correctly. Check off the server you want to deploy this Data Source to (AdminServer is the default). Click Finish.

9. Click the *Activate Changes* button on the left, above the Domain Structure tree.

10. In the Domain Structure tree, select *Mail Sessions.* Then click the *Lock & Edit* button again to enable modifying these settings.

11. Click the *New* button which is now enabled on the right side of the screen.

12. Give the Mail Session a name, such as LiferayMail.

13. Select your new LiferayMail session from the list by clicking on it.

14. On the screen that appears, define the JNDI name as *mail/MailSession.* Click the *Save* button.

15. Click the *Targets* tab. Check off the server you want to deploy this Data Source to (AdminServer is the default).

16. Click the *Activate Changes* button on the left side of the screen, above the Domain Structure tree.

17. Click the *Deployments* option in the Domain Structure tree on the left side of the screen.

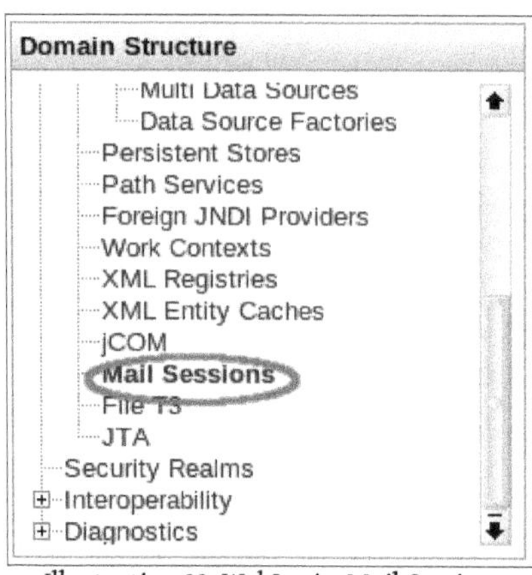

Illustration 22: WebLogic: Mail Sessions

18. Click the *Lock & Edit* button above the Domain Structure tree.

19. Click the *Install* button on the right side of the screen.

20. Click the *Upload your file(s)* link.

21. Browse to where you have stored the Liferay .war file, select it, and then click *Next.*

22. Select the Liferay .war file from the list and click *Next.*

23. Leave *Install this deployment as an application* selected and click Next.

24. Give the application a name (the default name is fine). Leave the other defaults selected and then click Finish.

25. WebLogic will now deploy Liferay. When it is finished, a summary screen is displayed. Click the *Activate Changes* link on the left above the Domain Struc-

ture tree.

26. In the Deployments screen, select the Liferay application and click the *Start* button. Select *Servicing All Requests* in the pop up.

27. Click *Yes* to continue on the next screen.

Liferay will start. You will be able to get to it by browsing to http://<server name>:7001. If your browser is running on the same machine upon which you have installed Liferay, the URL is http://localhost:7001.

WebSphere 6.0.X.X

Tip: WebSphere 6.0 does not support JDK 1.5. You will not be able to install Liferay 5.x and above on WebSphere 6.0. Liferay 4.x can be installed on WebSphere 6.0.

Installation

Tip: Throughout this installation and configuration process, WebSphere will prompt you to Click Save to apply changes to Master Configuration. Do so intermittently to save your changes.

1. Download Liferay Portal WAR file.
2. Download and extract these Liferay jars to *websphere/appserver/lib/ext*.
    - Dependency libraries (Liferay Portal Dependencies)
    - liferay-portal-jaas.jar (Liferay Portal Enterprise JAAS Libraries from Sourceforge)
    - mysql-connector-java-x.x.x-bin.jar (MySQL)

Set Up Database Service

1. Start WebSphere.
2. Open Administrative Console and login.
3. Click *Resources*, click *JDBC Providers*.

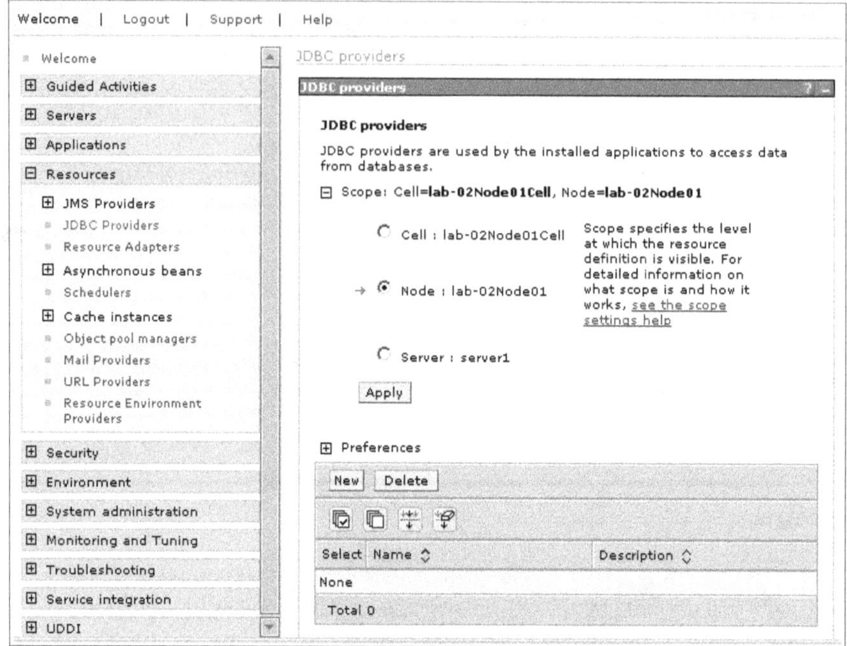

Illustration 23: WebSphere JDBC Providers

4. Click Next.
5. For name, enter name of JDBC provider, e.g. *liferayjdbc*.
6. Clear any text in class path.
7. For Implementation class name enter

```
com.mysql.jdbc.jdbc2.optional.MysqlConnectionPoolDataSource
```

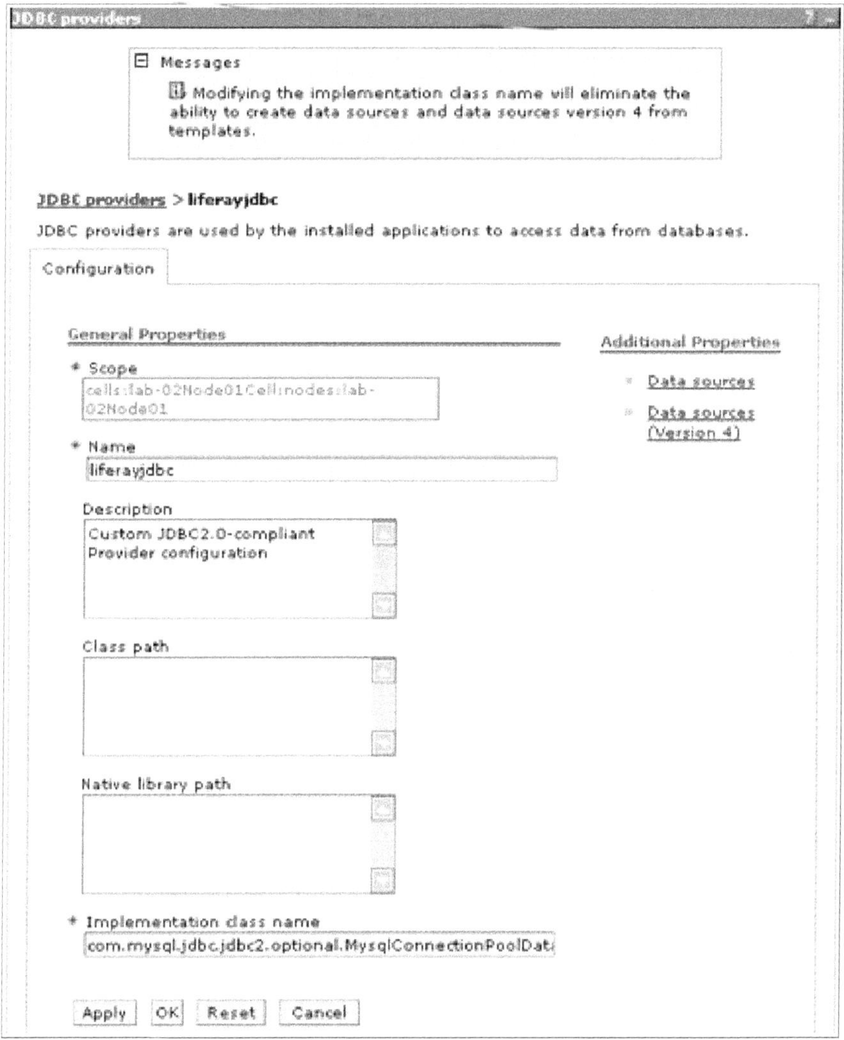

Illustration 24: WebSphere Liferay JDBC Provider

8. Click *OK*.
9. Click *Data sources* under *Additional Properties*.
10. Click *New*.
11. Enter a name: *liferaydatabasesource*.
12. Enter JNDI: *jdbc/LiferayPool*.
13. Everything else should stay at the default values.

14. Click *OK*.

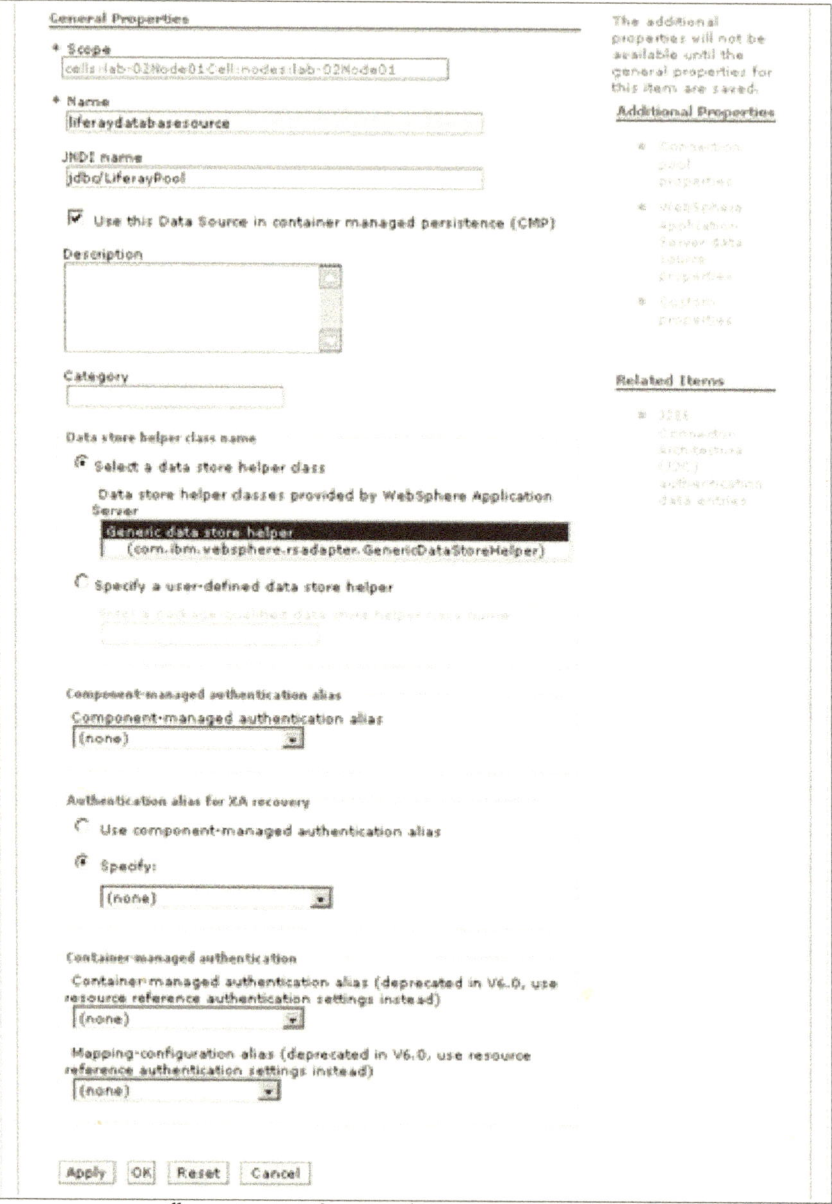

Illustration 25: Liferay Database Resource on WebSphere

15. Under *Additional Properties*, click *Custom properties*.

16. Click *New*.

17. Create three custom properties by entering Name, Value and clicking OK for each row in the following table:

Name	Value
1. user	root
2. serverName	localhost
3. databaseName	lportal

18. When done correctly, custom properties should look like this:

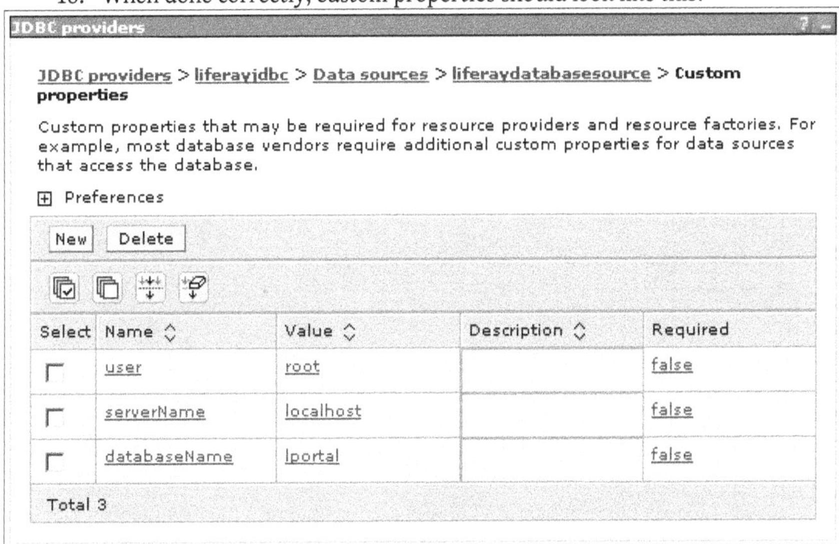
JDBC providers

JDBC providers > liferayjdbc > Data sources > liferaydatabasesource > **Custom properties**

Custom properties that may be required for resource providers and resource factories. For example, most database vendors require additional custom properties for data sources that access the database.

Preferences

New Delete

Select	Name	Value	Description	Required
	user	root		false
	serverName	localhost		false
	databaseName	lportal		false

Total 3

Illustration 26: All of the Liferay Custom Properties

19. Click Data Sources -> Test Connection to test.

Mail Configuration

1. Click *Resources -> Mail Providers.*
2. Click *Built-in Mail Provider.*
3. Click *Mail Sessions.*
4. Click *New.*
    1. **Name:** *liferaymail*
    2. **JNDI name:** *mail/MailSession*
5. Leave the other fields as they are and click *OK.*
6. Click *Security.*

7. Click *Global Security.*

8. Select *Enable Global Security.*

9. Deselect *Enforce Java 2 Security.*

10. In *Active User Registry*, select *Custom User Registry.*

11. Click *Apply* to go to Custom user registry page.

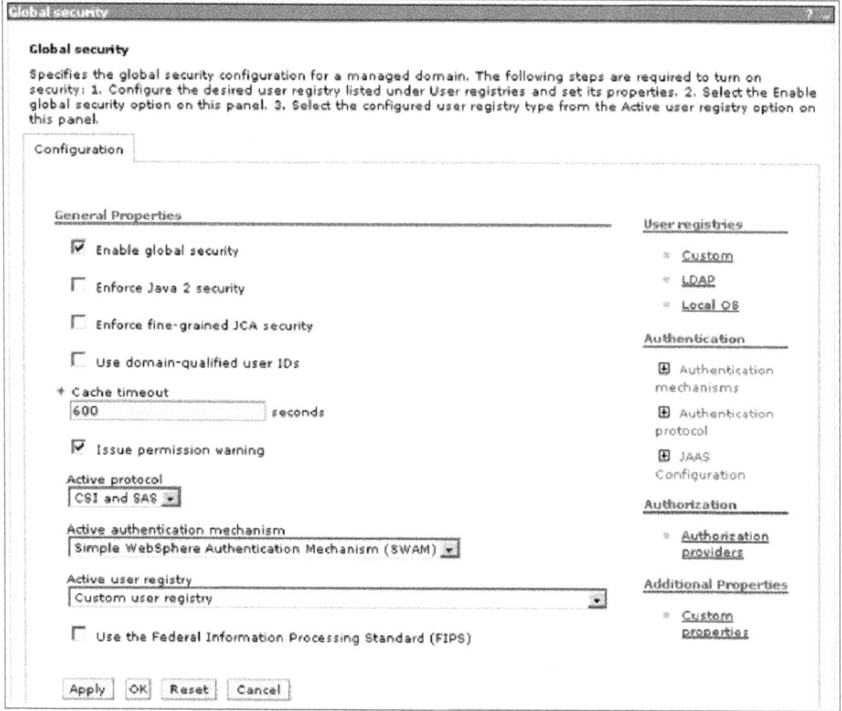

Illustration 27: WebSphere Global Security Settings

12. Enter *system* for server user ID.

13. Enter *password* for server user password.

14. Enter Custom registry class name *com.liferay.portal.security.jaas.ext.websphere.-PortalUserRegistry.*

15. Click *Apply.*

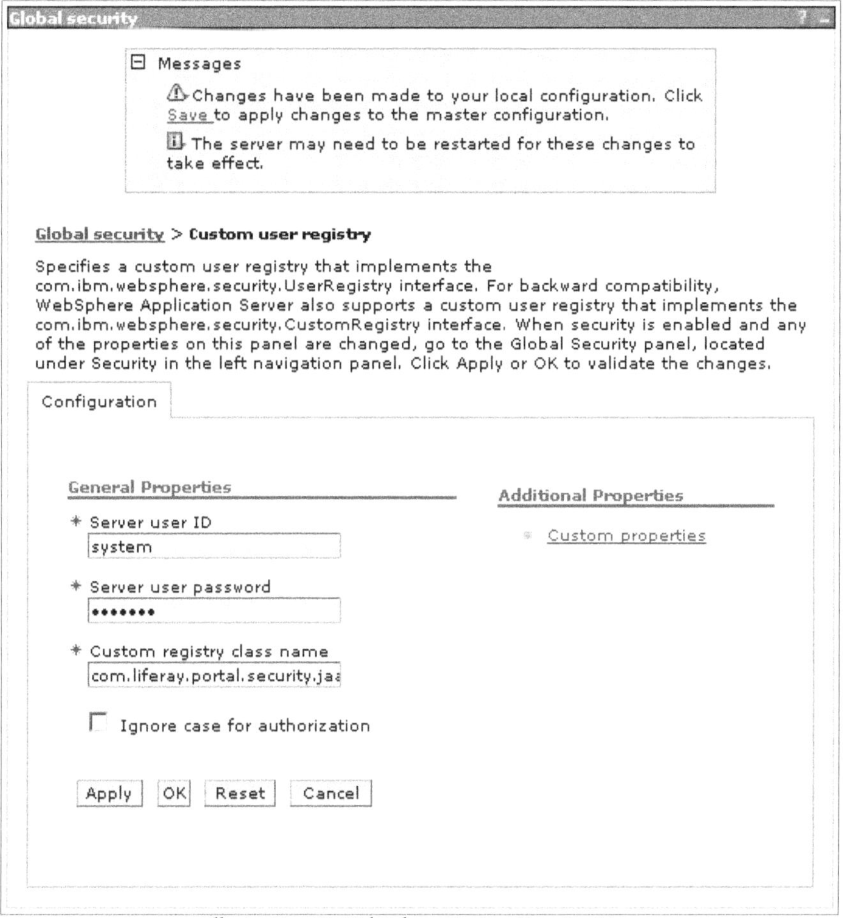

Illustration 28: WebSphere Custom User Registry

16. Insert user name/password into database:
    1. Open a MySQL console.
    2. Log in and select the Liferay database by typing *use lportal;*
    3. Enter the following SQL command:

```
Insert into User_ (companyId, userId, password_) values ('sys-
tem', 'system', 'password');
```

```
C:\WINDOWS\system32\cmd.exe - mysql
C:\>
C:\>
C:\>
C:\>
C:\>
C:\>
C:\>
C:\>
C:\>
C:\>
C:\>
C:\>
C:\>mysql
Welcome to the MySQL monitor.  Commands end with ; or \g.
Your MySQL connection id is 15 to server version: 4.1.20-community-nt

Type 'help;' or '\h' for help. Type '\c' to clear the buffer.

mysql> use lportal
Database changed
mysql> insert into User_ (companyId, userId, password_) values ('system', 'syste
m', 'password');
Query OK, 1 row affected (0.03 sec)

mysql>
```

Illustration 29: Insert Custom User Manually into Database

Install Liferay

1. Click *Applications -> Install New Application.*
2. Browse for liferay-portal-x.x.x.war.
3. Enter context root /.

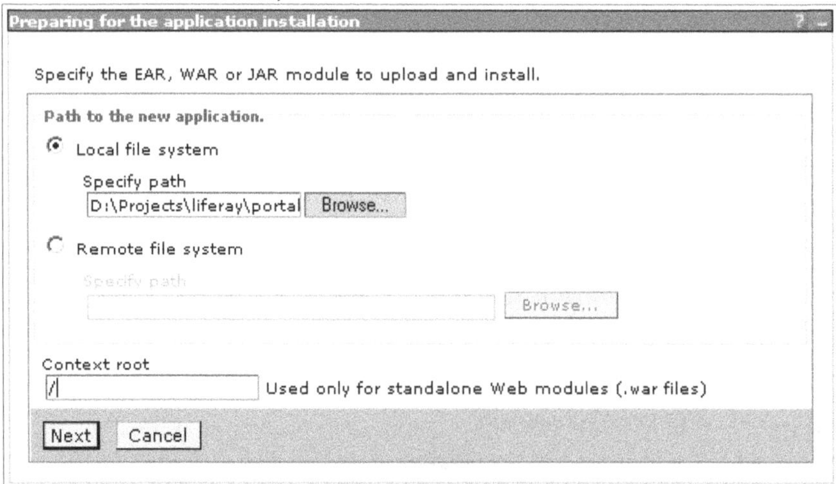

Illustration 30: Installing the Liferay .war file on WebSphere

4. Click *Next*
5. Select *Generate Default Bindings -> Override default bindings -> Use default virtual host name for web modules.*

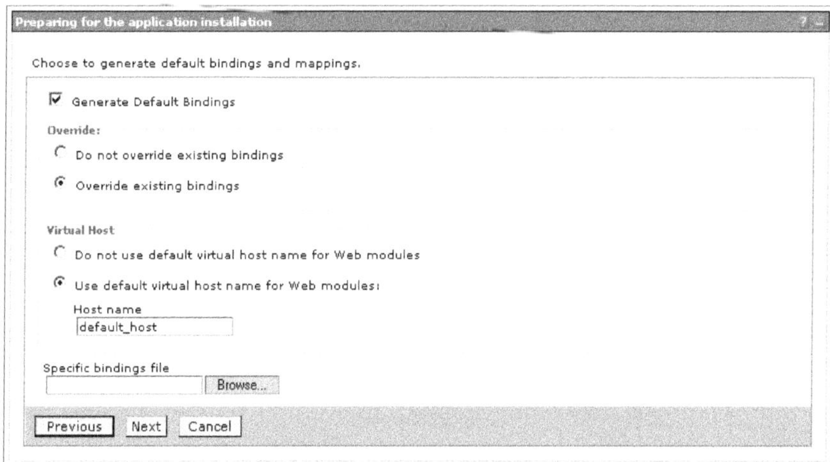

Illustration 31: Binding Liferay

6. Click *Next*. Click *Continue*. For Steps 1 to 4, click *Next* to apply defaults.

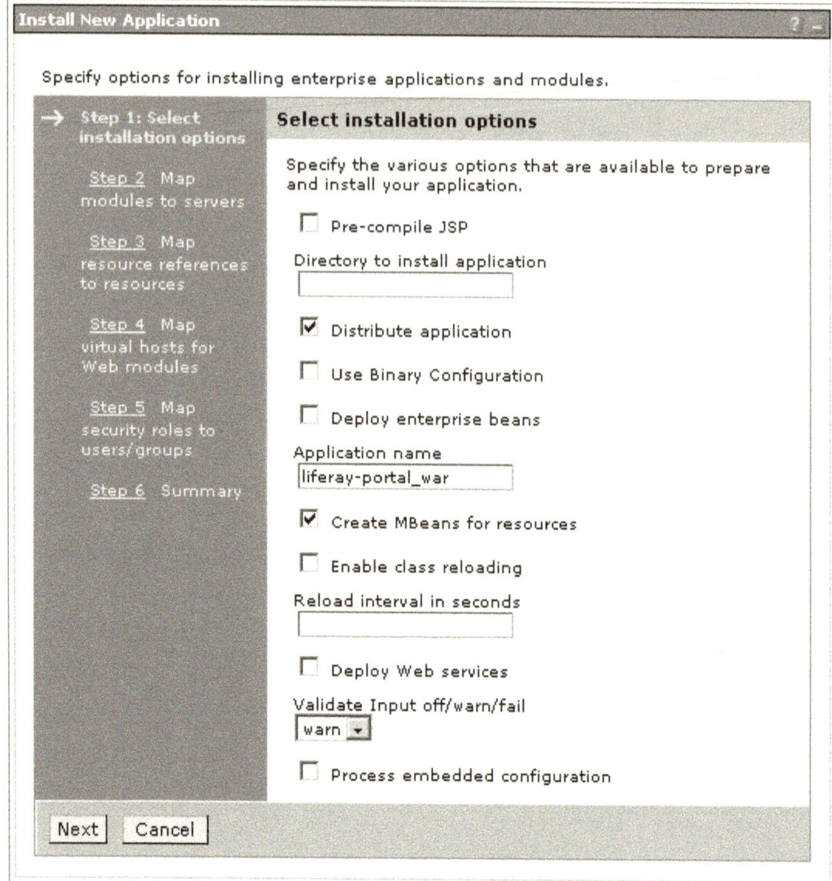

Illustration 32: The WebSphere Install wizard

7. In Step 5, check *all authenticated.*

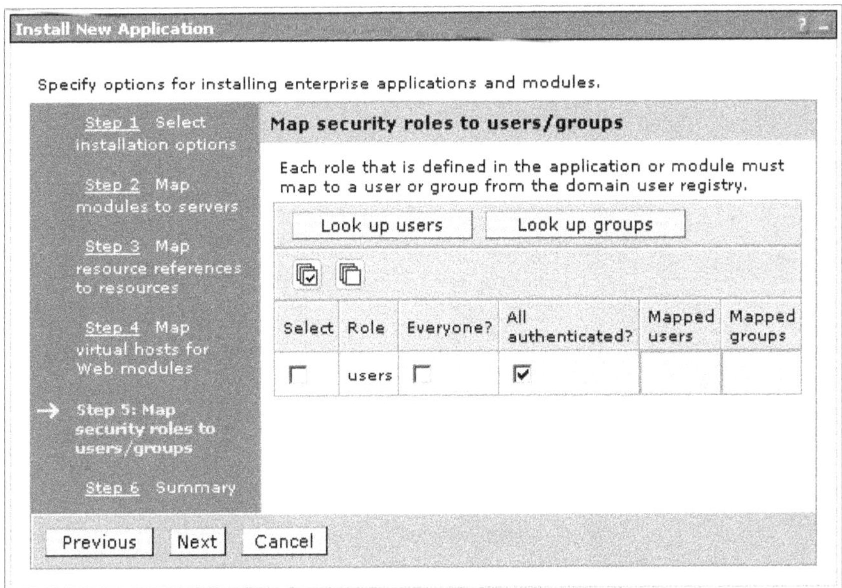

Illustration 33: Mapping Security Roles in WebSphere

8. Click *Next*.

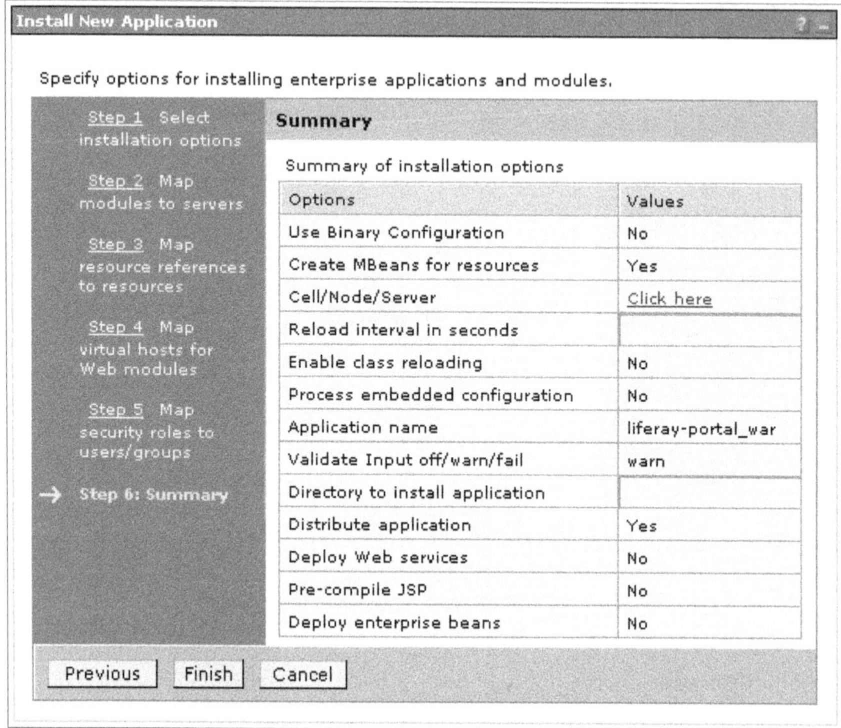

Illustration 34: Completing the installation wizard

9. Click *Finish*.
10. Wait for installation process.

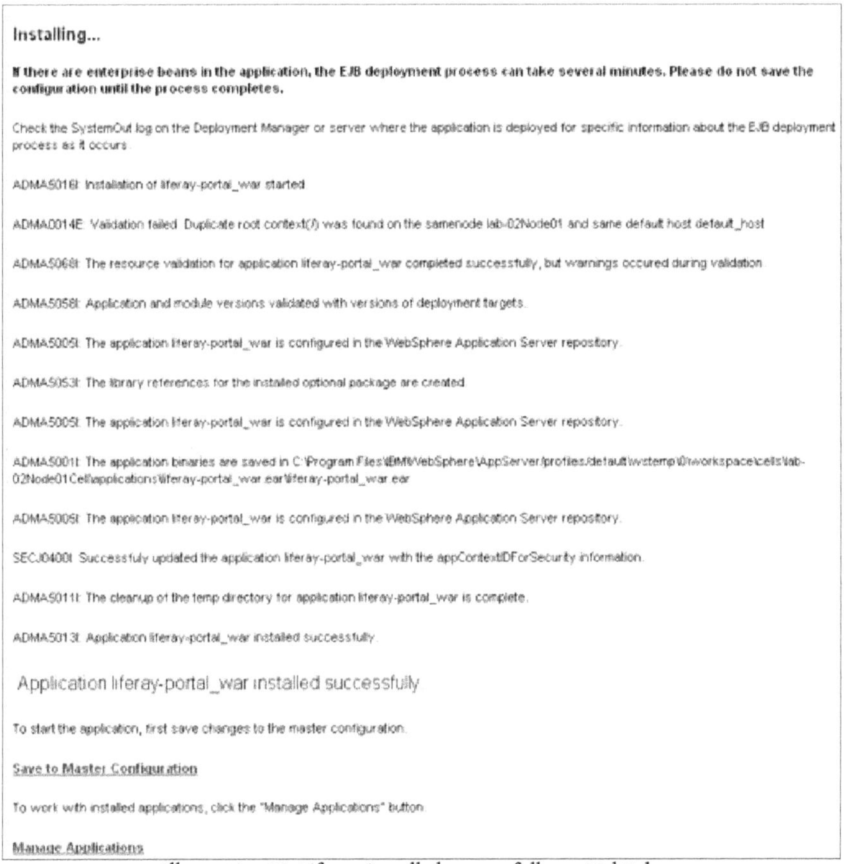

Installing...

If there are enterprise beans in the application, the EJB deployment process can take several minutes. Please do not save the configuration until the process completes.

Check the SystemOut log on the Deployment Manager or server where the application is deployed for specific information about the EJB deployment process as it occurs.

ADMA5016I: Installation of liferay-portal_war started.

ADMA0014E: Validation failed. Duplicate root context(/) was found on the samenode lab-02Node01 and same default host default_host

ADMA5068I: The resource validation for application liferay-portal_war completed successfully, but warnings occured during validation.

ADMA5058I: Application and module versions validated with versions of deployment targets.

ADMA5005I: The application liferay-portal_war is configured in the WebSphere Application Server repository.

ADMA5053I: The library references for the installed optional package are created.

ADMA5005I: The application liferay-portal_war is configured in the WebSphere Application Server repository.

ADMA5001I: The application binaries are saved in C:\Program Files\IBM\WebSphere\AppServer/profiles/default\wstemp\0\workspace\cells\lab-02Node01Cell\applications\liferay-portal_war.ear\liferay-portal_war.ear

ADMA5005I: The application liferay-portal_war is configured in the WebSphere Application Server repository.

SECJ0400I: Successfuly updated the application liferay-portal_war with the appContextIDForSecurity information.

ADMA5011I: The cleanup of the temp directory for application liferay-portal_war is complete.

ADMA5013I: Application liferay-portal_war installed successfully.

Application liferay-portal_war installed successfully.

To start the application, first save changes to the master configuration.

Save to Master Configuration

To work with installed applications, click the "Manage Applications" button.

Manage Applications

Illustration 35: Liferay installed successfully on WebSphere

11. Save this configuration to master configuration by clicking on *System administration* and *Save Changes to Master Repository*.

Start Liferay Portal

1. Click *Applications.*
2. Click *Enterprise Applications.*

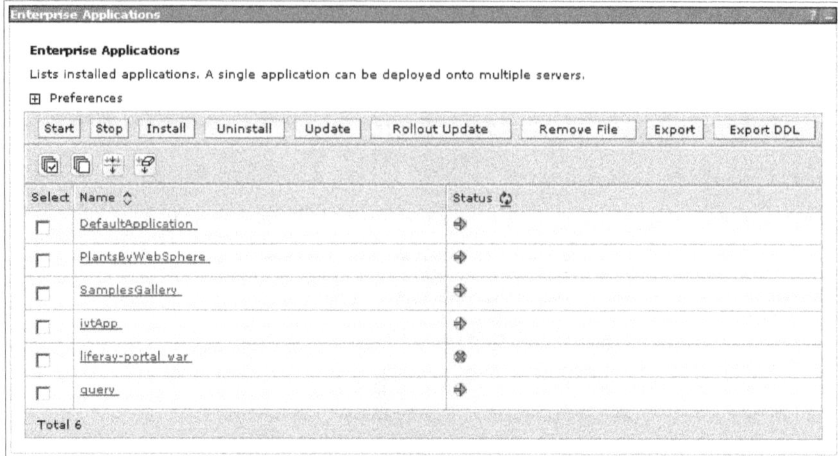

Illustration 36: Starting Liferay on WebSphere

3. Uninstall *DefaultApplication*, *PlantsByWebSphere* and *SamplesGallery*.
4. Select liferay-portal.war and click *Start*.
5. Open up browser and point to http://localhost:9080. You should see the default Liferay home page.
6. If you are running Windows, edit your Stop the Server shortcut to set the user id and password. If you don't do this, you will not be able to stop the server after you restart WebSphere:

```
"C:\Program Files\WebSphere\AppServer\bin\stopServer.bat" server1
-user system -password password
```

7. Stop WebSphere and restart it. Login on with *system* for user name and *password* for password.

WebSphere 6.1

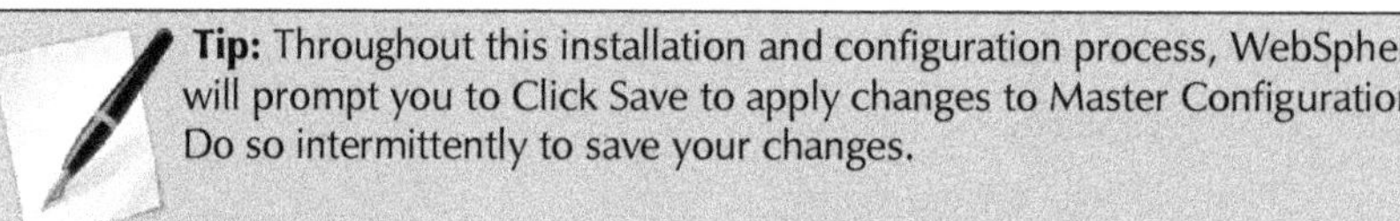

Tip: Throughout this installation and configuration process, WebSphere will prompt you to Click Save to apply changes to Master Configuration. Do so intermittently to save your changes.

Installation

1. Download the Liferay Portal WAR file.
2. Download and extract these Liferay jars to *websphere/appserver/lib/ext*.
   - Dependency libraries (Liferay Portal Dependencies)

- Currently you also need to copy *portlet.jar* from the Liferay Dependencies archive and *icu4j.jar* from the Liferay WAR file into *WebSphere/AppServer/java/lib/ext*, as WebSphere already contains older versions of these .jar files which must be overridden at the highest level of the class path. This issue may be fixed in future releases; check the Liferay Wiki for updates to this issue.
- mysql-connector-java-x.x.x-bin.jar (MySQL)

Set Up Database Service

1. Start WebSphere.
2. Open Administrative Console and login.
3. Click *Resources*, click *JDBC Providers*.

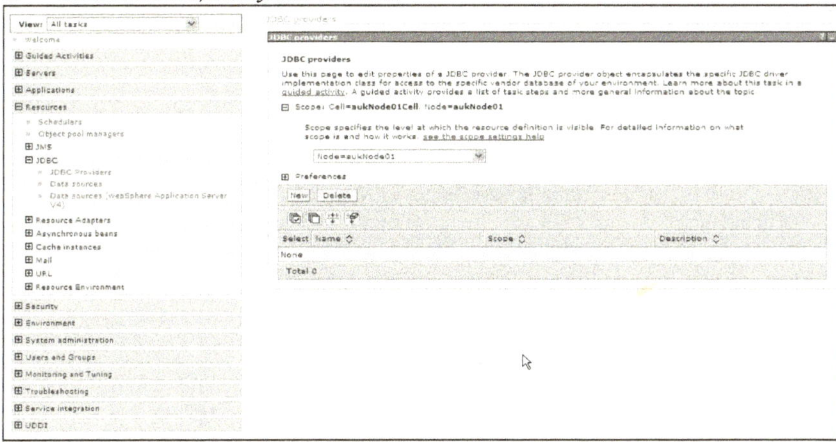

Illustration 37: WebSphere 6.1 JDBC Providers

4. Click *New*.
5. For name, enter name of JDBC provider, e.g. MySQL Jdbc Provider.
6. For Implementation class name, enter:

```
com.mysql.jdbc.jdbc2.optional.MysqlConnectionPoolDataSource
```

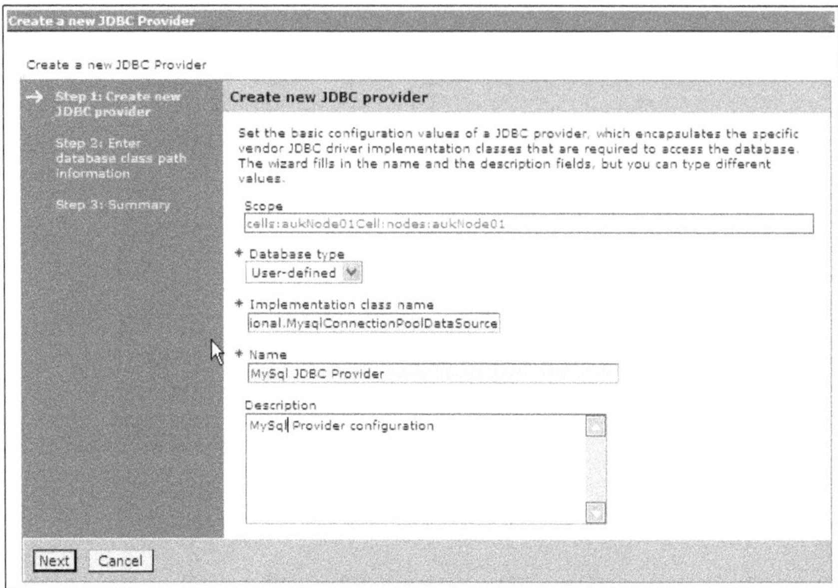

Illustration 38: WebSphere 6.1 New JDBC Provider

7. Click *Next.*

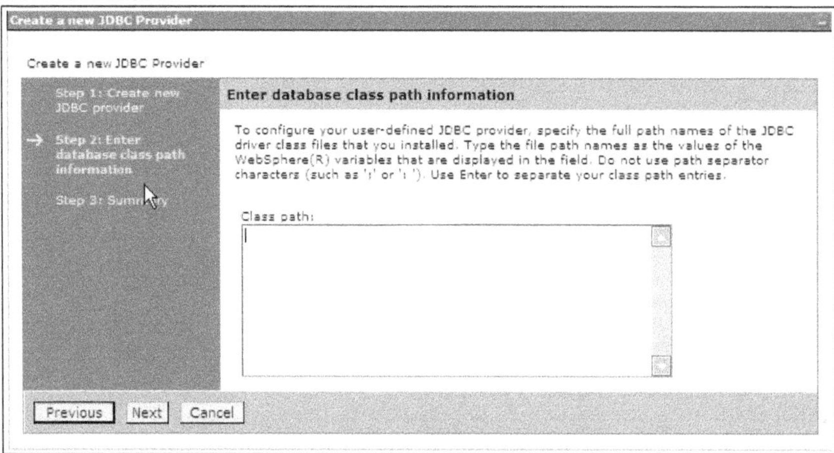

Illustration 39: Clear out anything in the class path.

8. Clear any text in class path. You already copied the necessary .jars to a location on the server's class path.

9. Click *Next.*

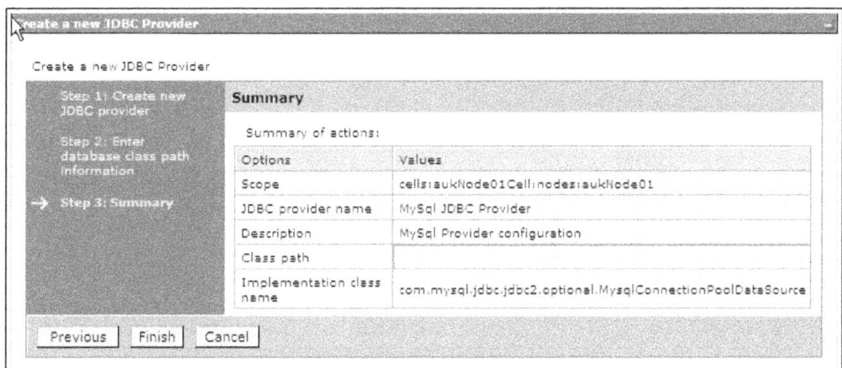

Illustration 40: JDBC Provider summary screen

10. Click *Finish.*
11. Click *Data Sources* under *Additional Properties.*
12. Click *New.*
13. Enter a name: *liferaydatabasesource.*
14. Enter JNDI: *jdbc/LiferayPool.*
15. Everything else should stay at the default values.

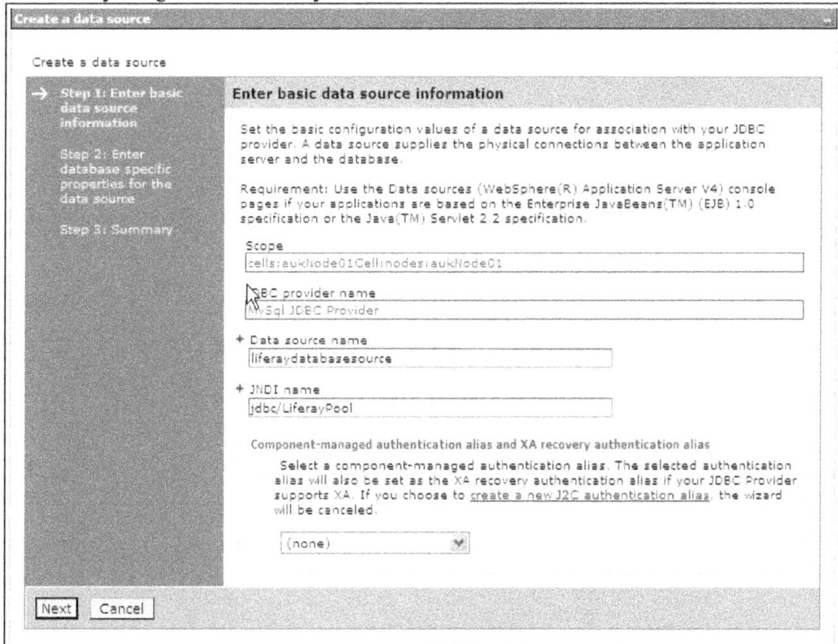

Illustration 41: Liferay data source on WebSphere 6.1

16. Click *Next.*

17. Under *Additional Properties*, click *Custom Properties.*
18. Click *New.*
19. Create three custom properties by entering Name, Value and clicking OK for each row in the following table.

Name	Value
1. user	root
2. serverName	localhost
3. databaseName	lportal

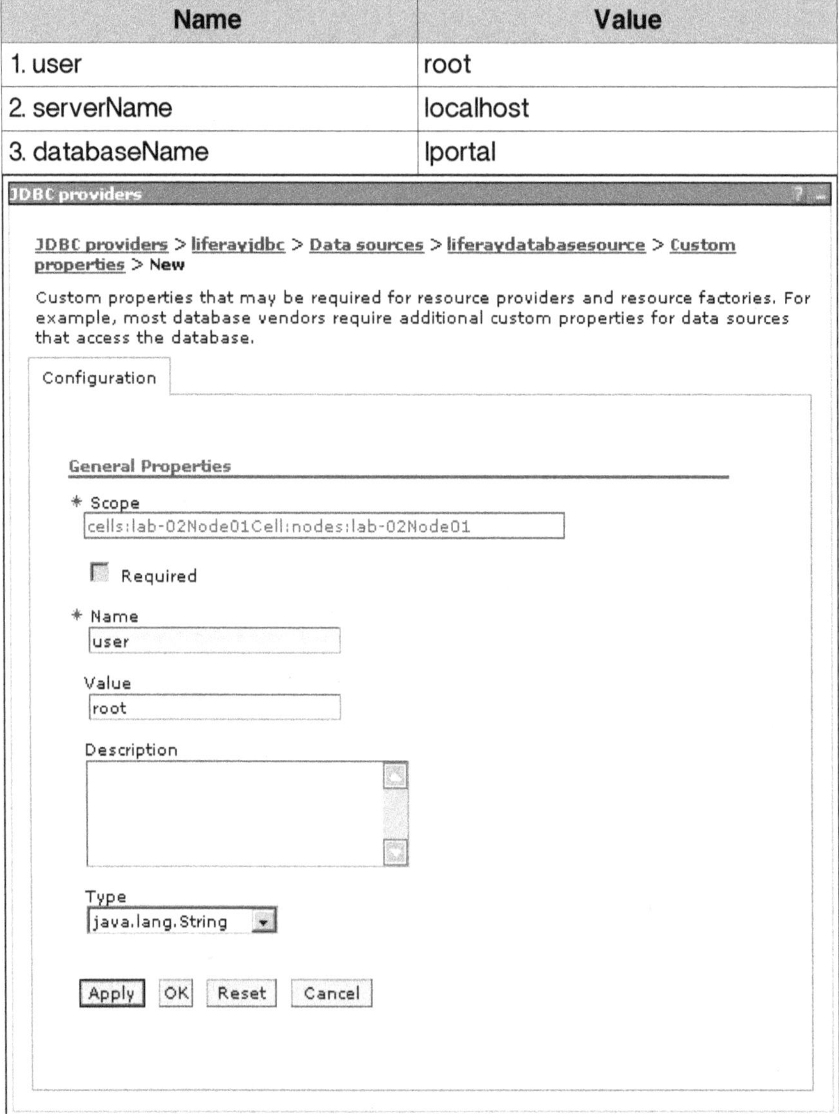

Illustration 42: WebSphere 6.1 Custom Properties Entry

20. When done correctly, custom properties should look like this:

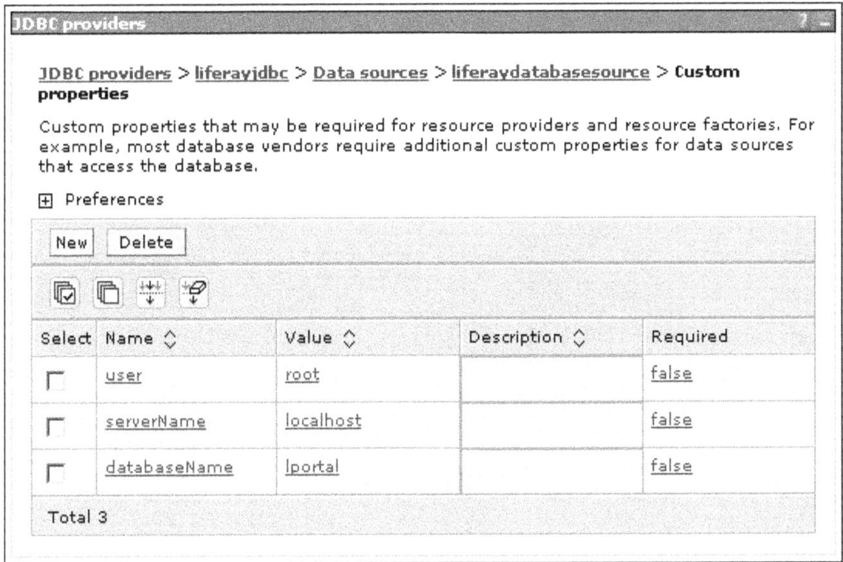

Illustration 43: Liferay Custom Properties

21. Click *Data Sources -> Test Connection* to test.

Mail Configuration

1. Click *Resources -> Mail Providers.*
2. Click *Built-in Mail Provider.*
3. Click *Mail Sessions.*
4. Click *New.*
    1. **Name:** *liferaymail*
    2. **JNDI Name:** *mail/MailSession*

Mail Providers > Built-in Mail Provider > Mail Sessions > **liferaymail**

Use this page to create mail sessions, which are collections of properties that define how your application sends mail and accesses the mail store. Configure mail sessions only after you configure the necessary protocol providers.

Configuration

General Properties

* Scope
cells:aukNode01Cell:nodes:aukNode01

* Provider
Built-in Mail Provider

* Name
liferaymail

* JNDI name
mail/MailSession

Description

Category

Mail transport host

Mail transport protocol
smtp

Mail transport user ID

Mail transport password

☑ Enable strict Internet address parsing

Mail from

Mail store host

Mail store protocol
pop3

Mail store user ID

Mail store password

☐ Enable debug mode

Apply | OK | Reset | Cancel

Additional Properties

- Custom properties

Illustration 44: Creating a Mail Session on WebSphere 6.1

5. Click *OK*.
6. Click *Security*.
7. Click *Secure administration, applications, and infrastructure*.
8. Select *Enable application security*.
9. Deselect *Use Java 2 security to restrict application access to local resources*.

Install Liferay

1. Click *Applications -> Install new applications.*
2. Browse for liferay-portal-x.x.x.war.

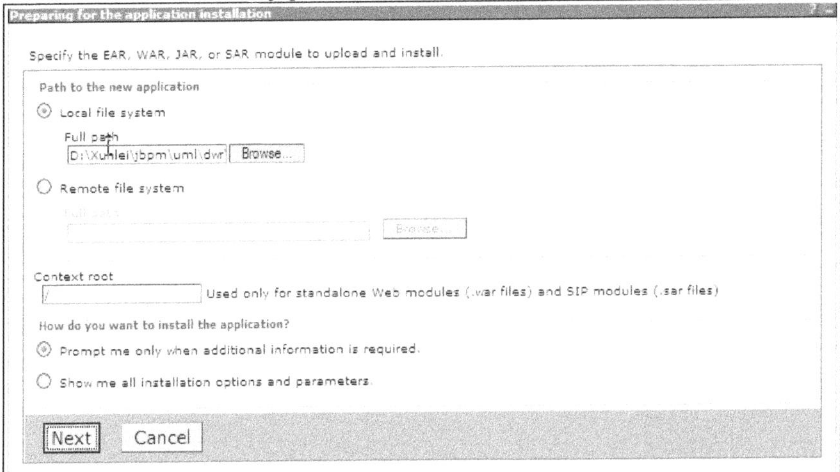

Illustration 45: Installing the Liferay .war file on WebSphere 6.1

3. Enter context root /.

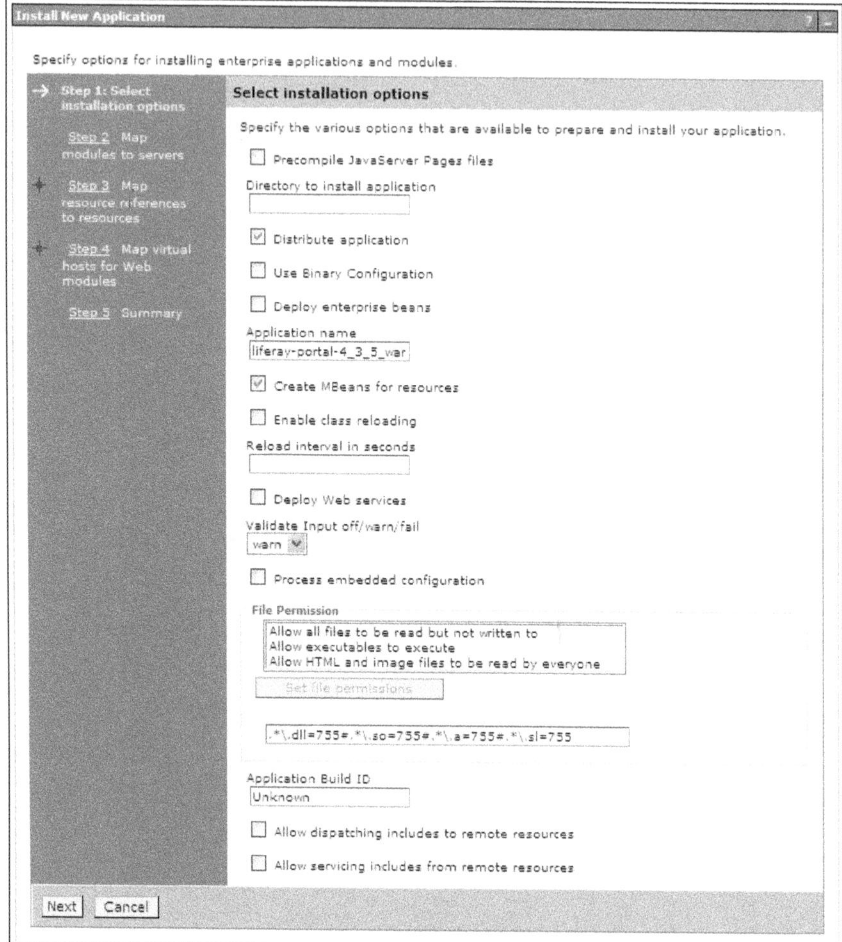

Illustration 46: Select the installation options

4. Click *Next*. For Steps 1 to 3, click *Next* to apply defaults.

5. Choose the Mail Session and Data Source, and then click *Next*

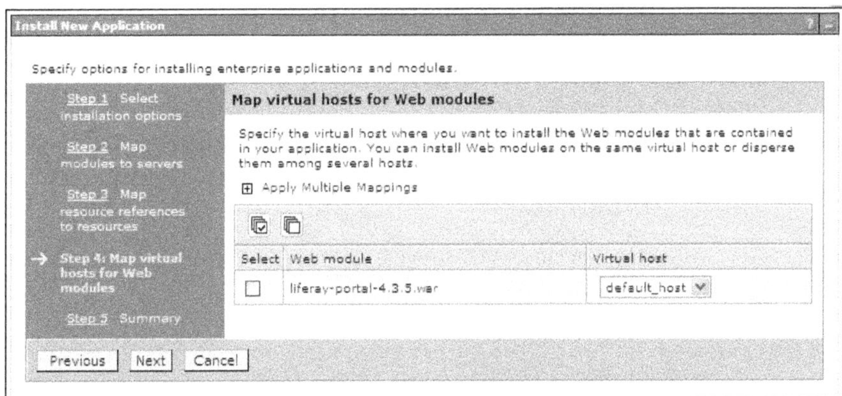

Illustration 47: Select the virtual host

6. Specify the virtual host upon which you want Liferay to run.
7. At the Summary Screen, click *Finish.*

Illustration 48: WebSphere 6.1 installation process

8. Wait for the installation process to complete.
9. Save this configuration to master configuration by clicking on *System administration* and *Save Changes to Master Repository*.

Start Liferay Portal

1. Applications.
2. Click *Enterprise Applications.*

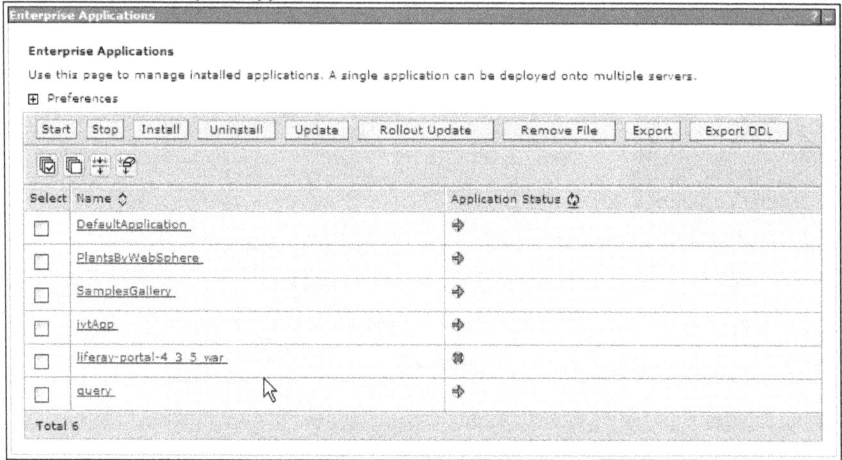

Illustration 49: Starting Liferay on WebSphere 6.1

3. Uninstall *DefaultApplication*, *PlantsByWebSphere* and *SamplesGallery*.
4. Select *liferay-portal.war*, click *Start.*
5. Open up browser and point to http://localhost:9080. The default Liferay home page will be displayed.

Making Liferay Coexist with Other Java EE Applications

Liferay Portal by default is configured to sit at the root (i.e., /) of your application server. Dedicating your application server to running only Liferay Portal is a good practice, allowing for separation between your portal environment and your web application environment. If, however, you want Liferay to share space on an application server with other applications, there is no reason why you cannot do that. In this instance, you may not want to make Liferay the default application in the root context of the server.

There are two steps to modifying this behavior:

1. Deploy Liferay in a context other than root (for example */portal*).
2. Modify the *portal-ext.properties* file to tell Liferay the context to which it has been deployed.

The order in which you take these steps depends on your application server. If your application server deploys Liferay in such a manner that you can browse its directory structure and modify files, then you would make this change in the order above (i.e., *after* deploying Liferay, but *before* starting it). If your application server does not deploy Liferay in this way, then you will have to modify the *portal-ext.properties* file inside the Liferay .war itself. You would extract the file from the .war file, modify it, and then put it back in the .war file. Then deploy the modified Liferay .war file to the server in the proper context.

To change the file, open it in a text editor. Place the *portal.ctx* property at the top of the file:

```
portal.ctx=/
```

This default setting defines Liferay Portal as the application that sits at the root context. If you change it to something else, say */portal*, for example, you can then deploy Liferay in that context and it will live there instead of at the root context.

A full discussion of the *portal-ext.properties* file appears in Chapter 4.

3. Configuration

Once Liferay is successfully installed, you can begin configuring it to fit it to your environment and your particular portal project. You can perform many of these configuration tasks through Liferay's portlet-driven user interface.

You will want to customize your portal by configuring various settings for it, such as email notifications, integration with services such as LDAP, creating users, user groups, organizations, and roles, and readying your portal to have its content and applications loaded by your developers. This chapter covers these activities:

- *Liferay's User Interface:* How to navigate around Liferay and make use of the administrative portlets.
- *Liferay Administration:* How to administer a Liferay portal.
- *Global Portal Settings:* Password policies, Settings, Monitoring, and more.

Liferay's User Interface

Liferay is a *portal server*. This means that it is designed to be a single environment where all of the applications a user needs can run, and these are integrated together in a consistent and systematic way. If an application lives outside of the portal, the portal should be able to consume some resource of the application (such as an RSS feed or a subset of functionality in a "dashboard" application) so that the end user can see everything he or she interacts with at a glance.

To achieve this, all of the application functionality within Liferay Portal is in fragments of the page called *portlets*. Portlets are web applications that run in a portion of a web page. The heart of any portal implementation is its portlets, because portlets are where all of the functionality is implemented. Liferay's core is a portlet container, and the container's job is to aggregate the set of portlets that are to appear on any particular page and display them properly to the user. In this way, one or many applications can reside on a page, and the user can (at the administrator's discretion) arrange them in the way that works best for the user.

Portlet applications, like servlet applications, have become a Java standard which various portal server vendors have implemented. The Java standard defines the portlet specification. A JSR-168 or JSR-286 standard portlet should be deployable on any portlet container which supports those standards. Portlets are placed on the page in a certain order by the end user and are served up dynamically by the portal server.

Portal applications come generally in two flavors: 1) multiple portlets can be written to provide small amounts of functionality and then are aggregated by the portal server into a larger application, or 2) whole applications can be written to reside in only one or a few portlet windows. The choice is up to those designing the application. Developers only have to worry about what happens inside of the portlet itself; the portal server handles building out the page as it is presented to the user.

Portlets are not difficult to build, and Java standard portlets can be written by any Java developer with experience in writing web applications. Liferay provides a Plugins Software Development Kit that makes creating portlet projects easy. For further information about the Plugins SDK, please see the *Liferay Developer's Guide*.

Additionally, Liferay supports portlets written in other programming languages, such as PHP, Ruby, Groovy, or Python. Sample portlets written in these languages are available to download from our Sourceforge site (http://sourceforge.net/projects/lportal) or can be checked out from our Subversion repository (https://lportal.svn.sourceforge.net/svnroot/lportal).

Navigating Liferay

When you see Liferay's default interface for the first time, you will see what we call the Dock in the upper right hand corner of the screen. The Dock is the key to navigating within the supplied Liferay themes: it provides links to all the global functions a user needs, such as logging in and out and switching between various community and organization pages. By default, it contains only two links: *Home* and *Sign In*. To show these links, all you need to do is roll your mouse cursor over the Dock, and it will expand.

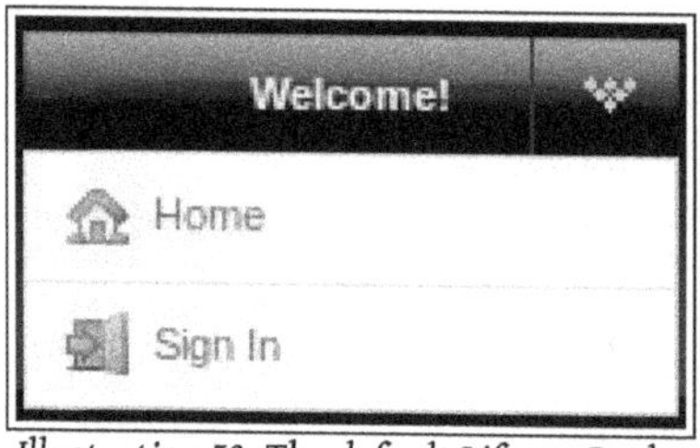

Illustration 50: The default Liferay Dock.

To sign into Liferay for the first time, you can click the *Sign In* link. You will then be presented with the **Sign In Portlet**. This portlet allows a user (or a prospective user) to do several things: sign in to Liferay, create a new account on the portal, or have a password reminder emailed if the user has forgotten his or her password. To sign in for the first time, don't create an account for yourself. We will do that later. If you were to create a new account on the portal for yourself now, it would be created using Liferay's defaults, which means the account would not have access to the administrative portlets you need in order to set up Liferay for your organization. For this reason, you will need to sign in as the default administrative user. This user's credentials are:

User Name: test@liferay.com

Password: test

Go ahead and sign into your new portal using these credentials. As you can see, Liferay by default uses one's email address as the user name. This can be changed later if you don't like this functionality, but it is generally a good practice to keep it this way. Users' email addresses are not normally things they will forget, and they are unique to each user, so they make good candidates for user IDs.

The first page that will be displayed when a user logs in for the first time is the Terms of Use page. This page is displayed to the user before he or she is allowed to access the portal. By default, your users will have to agree to your terms of service before they will be allowed to used the portal. This page can be customized to contain whatever text you want, or the feature can be disabled altogether. To continue, you will need to agree to the Terms of Service.

Once you log in as the administrative user, you will see that little has changed. The Sign In portlet now displays the name of the user (whose rather unimaginative name is Test Test) who is logged in, and the Dock now displays the text "Welcome, Test Test!" If you hover your mouse over the dock now, however, you will see that there are many more links in it:

Home: takes you to the home page.

Sign Out: logs you out of the portal.

Add Application: opens the Add Application window which allows you to add portlets to the page.

Layout Template: displays the Layout Template window which allows you to choose different layouts for the page.

Manage Pages: takes you to the page administration screen, where you can add and delete pages, change the order of the pages, and configure several other things about pages.

Toggle Edit Controls: This will let you turn on and off the edit controls in the top of the portlet windows. This is helpful for administrators who want to look at a page they're working on and see it the way a regular user would.

My Places: shows you the community and organization pages in the portal to which you can navigate.

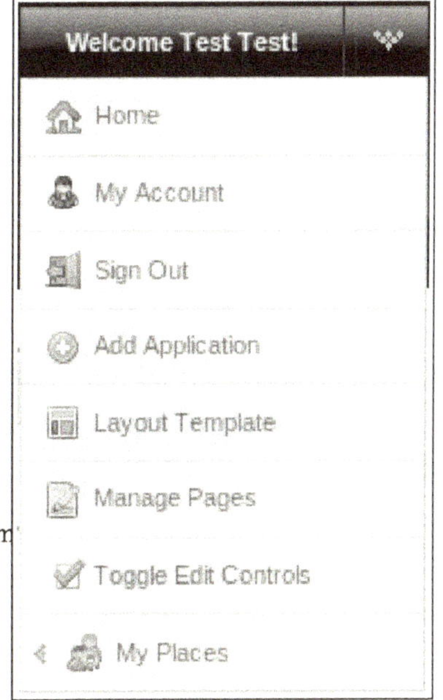

Illustration 51: Administrator's Dock

If you roll your mouse over *My Places*, the Dock will expand, showing all of the places in the portal to which you have access. Initially, the place you are on will be highlighted. You will see that you are in the Guest community, on the public pages. Liferay allows for various configurations of pages for end users: you can configure it so that some or all users have their own pages, public and private (or both), upon which they can place the portlets they need to use. The administrator account by default has its own pages. To administer Liferay, you will need to add the administrative portlets to a page somewhere. Since the Guest community is by default where the public pages for your web site will go, you do not want to put the administrative portlets there. Instead, it is better to put them on the administrator's private pages.

To navigate to these pages, you would go to the Dock, then My Places, then My Community, and then click on *Private Pages*. You will then be taken to the administrator's private pages.

Adding the Administrative Portlets

Liferay's administration interface is itself implemented as portlets. This means that there is no special area to go to in Liferay in order to begin administering your new portal. All you need to do is add the administrative portlets to a page and get to work! For our purposes, we will create a page in the administrative user's private page area called *Admin*. At the top right of the page you are viewing (under the Dock), you should see an *Add Page* link. Click it, and a field will appear, allowing you to type a name for the page. Type *Admin* and press the Enter key. The page has now been created. Go to the page by clicking on it.

You will see that the page is blank. We will be adding some of Liferay's administrative portlets to it so that we can begin configuring Liferay. First, though, we want to change the layout so that it is optimal for the portlets that we want to add. So go up to the Dock and click *Layout Template*. Select the *2 Column 70/30* layout and click *Save*. It won't look like anything has changed, but that's because you don't have any portlets on the page yet. We will now add the administrative portlets that we will need to begin configuring Liferay.

Go back up to the Dock and click *Add Application*. You will see a new window with application categories pop up on the left of your browser window. There are several ways you can use this window to find portlets to add to your page.

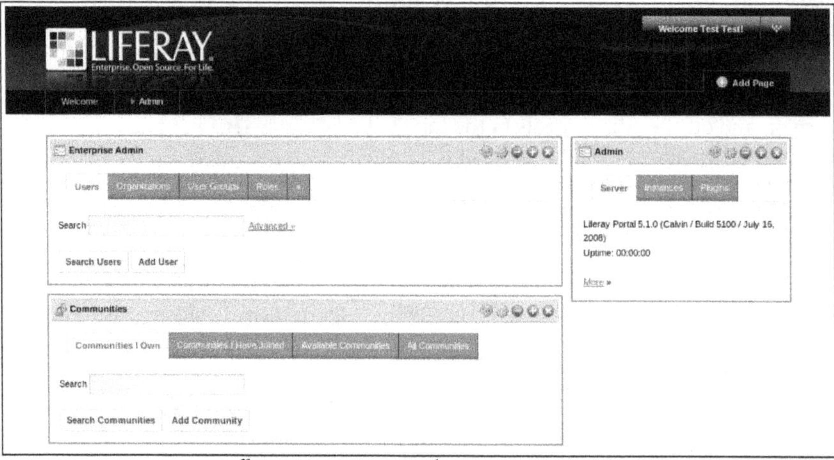

Illustration 52: Your Administrative Page.

If you know what you are looking for, you can begin typing the name of the portlet in the search bar at the top. The window will readjust itself as you type to display portlet titles that match your search. If you're not sure of the name of the portlet you want, you can click on the categories and they will expand and display the portlets that are inside those categories.

Click the *Admin* category. One of the portlets listed there is called **Enterprise Admin**. Drag the portlet title off the Add Application window and onto your Liferay workspace. You will see the columns for the layout you chose previously appear as you drag. Drop the portlet in the left most column, and it will appear there. Next, drag the portlet called **Admin** to the right most (smaller) column.

After this, open the *Community* category. One of the portlets in this category is called simply, **Communities.** Drag this portlet to the left most column underneath the Enterprise Admin portlet. After you have done all of this, you can close the Add Application window by clicking the red X that's in the top right corner of the window.

When you are finished, you should have a page that looks similar to what is pictured.

Portal Architecture

Before we dive into the user interface for adding and maintaining various portal resources, it is best to go over the concepts Liferay uses to organize a portal.

Portals are accessed by *Users.*

Users can be collected into *User Groups.*

Users can belong to *Organizations.*

Organizations can be grouped into hierarchies, such as Home Office -> Regional Office -> Satellite Office.

Users, Groups, and *Organizations* can belong to *Communities* that have a common interest.

The simplest way to think about this is that you have users and various ways those users can be grouped together. Some of these groupings follow an administratively organized hierarchy, and other groupings may be done by the users themselves (such as different users from multiple organizations starting a community called "Dog Lovers" that has a common interest in dogs). And other groupings may be done administratively via User Groups or Roles for other functions that may cut across the portal (such as a *Message Board Administrators* group made up of users from multiple communities and organizations, allowing those users to administer any message board in the portal).

This way of organizing portal concepts may be illustrated in the following manner:

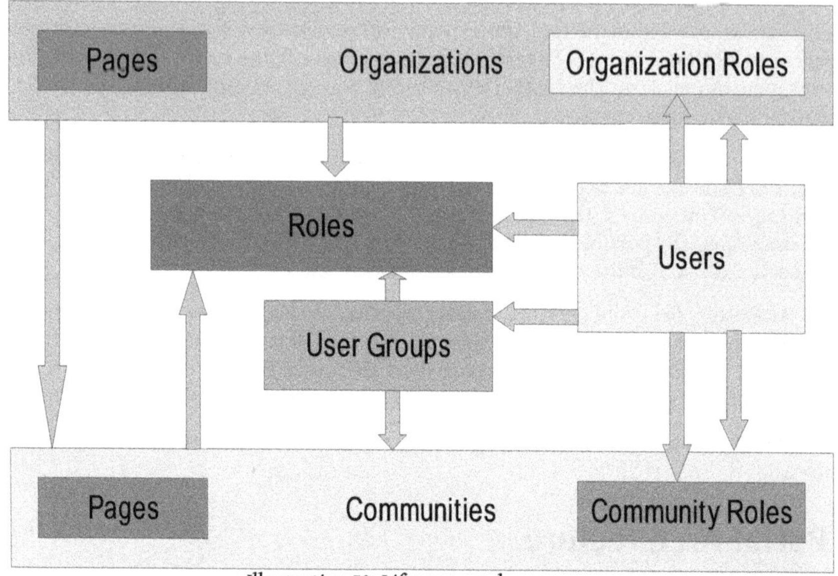

Illustration 53: Liferay portal resources

In the illustration above, each arrow may be read using the words "can be a member of." So this means that Organizations can be members of Communities, Communities can be members of Roles, Users can be members of anything, and so on. Though this seems very complex, it provides a powerful mechanism for portal administrators to configure portal resources and security in a consistent and robust manner.

Users

Users can be collected in multiple ways. They can be members of organization hierarchies, such as Liferay, Inc. -> Security -> Internet Security. They can be collected into arbitrary user groups, such as *Writers*, which would have access to enter content into the content management system. They can be members of communities which draw together common interests. And they can have roles which describe their functions in the system, and these roles can be scoped by Portal, Organization, or Community.

User Groups

User Groups are simple, arbitrary collections of users, created by administrators. They can be members of communities or roles. Permissions can be assigned to groups, granting access to all members of the group to certain portal resources. Though User Groups do not have pages like some of the other collections of users (such as Communities or Organizations), they do have page templates which can be used to customize users' personal set of pages. This will be fully described below.

Roles

There are three kinds of roles:

- Portal Roles
- Organization Roles
- Community Roles

These are called role *scopes*. Roles are used to define permissions across their scope: across the portal, across an organization, or across a community. For example, consider a role which grants access to create a Message Board category. A Portal role would grant that access across the portal, wherever there was a Message Board portlet. A Community role would grant that access only within a single community. An Organization role would grant that access only within an Organization.

Because Roles are used strictly for portal security, they also do not have pages, like Communities and Organizations.

Users, User Groups, Communities, or Organizations can be members of a role.

Organizations

Organizations are hierarchical collections of Users. They are one of the two types of portal resources that can have pages. There is also a special type of Organization called a *location*, which can define where users are specifically located.

Organizations are handy for defining where a user belongs in a particular hierarchy. For example, if you are implementing Liferay for a large organization, it may help to define user Joe Smith via his position in the organization chart. If Joe Smith is a Sales Engineer located in the New Jersey office, working in the North East division of the Sales department, he might be a member of the following organizations:

- Sales
- North East Division
- New Jersey Location

Now say that you have placed an Asset Publisher portlet as a static portlet on every user's home page (via a User Group page template) so that you can inform employees of various announcements via the content management system. If you tagged your content appropriately, you could ensure that Joe Smith gets any announcements that are meant for Sales, the North East Division, or the New Jersey location.

Organizations can be members of Communities.

Communities

Communities are collections of Users who have a common interest. Liferay's default pages are in the Guest community, because everyone—whether they are anonymous or members of the portal—has a common interest in the default, public pages of your site. There are three types of Communities:

- Open
- Restricted
- Hidden

An Open Community (the default) allows portal users to join and leave the Community whenever they want to, provided they have access to a Communities portlet from which to do this. A Restricted Community requires that users be added to the Community by a community administrator. Users may use the Communities portlet to request membership. A Hidden community is just like a Restricted community, with the added concept that it does not show up at all in the Communities portlet.

Using Liferay's Administrative Portlets

The **Enterprise Admin** portlet is used for most administrative tasks. You added this portlet to the top left of the *Admin* page you created in the administrator's private pages area. This portlet has an interface for the creation and maintenance of

- Users
- Organizations
- User Groups
- Roles

Additionally, it allows you to configure many server settings, including:

- Information about the site
- Authentication options, including Single Sign-On and LDAP integration
- Default User Associations
- Reserved Screen Names
- Mail Host Names
- Email Notifications

You will use the Enterprise Admin portlet to create your portal structure, implement security, and administer your users. Note that only users with the Administrator role—a portal scoped role—have permission to add the Enterprise Admin portlet to a page.

Adding Users

Let's begin by adding a user account for yourself. We will then configure this account so that it has the same administrative access as the default administrator account. Click the *Add User* button in the Enterprise Admin portlet.

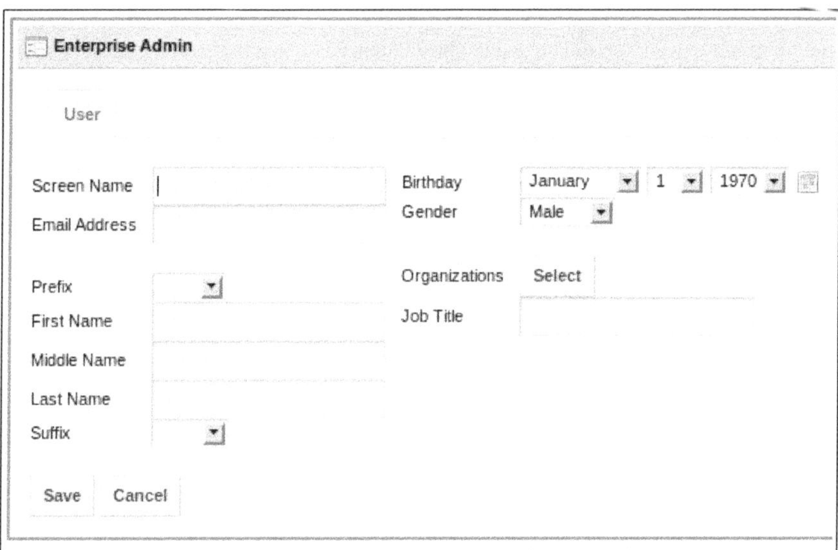

Illustration 54: The Add User screen.

The portlet will maximize to take up the whole screen and then present you with the Add User form. Fill out the form using your name and email address. When you are finished, click *Save*.

The portlet will then reappear with a message saying that the save was successful, and there will now be an expanded form which allows you to fill out a lot more information about the user. You don't have to fill anything else out right now, but one thing is important to note: when the user ID was created, a password was automatically generated and, if Liferay has been correctly installed (see Chapter 2), an email message with the password in it was sent to the user. This of course requires that Liferay can properly communicate with your SMTP mail server in your organization.

If you have not yet set up your mail server, you will need to use this screen to change the default password for the user ID to something you can remember. You can do this by clicking on the *Password* tab, entering the new password in the two fields, and clicking *Save*.

Next, you will want to give your user account the same administrative rights as the default administrator's account. This will allow you to perform administrative tasks with your own ID instead of having to use the default ID. And this allows you to make your portal more secure by deleting or disabling the default ID.

Click the *Regular Roles* tab, and then click the *Assign Regular Roles* button. You will then be taken to a screen which shows the regular roles to which your ID is currently assigned. By default, these are *User* and *Power User*. A User role is held by anyone in

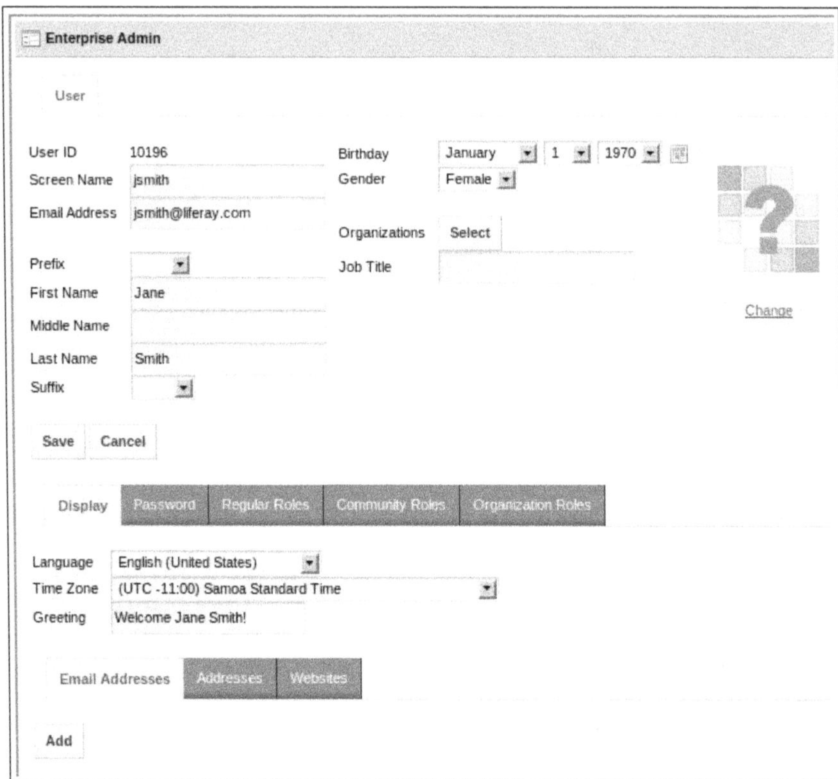

Illustration 55: Liferay's User Account editor.

the system: it defines the difference between a Guest and a person who has a user ID in the portal. By default, all users are also assigned the Power User role. This role by default gives users their own personal pages (both public and private) where they can place portlets, though this functionality can now be changed in Liferay 5.1. You can define the default roles a new user receives in the Enterprise Admin portlet; we will go over this later.

To make yourself an Administrator, click the *Available* tab. You will see a list of all the roles in the system. Check off the Administrator role and then click the *Update Associations* button. You are now an administrator of the portal. Log out of the portal and then log back in with your own user ID. You can now create a private page for the administration portlets and set them up in your own space.

User Management

If you click the *Users* tab in the Enterprise Admin portlet, you will see that there are now two users in the list of users. If you wanted to change something about a particular user, you can click the *Actions* button next to that user.

Edit User: This takes you back to the Edit User page, where you can modify anything about the user.

Permissions: This allows you to define which Users, User Groups, or Roles have permissions to edit the user.

Manage Pages: If the user has pages, this allows you to edit them.

Impersonate User: This opens another browser window which allows you to browse the site as though you were the user.

Deactivate: Clicking this will deactivate the user's account.

Note that most users will not be able to perform most of the above (in fact, they won't even have access to the Enterprise Admin portlet). Because you have administrative access, you can perform all of the above functions.

Organizations

Organizations in Liferay are meant to model organizations in real life. They can be used to represent different companies, non-profit organizations, churches, schools, clubs, and so on. The example we use in our Lifecasts uses them to represent a sports league, with various sports (soccer, baseball, basketball, etc.) and their teams as sub-organizations. If you have a collection of users that all belong to the same grouping, you may be able to model that as an organization.

Your portal may have only one organization or several, depending on what kind of site you are building. For example, a corporate site may model its own organization hierarchy in Liferay, while a social networking site may have users from many separate organizations who access the site. Organizations can have a hierarchy to unlimited levels, and Users can be members of one or many organizations—inside of a hierarchy or across hierarchies.

Additionally, Organizations can be granted permissions over portal resources, and can also be associated with Roles. One application of this in a corporate setting could be an IT Security group. You may have an organization within your IT organization that handles security for all of the applications company-wide. If you had users as members of this organization, you could grant the Administrator role you just granted to your own ID to the whole Organization, thereby giving the members of the IT Security organization administrative access to the portal. If a user in this organization later was hired by the Human Resources department, the simple administrative act of moving the user from the IT Security organization to the HR organization would remove this privilege from the user, since the user would no longer be in an organization that has the Administrator role. By adding the user to the HR organization, any roles the HR organization has (such as access to a benefits system in the portal) would be transferred to the user. In this manner, you can design your portal to correspond with your existing organization chart, and have users' permissions reflect their positions in the chart.

Of course, this is only one way to design it. If you have more complex requirements, you can combine Organizations with User Groups and Roles to assemble the sets of permissions you wish to grant to particular users.

Organizations are one of two types of Liferay resources (the other being Communities) that can have its own pages. This allows members of the organizations (if they are granted the *Manage Pages* permission) to maintain their own pages. They can have a set of public pages which include information and applications appropriate for guests or logged in users to make use of (such as a help desk ticket entry system for an IT page), and they can have a set of private pages with applications for the organization's own use (such as the back-end portlets of the same ticketing system).

To add an organization, click the *Organizations* tab in the Enterprise Admin portlet, and then click the *Add Organization* button.

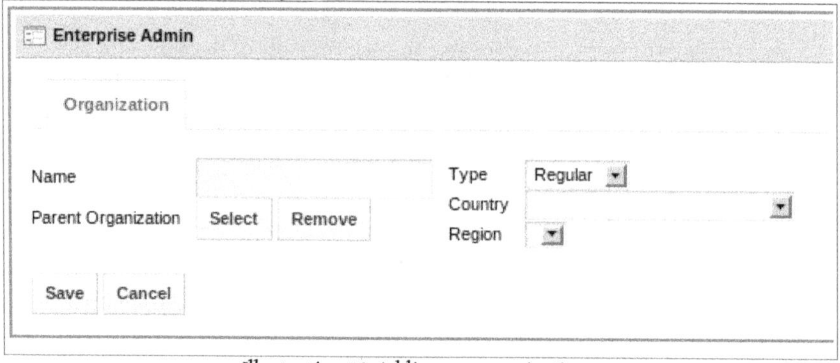

Illustration 56: Adding an organization.

Name: The name of the organization.

Parent Organization: Click the *Select* button to bring up a window which allows you to select the organization in the system that is the direct parent of the organization you are creating. Click the *Remove* button to remove the currently configured parent.

Type: Use this to choose whether this is a regular organization or a location.

Country: Choose the country where this organization is located.

Region: Select the region within the country where this organization is located.

Fill out the information for your organization and click *Save*.

As before with users, the form reappears and you can enter more information about the organization. Organizations can have multiple email addresses, postal addresses, web sites, and phone numbers associated with them. The *Services* tab can be used to indicate the operating hours of the organization, if any.

For now, click the *Back* button. This will take you back to the list of organizations.

Click the *Actions* button next to the new organization you have created. You will then see the many actions you can take to manipulate this organization.

Edit: Lets you edit the organization.

Permissions: This allows you to define which Users, User Groups, or Roles have permissions to edit the Organization.

Manage Pages: Lets you create and manage public and private pages for the Organization.

Assign User Roles: Lets you assign Organization-scoped roles to users. By default, Organizations are created with three roles: Organization Administrator, Organization Member, and Organization Owner. You can assign one or more of these roles to users in the organization. All members of the Organization get the Organization Member role.

Assign Members: Takes you to a screen where you can search and select users in the portal to be assigned to this organization as members.

Add User: Adds a new user in the portal who will be a member of this organization.

View Users: Shows a list of users who are members of this organization.

Add Suborganization: Lets you add a child organization to this organization. This is how you create hierarchies of organizations with parent-child relationships.

View Suborganizations: Shows a list of all the organizations that are children of this organization.

Delete: Deletes this organization from the portal. You will have to ensure that the organization has no users in it first.

Tip: Note that you are already a member of the organization you created, because you created it. By creating an organization, you become both a member and have the Organization Owner role, which gives you full rights to the organization.

User Groups

User Groups are arbitrary groupings of users. These groups are created by portal administrators to group users together who don't have an obvious organizational or community-based attribute or aspect which brings them together. Groups can have permissions, much like roles. You would therefore use a User Group to grant permissions to any arbitrary list of users.

For example, a User Group called *People Who Have Access to My Stuff* could be created, and permission to a particular Document Library folder could be granted to that User Group. This list of users could be members of separate Organizations, Communities, or Roles, who happen to also have access to this Document Library folder which is on some personal, community, or organization page that is accessible to them in the portal.

Creating a User Group is easy. Click the *User Groups* tab and then click the *Add User Group* button. There are only two fields to fill out: Name (the name of the User Group) and Description (an optional description of what the group is for). Click *Save* and you will then be back to the list of groups.

As with the other resources in the portal, you can click the *Actions* button to perform various operations on User Groups.

Edit: Allows you to modify the name or description of the User Group.

Permissions: This allows you to define which Users, User Groups, or Roles have permissions to edit the User Group.

Manage Pages: Though User Groups don't have pages of their own, you can create *page templates* for a group. When a User Group has page templates, any users added to the group will have the group's pages copied to their personal pages. This allows you to do things like create a *Bloggers* user group with a page template that has the Blogs and Recent Bloggers portlets on it. The first time users who are added to this group log in to the portal, this page will get copied to their personal pages. They will then automatically have a blog page that they can use.

Assign Members: Takes you to a screen where you can search for and select users in the portal to be assigned to this User Group.

View Users: Lets you view the users who are in the User Group.

Delete: Deletes the User Group.

User Groups and Page Templates

Liferay allows users to have a personal set of public and private pages that each user can customize at will. The default configuration of those pages can be determined by the portal administrator through the *portal.properties* file and optionally by providing the configuration in a LAR file. Though this has been a long-time feature of Liferay, it was not very flexible or easy to use.

Liferay version 5.1 introduces the concept of *page templates* which are tied to User Groups. This enables administrators to provide the same configuration for the personal pages of all (or just a subset of) users. In some cases you may want to provide a different configuration for each user depending on his or her profile. For example, in a portal for University students, staff and undergraduates would get different default pages and portlets. You can also set it up so that different groups are combined together to create the desired default configuration. When a user is assigned to a user group, the configured pages templates are copied directly to the user's personal pages.

Tip: The screen shots in this section show the old classic theme because they were taken right before it was revamped for 5.1. For that reason they'll be slightly different from what you'll find in an out-of-the-box Liferay 5.1 version. We thought it was more important to get the information to you as fast as possible.

User Group Page Templates: Defining page templates for a user group

The a User Group's page templates can be administered using the **Enterprise Admin** portlet. The *User Groups* tab lists all the existing user groups and allows you to perform several actions on each of them.

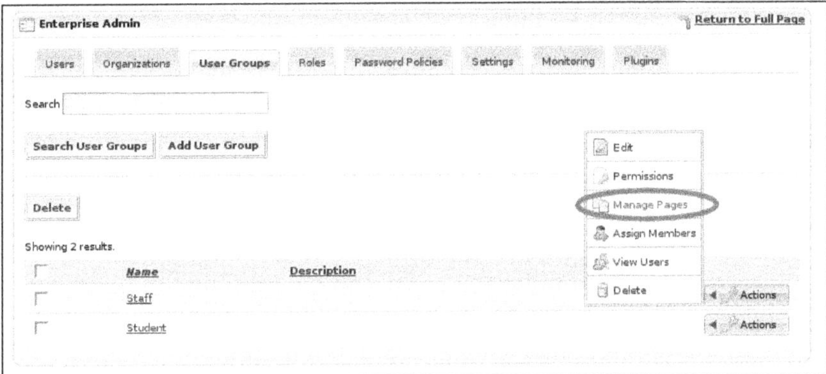

Illustration 57: Manage Pages action on a User Group.

By selecting the new *Manage Pages* action the administrator will access the common Liferay UI for creating pages and organizing them in a hierarchy.

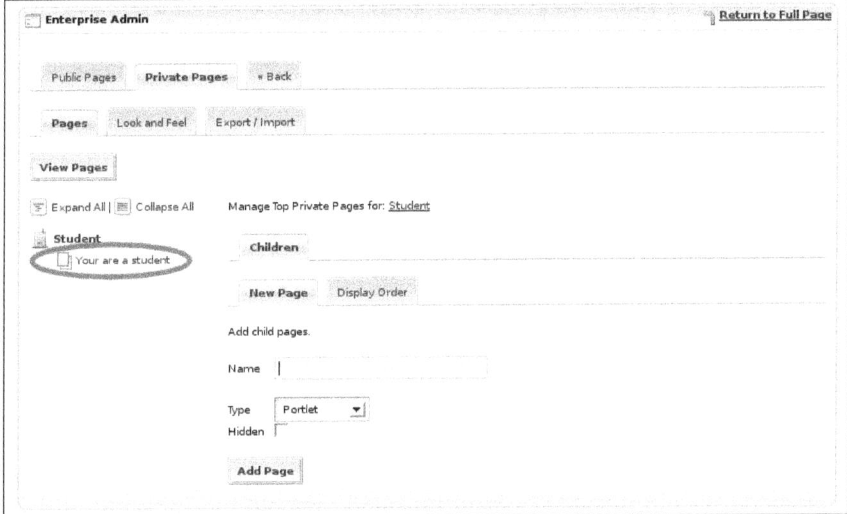

Illustration 58: Adding a Page Template.

Note that it is possible to create both public and private pages. Each set will be used as templates to be copied to the user's personal public or private page sets respectively when the user becomes a member of the user group.

In the screen shot above, the administrator has created a new private page called *You are a student* within the *Student2* user group. Since the page created is a portlet page, the administrator can now click the *View Pages* button to open the page and add as many portlets as desired to that page and configure them as needed. Let's assume for this example that the **Loan Calculator** and **Calendar** portlets are selected.

Applying the page templates by assigning members to the user group

The next step will be to assign an existing user to that group to verify that the page template is copied as a user's private page. To that end, the *Assign Members* action has to be selected in the list of available user groups.

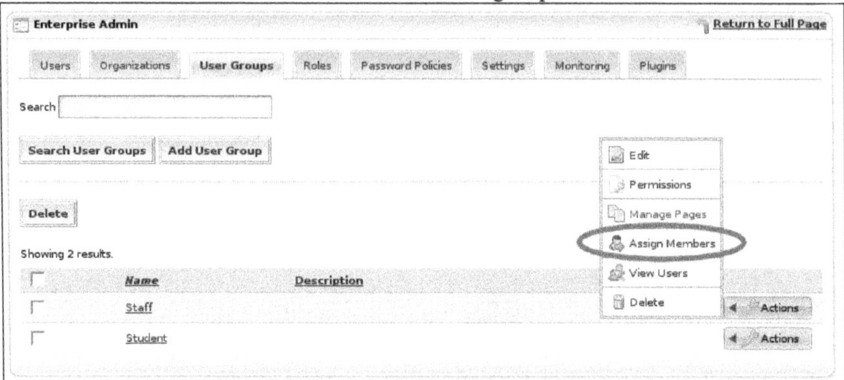

Illustration 59: Assigning Members to a User Group

By clicking the *Available* tab in the next screen, a list of all available users is shown. From that list, one or more users can be selected to make them members of the user group. When the *Update Associations* button is clicked, the users become members of the group and copies of any public or private page templates which are configured for the user group are copied to their page sets.

In the previous example, a user that already had an existing page called *Welcome* will now have a new page called *You Are A Student* the next time she accesses her private pages. That page will contain two portlets: *Loan Calculator* and *Calendar* as configured by the User Group administrator:

Illustration 60: Template copied to a user's page set.

Additional details

Because the pages are copied to a user's set of pages, once copied, they can be changed at any time. When a user is removed from a user group the associated pages won't be removed: they have become that user's pages. The system is smart enough, however, to detect when a user is added again to a group of which he or she was already a part, and the pages are not added again.

If an administrator modifies page templates for a User group after users have already been added to the group, those changes will be used when new users are assigned to the user group. Since the pages are templates, however, the changes won't be applied to users that were already members of the user group.

Users can belong to many User Groups. If you have templates defined for a number of groups, this may result having many page templates copied to users' pages. To prevent this, you can combine pages from different user groups into a single page. This will be covered in the next section.

Composing A Page Out of Several User Groups

While the functionality described so far is quite powerful, in some complex scenarios it might not be enough. This section describes how more even flexibility can be achieved by combining the pages from different user groups into a single user page when he or she belongs to more than one of them.

Let's expand our previous example by dividing the Students into *First Year Students*, *Second Year Students*, *Third Year Students*, *International Students*, and *Prospective Students*. For each of these types of students we want them to have a page with the **Loan Calculator** and **Calendar**, but depending on which type we also want other different portlets to be on that page too.

This can be achieved by a naming convention for the pages. If two or more pages of different user groups have the same name, they will be combined into a single page when they are copied to a user's personal pages set.

In the example above, a User was added to a *Students* group which had a page called *You are a Student*. If the administrator creates a page template with the same name (*You are a Student*) in the *First Year Students* group and puts in it an RSS portlet pointing to information interesting for them, that page would be combined with the *You are a Student* page that's in the *Students* group, and the resulting page would contain the portlets configured for both User Groups:

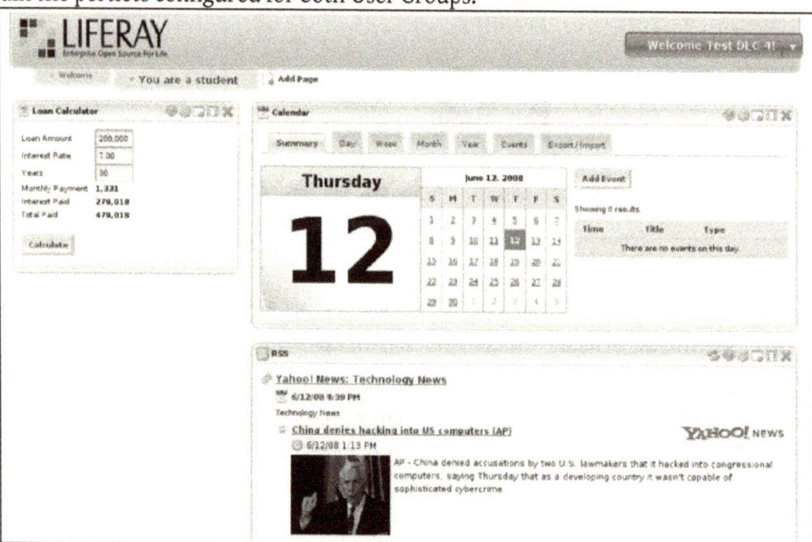

Illustration 61: Combined portlet pages.

Page Combination Rules

The following rules are used when composing a page by combining pages from different user groups:

- If a user becomes a member of a User Group that has a page template with the same name in the same set (public or private) as a page that the user already has, those pages will be combined.
- If any of the pages has the name translated to several languages, only the default language is considered in the comparison.
- The portlets on the new page will be copied to the bottom of the equivalent columns of the existing page.
- If the existing and the new pages have different layout templates, the existing one is preserved.
- If the new layout template has portlets in columns that do not exist in the existing page, those portlets will be automatically copied to the first column of the existing layout template.

As you can see, it is possible to have a very flexible configuration for the default pages of portal users. Furthermore, that configuration can be changed at any time using the UI administrators are used to and then assigning users to new user groups.

While these examples are somewhat simple, the system allows for as many user groups as desired. By using the convention of matching the page names it is possible to build any default page composition that you want for your users.

Roles

Roles are groupings of users that share a particular function within the portal, according to a particular scope. Roles can be granted permissions to various functions within portlet applications. Think of a role as a description of a function, such as Message Board Administrators. A role with that name is likely to have permissions to functions of the Message Board portlet delegated to it. Users who are placed in this role then inherit those permissions.

Roles are scoped by Portal, Organization, or Community. Because the Enterprise Admin portlet by definition is operating on the portal as a whole, you can create Organization or Community roles and assign permissions to them, but you can't assign users to them in the Roles tab. For that, you would need to go to the Community (in the **Communities Portlet**) or the Organization (on the *Organizations* tab of the Enterprise Admin portlet or the **Organization Admin** portlet).

To create a Role, click the *Roles* tab, and then click the *Add Role* button. Type a name for your role and an optional description. The drop down box at the bottom of the form lets you choose whether this is a Regular, Community, or Organization role. When you have finished, click *Save*.

You will be back at the list of roles. To see what functions you can perform on your new role, click the *Actions* button.

Edit: Click this action to edit the role. You can change its name or description.

Permissions: This allows you to define which Users, User Groups, or Roles have permissions to edit the Role.

Define Permissions: Click this to define what permissions this role has. This is outlined in the next section.

Assign Members: Takes you to a screen where you can search and select users in the portal to be assigned to this role. These users will inherit any permissions given to the role.

View Users: Lets you view the users who are in the Role.

Delete: Deletes the Role.

Defining Permissions on a Role

Roles exist as a bucket for granting permissions to the users who are members of them. So one of the main tasks you will be doing with a role is granting it the permissions that you want members of the role to have.

When you click the *Define Permissions* action, you are given a choice of two kinds of permissions that can be defined for this role: *Portal Permissions* and *Portlet Permissions.*

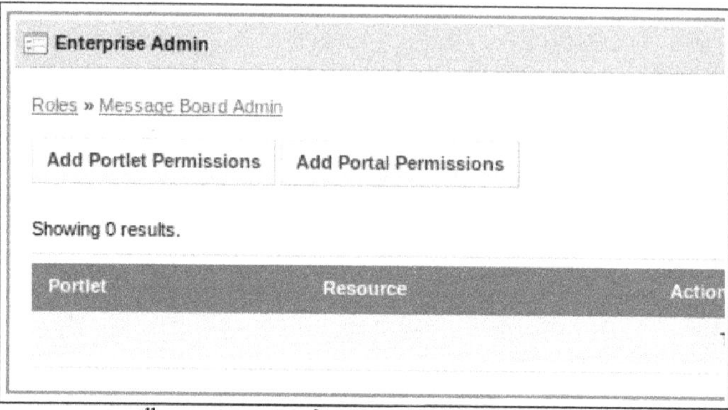

Illustration 62: Defining Permissions on a Role.

Portal permissions cover portal-wide activities that are in several categories, such as Community, Location, Organization, Password Policy, etc. This allows you to create a Role that, for example, can create new Communities in the portal. This would allow you to grant users that particular permission without making them overall portal administrators.

Portlet permissions cover permissions that are defined within various portlets. Clicking the *Portlet Permissions* button brings you to a page where you can browse the names of the portlets that are currently installed in your portal. Once you choose a portlet, you can then define the actions within this portlet that the role will have permission to perform.

If we stick with our example of a *Message Boards Admin* role, we would then find the **Message Boards** portlet in the list and click on it. A new page with configurable permissions would then be displayed (see right).

Each possible action to which permissions can be granted is listed. To grant a permission, choose the scope of the permission. You have two choices: *Enterprise* and *Communities.* Granting Enterprise permissions means that permission to the action will be granted across the portal, in any community or organization where there is a Message Boards portlet.

If you choose Communities, a button appears next to the permission allowing you to choose one or more communities in which the permission will be valid. This lets you pick and choose specific communities (for a portal scoped role) in which these permissions are valid for users in this role.

Once you have chosen the permissions granted to this role, click *Save.* For a Message Boards Admin role, you would likely grant Enterprise permissions to every action listed. After you click *Save*, you will see a list of all permissions that are currently granted to this role. From here, you can add more permissions (by clicking *Add Portlet Permissions* or *Add Portal Permissions*), or go back by clicking a link in the breadcrumb list or the *Return to Full Page* link.

Roles are very powerful, and allow portal administrators to define various permissions in whatever combinations they like. This gives you as much flexibility as possible to build the site you have designed.

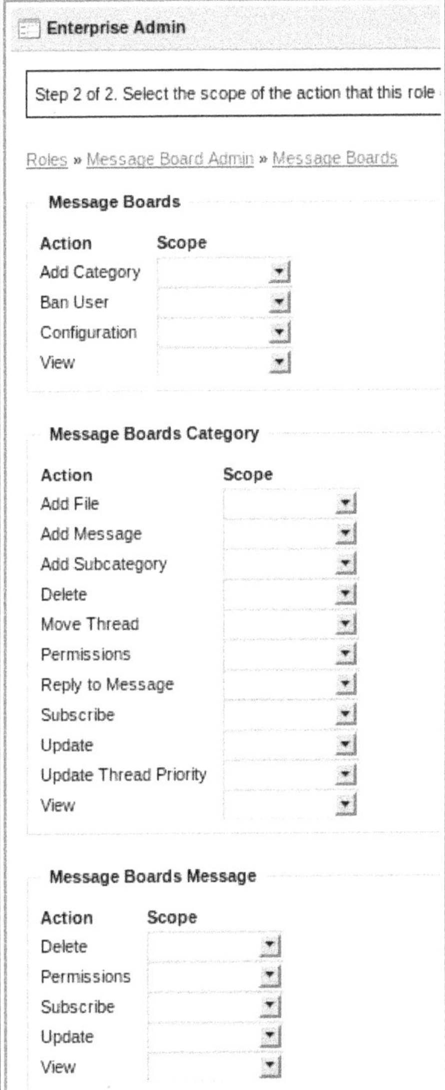

Illustration 63: Message Boards permissions.

Global Server Settings

Now that you have navigated in the Enterprise Admin portlet, you know that there are more tabs in it than it initially shows. While the first four tabs focus on the maintenance of users and portal security, the remaining tabs focus on various portal settings which cover how the portal operates and integrates with other systems you may have.

Password Policies

Password policies can help to enhance the security of your portal. Using password policies, you can set password rules such as password strength, frequency of password expiration, and more. Additionally, you can apply different rule sets to different sets of portal users.

If you are viewing the Enterprise Admin portlet in its Restored state (i.e., not maximized), click the tab with the two arrows on it (>>). This will expand the portlet so you can see the rest of the tabs. Next, click on the *Password Policies* tab. You will see that there is already a default password policy in the system. You can edit this in the same manner as you edit other resources in the portal: click *Actions* and then click *Edit*.

You will then see the Password Policy settings form:

Changeable: Selects whether a user can change his or her password.

Change Required: Selects whether a user must change his or her password upon first log in.

Minimum Age: You can choose how long a password must remain in effect before it can be changed.

Syntax Checking: Allows you to choose whether dictionary words can be in passwords as well as the minimum password length.

Password History: Keeps a history (with a defined length) of passwords and won't allow users to change their passwords to one that was previously used.

Password Expiration: Lets you choose an interval where passwords can be active before they expire. You can select the age, the warning time, and a grace limit.

Lockout: Allows you to set the number of failed log in attempts before a user's account becomes locked. You can choose whether an administrator needs to unlock the account or if it becomes unlocked after a specific duration.

From the list of password policies, you can perform several other actions.

Edit: Brings you to the form above and allows you to modify the password policy.

Permissions: This allows you to define which Users, User Groups, or Roles have permissions to edit the Password Policy.

Assign Members: Takes you to a screen where you can search and select users in the portal to be assigned to this password policy. The password policy will be enforced for any users who are added here.

Delete: This shows up for any password policies that you add beyond the default policy. You cannot delete the default policy.

Settings

The Settings tab is where most of the global portal settings are:

General: This lets you configure global settings, such as the company name, domain, the virtual host, a global portal logo, and more.

Authentication: Allows you to configure login IDs, connection to LDAP, and Single Sign-On.

Default User Associations: Lets you configure default membership to Roles, User Groups, and Communities for new users.

Reserved Screen Names: Lets you reserve screen names and email addresses so that users cannot register using them. You might use this to prevent users from registering with the portal with user names that contain profanity or that sound official, such as *admin* or *president*.

Mail Host Names: You can add a list of other mail servers besides your main one here.

Email Notifications: Liferay sends email notifications for certain events, such as user registrations, password changes, etc. You can customize those messages here.

We will go over these settings in detail below.

General

The *General* tab allows you to set the name of the company / organization / site which is running the portal. You can also set the default domain name, virtual host, language and time zone, as well as a number of other data about the organization.

You can also set the portal-wide logo which appears in the top left corner of themes that are configured to display it. Be careful when using this option to choose an image file that fits the space. If you pick something that is too big, it will mess up the navigation.

Authentication: General Settings

The *Authentication* tab has several tabs under it. All of these are used for configuring how users will authenticate to Liferay. Because Liferay supports a number of authentication methods, there are settings for each.

The general settings affect only Liferay functionality, and don't have anything to do with any of the integration options on the other tabs. This tab allows you to customize Liferay's out-of-box behavior regarding authentication. Specifically, the *General* tab allows you to select from several global authentication settings:

- Authenticate via email address (default), screen name, or user ID (a numerical ID auto-generated in the database—not recommended).
- Enable / Disable Forgot Password functionality.
- Enable / Disable account creation by strangers. If you are running an Internet site, you will probably want to leave this on so that visitors can create

accounts on your site.

- Enable / Disable account creation by those using an email address in the domain of the company running the site (which you just set on the General tab).
- Enable / Disable email address verification. If you enable this, Liferay, will send users a verification email with a link back to the portal to verify the email address they entered is a valid one they can access.

By default, all settings except for the last are enabled by default. One default that is important is that users will authenticate by their email address. Liferay defaults to this for several reasons:

1. An email address is, by definition, unique to the user who owns it.
2. People can generally remember their email addresses. If you have a user who hasn't logged into the portal for a while, it is possible that he or she will forget his or her screen name, especially if the user was not allowed to use his or her screen name of choice (because somebody else already used it).
3. If a user changes his or her email address, if it is not used to authenticate, it is more likely that the user will forget to update his or her email address in his or her profile. If the user's email address is not updated, all notifications sent by the portal will fail to reach the user. So it is important to keep the email address at the forefront of a user's mind when he or she logs in to help the user keep it up to date.

For these reasons, Liferay defaults to using the email address as a user name.

Authentication: LDAP

Connecting Liferay to an LDAP directory has become much easier and is now a straightforward process through the Enterprise Admin portlet. There are still, however, two places in which you can configure the LDAP settings: the *portal-ext.properties* file (which will be covered in the next chapter) and the Enterprise Admin portlet—where the settings will get stored in the database. Note that if you use both, the settings in the database will override the settings in *portal-ext.properties*. For this reason, we recommend for most users that you use the Enterprise Admin portlet to configure the LDAP settings—it's easier and does not require a restart of Liferay. The only compelling reason to use the *portal-ext.properties* file is if you have many Liferay nodes which will be configured to run against the same LDAP directory. In that case, for your initial deployment, it may be easier to copy the *portal-ext.properties* file to all of the nodes so that the first time they start up, the settings are correct. Regardless of which method you use, the settings are the same.

The LDAP settings screen is very detailed, so we will look at it in chunks.

Global Values

There are two global LDAP settings.

Enabled: Check this box to enable LDAP Authentication.

Required: Check this box if LDAP authentication is required. Liferay will then not allow a user to log in unless he or she can successfully bind to the LDAP directory first. Uncheck this box if you want to allow users that have Liferay accounts but no LDAP accounts to log in to the portal.

Default Values

Several leading directory servers are listed here. If you are using one of these, select it and the rest of the form will be populated with the proper default values for that directory.

Connection

These settings cover the basic connection to LDAP.

Base Provider URL: This tells the portal where the LDAP server is located. Make sure that the machine on which Liferay is installed can communicate with the LDAP server. If there is a firewall between the two systems, check to make sure that the appropriate ports are opened.

Base DN: This is the Base Distinguished Name for your LDAP directory. It is usually modeled after your organization. For a commercial organization, it may look something like: *dc=companynamehere,dc=com.*

Principal: By default, the administrator ID is populated here. If you have removed the default LDAP administrator, you will need to use the fully qualified name of the administrative credential you do use. You need an administrative credential because Liferay will be using this ID to synchronize user accounts to and from LDAP.

Credentials: This is the password for the administrative user.

This is all you need in order to make a regular connection to an LDAP directory. The rest of the configuration is optional: generally, the default attribute mappings are sufficient data to synchronize back to the Liferay database when a user attempts to log in. To test the connection to your LDAP server, click the *Test LDAP Connection* button.

If you are running your LDAP directory in SSL mode to prevent credential information from passing through the network unencrypted, you will have to perform extra steps to share the encryption key and certificate between the two systems.

For example, assuming your LDAP directory happens to be Microsoft Active Directory on Windows Server 2003, you would take the following steps to share the certificate:

On the Windows 2003 Domain Controller, open the *Certificates* MMC snapin. Export the Root Certificate Authority certificate by selecting *Certificates (Local Computer) mmc snapin -> Trusted Root Certification Authorities -> MyRootCACertificateName.* Right click this certificate and select *All Tasks -> export -> select DER encoded binary X.509 .CER.* Copy the exported *.cer* file to your Liferay Portal server.

As with the CAS install (see the below section entitled **Single Sign-On**), you will need to import the certificate into the *cacerts keystore.* The import is handled by a command like the following:

```
keytool -import -trustcacerts -keystore /some/path/jdk1.5.0_11/jre/lib/secu-
rity/cacerts -storepass changeit -noprompt
-alias MyRootCA -file /some/path/MyRootCA.cer
```

Once this is done, go back to the LDAP page in the Enterprise Admin portlet by selecting *Settings -> Authentication -> LDAP*. Modify the LDAP URL in the **Base DN** field to the secure version by changing the protocol to *https* and the port to 636 like the following:

```
ldaps://myLdapServerHostname:636
```

Save the changes. Your Liferay Portal will now use LDAP in secure mode for authentication.

Users

This section contains settings for finding users in your LDAP directory.

Authentication Search Filter: The search filter box can be used to determine the search criteria for user logins. By default, Liferay uses the email address as a user login name. If you have changed this setting—which can be done on the *General* tab that's next to the *LDAP* tab in the Enterprise Admin portlet—you will need to modify the search filter here, which has by default been configured to use the email address attribute from LDAP as search criteria. For example, if you changed Liferay's authentication method to use the screen name instead of the email address, you would modify the search filter so that it can match the entered login name:

```
(cn=@screen_name@)
```

Import Search Filter: Depending on the LDAP server, there are different ways to identify the user. Generally, the default setting (*objectClass=inetOrgPerson*) is fine, but if you want to search for only a subset of users or users that have different object classes, you can change this.

User Mapping: The next series of fields allows you to define mappings from LDAP attributes to Liferay fields. Though your LDAP user attributes may be different from LDAP server to LDAP server, there are five fields that Liferay requires to be mapped in order for the user to be recognized. You must define a mapping to the corresponding attributes in LDAP for the following Liferay fields:

- Screen Name
- Password
- Email Address
- First Name
- Last Name

The Enterprise Admin portlet provides default mappings for commonly used LDAP attributes. You can also add your own mappings if you wish.

Test LDAP Users: Once you have your attribute mappings set up (see above), click the *Test LDAP Users* button, and Liferay will attempt to pull LDAP users and match them up with their mappings as a preview.

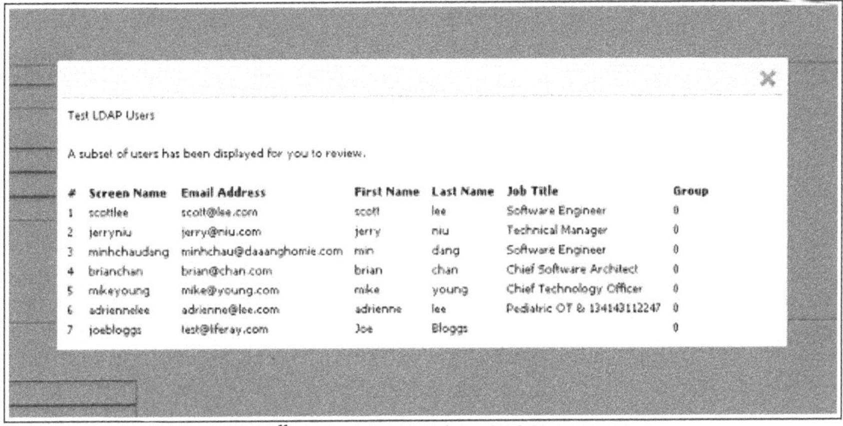

Illustration 64: Testing LDAP Users

Groups

This section contains settings for mapping LDAP groups to Liferay.

Import Search Filter: This is the filter for finding LDAP groups that you want to map to Liferay. Enter the LDAP group attributes that you want retrieved for this mapping. The following attributes can be mapped:

- Group Name
- Description
- User

Test LDAP Groups: Click the *Test LDAP Groups* to display a list of the groups returned by your search filter.

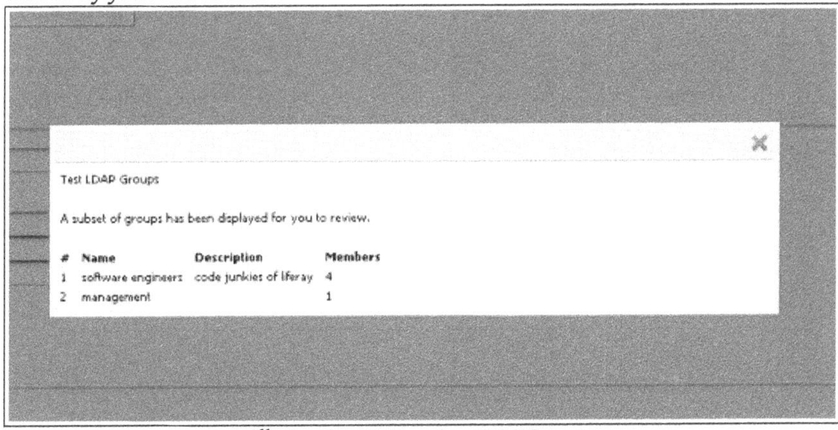

Illustration 65: Mapping LDAP Groups.

Import/Export

Import Enabled: Check this box to cause Liferay to do a mass import from your LDAP directory. If you want Liferay to only synchronize users when they log in, leave this box unchecked. Definitely leave this unchecked if you are working in a clustered environment.

If you check the box, several other options will become available.

Import on Startup Enabled: Check this box to have Liferay run the import when it starts up.

Import Interval: The import runs on a schedule. Select how often you want the import to run.

Export Enabled: Check this box to enable Liferay to export user accounts from the database to LDAP. Liferay uses a listener to track any changes made to the User object and will push these changes out to the LDAP server whenever the User object is updated. Note that on every login, fields such as *LastLoginDate* are updated. When export is enabled, this has the effect of causing a user export every time the user logs in.

Users DN: Enter the location in your LDAP tree where the users will be stored. When Liferay does an export, it will export the users to this location.

User Default Object Classes: When a user is exported, the user is created with the listed default object classes. To find out what your default object classes are, use an LDAP browser tool such as *JXplorer* to locate a user and view the Object Class attributes that are stored in LDAP for that user.

Groups DN: Enter the location in your LDAP tree where the groups will be stored. When Liferay does an export, it will export the groups to this location.

Use LDAP Password Policy: Liferay uses its own password policy by default. This can be configured on the *Password Policies* tab of the Enterprise Admin portlet. If you want to use the password policies defined by your LDAP directory, check this box. Once this is enabled, the *Password Policies* tab will display a message stating that you are not using a local password policy. You will now have to use your LDAP directory's mechanism for setting password policies. Liferay does this by parsing the messages in the LDAP controls that are returned by your LDAP server. By default, the messages in the LDAP controls that Liferay is looking for are the messages that are returned by the Fedora Directory Server. If you are using a different LDAP server, you will need to customize the messages in Liferay's *portal-ext.properties* file, as there is not yet a GUI for setting this. See below for instructions describing how to do this.

Once you have completed configuring LDAP, click the *Save* button.

LDAP Options Not Available in the GUI

Though most of the LDAP configuration can be done from the Enterprise Admin portlet, there are several configuration parameters that are only available by editing *portal-ext.properties*. These options will be available in the GUI in future versions of Liferay Portal, but for now they can only be configured by editing the properties file.

If you need to change any of these options, copy the LDAP section from the *portal.properties* file into your *portal-ext.properties* file. Note that since you have already configured LDAP from the GUI, any settings from the properties file that match settings already configured in the GUI will be ignored. The GUI, which stores the settings in the database, always takes precedence over the properties file.

```
ldap.import.method=[user,group]
```

If you set this to *user,* Liferay will import all users from the specified portion of the LDAP tree. If you set this to *group*, Liferay will search all the groups and import the users in each group. If you have users who do not belong to any groups, they will not be imported.

```
ldap.error.password.age=age
ldap.error.password.expired=expired
ldap.error.password.history=history
ldap.error.password.not.changeable=not allowed to change
ldap.error.password.syntax=syntax
ldap.error.password.trivial=trivial
ldap.error.user.lockout=retry limit
```

These properties are a list of phrases from error messages which can possibly be returned by the LDAP server. When a user binds to LDAP, the server can return *controls* with its response of success or failure. These controls contain a message describing the error or the information that is coming back with the response. Though the controls are the same across LDAP servers, the messages can be different. The properties described here contain snippets of words from those messages, and will work with Red Hat's Fedora Directory Server. If you are not using that server, the word snippets may not work with your LDAP server. If they don't, you can replace the values of these properties with phrases from your server's error messages. This will enable Liferay to recognize them.

Single Sign-On

Single Sign-On solutions allow you to provide a single log in credential for multiple systems. This allows you to have people authenticate to the Single Sign-On product and they will be automatically logged in to Liferay and to other products as well.

Liferay at the time of this writing supports several single sign-on solutions. Of course if your product is not yet supported, you may choose to implement support for it yourself by use of the extension environment—or your organization can choose to sponsor support for it. Please contact sales@liferay.com for more information about this.

Authentication: Central Authentication Service (CAS)

CAS is an authentication system that was originally created at Yale University. It is a widely-used open source single sign-on solution, and was the first SSO product to be supported by Liferay.

Please follow the documentation for CAS to install it on your application server of choice. You can use the version that Liferay provides on our web site or the official version from the JA-SIG web site. The reason for the difference is simply that newer versions require JDK 5 and above only. We provide the older ones for use with Liferay 4.4.2 and below, so that users can have a full environment that runs on JDK 1.4.

Tip: If you are using Liferay 5.x, use the newer versions of CAS from the JA-SIG web site. If you are using Liferay 4.x, use the older Yale versions of CAS from Liferay's Sourceforge archives.

Your first step will be to copy the CAS client .jar file to Liferay's library folder. On Tomcat, this is in *<Tomcat Home>/webapps/ROOT/WEB-INF/lib*. Once you've done this, the CAS client will be available to Liferay the next time you start it.

The CAS Server application requires a properly configured Secure Socket Layer certificate on your server in order to work. If you wish to generate one yourself, you will need to use the *keytool* utility that comes with the JDK. Your first step is to generate the key. Next, you export the key into a file. Finally, you import the key into your local Java key store. For public, Internet-based production environments, you will need to either purchase a signed key from a recognized certificate authority (such as Thawte or Verisign) or have your key signed by a recognized certificate authority. For Intranets, you should have your IT department pre-configure users' browsers to accept the certificate so that they don't get warning messages about the certificate.

To generate a key, use the following command:

```
keytool -genkey -alias tomcat -keypass changeit -keyalg RSA
```

Instead of the password in the example (*changeit*), use a password that you will be able to remember. If you are not using Tomcat, you may want to use a different alias as well. For First and Last name, enter *localhost,* or the host name of your server. It cannot be an IP address.

To export the key to a file, use the following command:

```
keytool -export -alias tomcat -keypass changeit -file server.cert
```

Finally, to import the key into your Java key store, use the following command:

```
keytool -import -alias tomcat -file %FILE_NAME% -keypass changeit
-keystore $JAVA_HOME/jre/lib/security/cacerts
```

If you are on a Windows system, replace *$JAVA_HOME* above with *%JAVA_HOME%*. Of course, all of this needs to be done on the system on which CAS will be running.

Once your CAS server is up and running, you can configure Liferay to use it. This is a simple matter of navigating to the *Settings -> Authentication -> CAS* tab in the **Enterprise Admin** portlet. Enable CAS authentication, and then modify the URL properties to point to your CAS server.

Enabled: Set this to true to enable CAS single sign-on.

Import from LDAP: A user may be authenticated from CAS and not yet exist in the portal. Select this to automatically import users from LDAP if they do not exist in the portal.

The rest of the settings are various URLs, with defaults included. Change *localhost* in the default values to point to your CAS server. When you are finished, click *Save*.

After this, when users click the *Sign In* link from the Dock, they will be directed to the CAS server to sign in to Liferay.

Authentication: NTLM

NTLM is a Microsoft protocol that can be used for authentication through Microsoft Internet Explorer. Though Microsoft has adopted Kerberos in modern versions of Windows server, NTLM is still used when authenticating to a workgroup.

Enabled: Check the box to enable NTLM authentication.

Domain Controller: Enter the IP address of your domain controller. This is the server that contains the user accounts you want to use with Liferay.

Domain: Enter the domain / workgroup name.

Authentication: OpenID

OpenID is a new single sign-on standard which is implemented by multiple vendors. The idea is that multiple vendors can implement the standard, and then users can register for an ID with the vendor they trust. The credential issued by that vendor can be used by all the web sites that support OpenID. Some high profile OpenID vendors are AOL (http://openid.aol.com/screenname), LiveDoor (http://profile.livedoor.com/username), and LiveJournal (http://username.livejournal.com). Please see the OpenID site (http://www.openid.net) for a more complete list.

The obvious main benefit of OpenID for the user is that he or she no longer has to register for a new account on every site in which he or she wants to participate. Users can register on *one* site (the OpenID provider's site) and then use those credentials to authenticate to many web sites which support OpenID. Many web site owners often struggle to build communities because end users are reluctant to register for so many different accounts. Supporting OpenID makes it easier for site owners to build their communities because the barriers to participating (i.e., the effort it takes to register for and keep track of many accounts) are removed. All of the account information is kept with the OpenID provider, making it much easier to manage this information and keep it up to date.

Liferay Portal can act as an OpenID consumer, allowing users to automatically register and sign in with their OpenID accounts. Internally, the product uses OpenID4-Java (http://code.google.com/p/openid4java/) to implement the feature.

OpenID is enabled by default in Liferay, but can be disabled on this tab.

Atlassian Crowd

Atlassian Crowd is a web-based Single Sign-On product similar to CAS. Crowd can be used to manage authentication to many different web applications and directory servers.

Because Atlassian Crowd implements an OpenID producer, Liferay works and has been tested with it. Simply use the OpenID authentication feature in Liferay to log in using Crowd.

Authentication: OpenSSO

OpenSSO is an open source single sign-on solution that comes from the code base of Sun's System Access Manager product. Liferay integrates with OpenSSO, allowing you to use OpenSSO to integrate Liferay into an infrastructure that contains a multitude of different authentication schemes against different repositories of identities.

You can set up OpenSSO on the same server as Liferay or a different box. Follow the instructions at the OpenSSO site (http://opensso.dev.java.net) to install OpenSSO. Once you have it installed, create the Liferay administrative user in it. Users are mapped back and forth by screen names. By default, the Liferay administrative user has a screen name of *test*, so in OpenSSO, you would register the user with the ID of *test* and an email address of *test@liferay.com*. Once you have the user set up, log in to Open SSO using this user.

In the same browser window, go to the URL for your server running Liferay and log in as the same user, using the email address *test@liferay.com*. Go to the **Enterprise Admin** portlet and the *Settings -> Authentication -> OpenSSO* tabs. Modify the three URL fields (Login URL, Logout URL, and Service URL) so that they point to your OpenSSO server (i.e., only modify the host name portion of the URLs), click the *Enabled* check box, and then click *Save*. Liferay will then redirect users to OpenSSO when they click the *Sign In* link.

Default User Associations

The *Default User Associations* tab has three fields allowing you to list (one per line) communities, roles, and user groups that you want new users to be members of by default. Liferay's default is to have new users be members of both the Users role and the Power Users role.

The Power Users role allows users to have their own set of pages where they can add their own portlets, such as blogs, mail, or calendar.

This is generally appropriate for an Intranet, but not an Internet, so you may want to change this for your own implementations. If you have defined other user groups, communities, or roles that you want newly created users to be members of by default, enter them here. For example, you may have defined page templates in certain user groups to pre-populate end users' private pages. If there is a particular configuration that you want everyone to have, you may want to enter those user groups here.

Reserved Screen Names

The next tab is *Reserved Screen Names*. You can enter screen names and email addresses here that you don't want others to use. Liferay will then prevent users from registering with these screen names and email addresses. You might use this feature to prevent users from creating IDs that look like administrative IDs or that have reserved words in their names.

Mail Host Names

The next tab is *Mail Host Names*. You can enter (one per line) other mail host names besides the one you configured on the General tab. Liferay will fail over to these host names in the event that the connection to the main one fails.

Email Notifications

There are three tabs under the *Email Notifications* tab. The *General* tab allows you to set the portal administration name and email address. By default, this is *Joe Bloggs* and *test@liferay.com*. You can change it to anything you want. This name and address will appear in the From field in all email messages sent by the portal.

The other two tabs (*Account Created Notification* and *Password Changed Notification*) allow you to customize the email messages that are sent to users on those two events. A list of tokens for inserting certain values (such as the portal URL) is given if you wish to use those.

The Admin Portlet

The Admin portlet lets you perform various administrative tasks relating to server administration, as opposed to administering resources in the portal. Clicking the first tab (the *Server* tab) of the Admin portlet makes this abundantly clear: you're immediately presented with a graph showing the resources available in the JVM.

Resources

The first tab under the *Server* tab is called *Resources*. This tab contains the aforementioned graph plus several server wide actions that an administrator can execute. These are:

- **Garbage collection:** You can send in a request to the JVM to begin the garbage collection task.
- **Clearing caches:** You can send in a request to the JVM to clear a single VM cache, the cluster cache, or the database cache.
- **Reindex:** You can send in a request to regenerate all search indexes. This will impact portal performance, so try not to do this except at non-peak times.
- **Generate Thread Dump:** If you are performance testing, you can generate a thread dump which can be examined later to determine if there are any deadlocks and where they might be.

Log Levels

Here you can dynamically modify the log levels for any class hierarchy in the portal. If you have custom code that you have deployed which isn't in the list, you can use the *Add Category* tab to add it. If you change the log level near the top of the class hierarchy (such as at *com.liferay*), all the classes under that hierarchy will have their log levels changed. If you are testing something specific, it is much better to be as specific as you can when you change log levels, as by modifying them too high in the hierarchy you can generate a lot more log messages than you probably need.

System Properties

This tab shows an exhaustive list of system properties for the JVM, as well as many Liferay system properties. This information can be used for debugging purposes or to check the configuration of the currently running portal.

Portal Properties

This tab shows an exhaustive list of the portal properties. These properties can be customized as will be seen in the next chapter. If you need to check the current value of a particular property, it can be viewed from this screen without having to shut down the portal or open any properties files.

Shutdown

If you ever need to shut down your Liferay Portal server while users are logged in, you can use the Shutdown tab to inform your logged-in users of the impending shutdown. You can define the number of minutes until the shutdown and a custom message that will be displayed.

Users will see your message at the top of their portal pages for the duration of time you specified. When the time expires, all portal pages will display a message saying the portal has been shut down. At this point, the server will need to be restarted to restore access.

OpenOffice

Liferay Portal contains a JSR-170 compliant document repository. This repository allows users to upload documents in many formats into a folder structure that they define.

OpenOffice.org is an open source office suite which is normally run in graphical mode to create documents, but it can be run in “server” mode. When run in server mode, OpenOffice.org can be used to convert documents to and from all of the file types it supports. Liferay's Document Library portlet can make use of this feature to automatically convert documents on the fly.

You would use this tab to tell Liferay how to connect to your running instance of OpenOffice.org. You can install OpenOffice.org on the same server upon which Liferay is running. Once you have it installed, you can start OpenOffice.org in server mode with the following command:

```
soffice -headless -accept="socket,host=127.0.0.1,port=8100;urp;" -nofirst-
startwizard
```

As you can see, the command above specifies that OpenOffice.org will run on port 8100, which is the default port in the Admin portlet. If you can use this port, all you need to do is check the *Enabled* box, and Liferay will be integrated with OpenOffice.org.

If you have something else running on this port, find a port that is open and specify it both in the command above and on the Admin portlet's OpenOffice.org configuration page. When you are finished, click *Save*.

Instances

Liferay Portal allows you to run more than one portal instance on a single server. Data for each portal instance are kept separate from every other portal instance. All portal data, however, is kept in the same database.

Each portal instance requires its own domain name. Liferay will direct users to the proper portal instance based on this domain name. So before you configure an instance, configure its domain name in your network first. When you're ready to add an instance, click the *Add* button on the *Instances* tab.

You'll be prompted for three fields:

Web ID: A general convention is to use the domain name for this. It's a user-generated ID for the instance.

Virtual Host: Put the domain name you configured in your network here. When users are directed to your Liferay server via this domain name, Liferay will then be able to send them to the proper portal instance.

Mail Domain: Enter the domain name for the mail host for this instance. Liferay will use this to send email notifications from the portal.

When you are finished filling out the form, click *Save*. Now navigate to the portal using your new domain name. You will see that you are brought to what looks like a clean install of Liferay. This is your new portal instance which can now be configured any way you like.

Plugins

The *Plugins* tab shows all of the plugins that are currently installed. These are divided into tabs for portlets, themes, layout templates, and web applications. If you want to install a new plugin, click the *Install More Portlets* button. You will then be brought to the **Plugin Installer**, where you can browse Liferay's repository of portlets or install your own plugins. The Plugin Installer will be covered in the next chapter.

Summary

This chapter has described the resources in Liferay Portal that can be configured to build the site you need to build. We have seen how to navigate Liferay's user interface so that you can get anywhere you need to in the portal. We have also looked at overall portal architecture and how you might go about designing your site using Liferay.

Next, we went in-depth through two of Liferay's administrative portlets: **Enterprise Admin** and **Admin**. Using these two portlets, we learned how to manage users, organizations, user groups, and roles. We also learned how to configure various server settings, such as authentication, LDAP integration, and single sign-on. We also learned how to associate users by default with different user groups, communities, and roles, and we saw how to reserve screen names and email addresses so that users cannot register in the portal with them.

Next, we saw how to view and configure overall server settings. We saw how to view the memory currently being used by the server, as well as how to initiate garbage collection, a thread dump, search engine re-indexing, and the clearing of various caches. We learned how to debug parts of the portal by changing log levels, and by viewing the various properties that are defined in the portal.

Finally, we learned how to properly notify users that the portal is about to shut down and how to enable the OpenOffice.org integration. The ability to run multiple portal instances on one installation of Liferay was covered, and we saw how to view the plugins that are currently installed.

All of this information should help to bring you well on your way to becoming a seasoned Liferay Portal Administrator.

4. Advanced Liferay Configuration

Liferay is configured by a combination of settings which are stored in the database (configured by the use of the various administration portlets) and settings which are stored in properties (text) files. These files can be modified to change Liferay's behavior in certain ways. There are a large number of configuration options that can be set, and so this section will have a wide-ranging set of topics. We will first go over the main configuration file, which is stored in *<Liferay Home>/WEB-INF/classes*, and is called *portal-ext.properties.*

There are also some lower level settings that you may want to further customize. They include changing certain out-of-box defaults, security configuration, and adding features to Liferay through plugin management. We will examine specifically these topics:

- *Advanced Liferay Configuration:* This includes the customization of the *portal-ext.properties* file.
- *Plugin Management:* You will learn how to install Plugins (portlets and themes) from Liferay's Official Repository and Liferay's Community Repository, as well as how to create your own plugin repository.
- *Liferay SOA:* Accessing Liferay services remotely, from outside the portal, will be discussed, as well as how to configure the security settings for these services.

The *portal-ext.properties* File

Liferay's properties files differ from the configuration files of most other products in that changing the default configuration file is discouraged. In fact, the file that contains all of the defaults is stored inside of a .jar file, making it more difficult to customize. Why is it set up this way? Because Liferay uses the concept of *overriding* the defaults in a separate file, rather than going in and customizing the default configuration file. You put just the settings you want to customize in your own configuration file, and then the configuration file for your portal is uncluttered and contains only the settings you need. This makes it far easier to determine whether a particular setting has been customized, and it makes the settings more portable across different instances of Liferay.

The default configuration file is called *portal.properties*, and it resides inside of the *portal-impl.jar* file. The file which is used to override the configuration is *portal-ext.properties*. This file is readily accessible inside of the *<Liferay Home>/WEB-INF/classes* folder in Liferay's installed location in your application server. By default, it has very little information in it, or it may not exist at all, depending on the version of Liferay you are running. What follows is a brief description of the options that can be placed there, thus overriding the defaults from the *portal.properties* file. These are presented in a logical order, not an alphabetical one, as many properties relate to other properties in the system.

Properties Override

This property specifies where to get the overridden properties. By default, it is *portal-ext.properties.* Updates should not be made on the original file (*portal.properties*) but on the overridden version of this file. Furthermore, each portal instance can have its own overridden property file following the convention portal-companyid.properties.

For example, one read order may be: portal.properties, then portal-ext.properties, and then portal-test.properties.

Examples:

```
include-and-override=portal-ext.properties
include-and-override=portal-${easyconf:companyId}.properties
include-and-override=portal-test.properties
```

You can add additional property files that overwrite the default values by using the *external-properties* system property.

A common use case is to keep legacy property values when upgrading to newer versions of Liferay. For example:

```
java ... -Dexternal-properties=portal-legacy-4.4.properties
include-and-override=${external-properties}
```

Portal Context

This specifies the path of the portal servlet context. This is needed because javax.servlet.ServletContext does not have access to the context path until Java EE 5.

Set this property if you deploy the portal to another path besides root.

Examples:

```
portal.ctx=/
portal.ctx=/portal
```

Resource Repositories Root

Specifies the default root path for various repository and resource paths. Under this path several directories will be created for the hot deploy feature, JCR, etc.

Examples:

```
resource.repositories.root=${user.home}/liferay
resource.repositories.root=/home/liferay
```

Technology Compatibility Kit

Set the following to true to enable programmatic configuration to let the Portlet TCK obtain a URL for each test. This should never be set to true unless you are running the TCK tests.

```
tck.url=false
```

Schema

Set this to true to automatically create tables and populate with default data if the database is empty.

```
schema.run.enabled=true
```

Set this to to true to populate with the minimal amount of data. Set this to false to populate with a larger amount of sample data.

```
schema.run.minimal=true
```

Upgrade

Input a list of comma delimited class names that implement com.liferay.portal.upgrade.UpgradeProcess. These classes will run on startup to upgrade older data to match with the latest version.

```
upgrade.processes=\
    com.liferay.portal.upgrade.UpgradeProcess_4_3_0,\
    com.liferay.portal.upgrade.UpgradeProcess_4_3_1,\
    com.liferay.portal.upgrade.UpgradeProcess_4_3_2,\
    com.liferay.portal.upgrade.UpgradeProcess_4_3_3,\
    com.liferay.portal.upgrade.UpgradeProcess_4_3_4,\
    com.liferay.portal.upgrade.UpgradeProcess_4_3_5,\
    com.liferay.portal.upgrade.UpgradeProcess_4_4_0,\
    com.liferay.portal.upgrade.UpgradeProcess_5_0_0,\
    com.liferay.portal.upgrade.UpgradeProcess_5_1_0
```

Verify

Input a list of comma delimited class names that implement com.liferay.portal.integrity.VerifyProcess. These classes will run on startup to verify and fix any integrity problems found in the database.

```
verify.processes=com.liferay.portal.verify.VerifyProcessSuite
```

Specify the frequency for verifying the integrity of the database.

Constants in VerifyProcess:

public static final int ALWAYS = -1;

public static final int NEVER = 0;

public static final int ONCE = 1;

```
verify.frequency=1
```

Auto Deploy

Input a list of comma delimited class names that implement *com.liferay.portal.kernel.deploy.auto.AutoDeployListener*. These classes are used to process the auto deployment of WARs.

```
auto.deploy.listeners=\
  com.liferay.portal.deploy.auto.LayoutTemplateAutoDeployListener,\
  com.liferay.portal.deploy.auto.PortletAutoDeployListener,\
  com.liferay.portal.deploy.auto.ThemeAutoDeployListener,\
  com.liferay.portal.deploy.auto.WebAutoDeployListener,\
  com.liferay.portal.deploy.auto.exploded.tomcat.LayoutTemplateExplodedTom-
catListener,\
  com.liferay.portal.deploy.auto.exploded.tomcat.PortletExplodedTomcatLis-
tener,\
  com.liferay.portal.deploy.auto.exploded.tomcat.ThemeExplodedTomcatListener
```

Set the following to true to enable auto deploy of layout templates, portlets, and themes.

```
auto.deploy.enabled=true
```

Set the directory to scan for layout templates, portlets, and themes to auto deploy.

```
auto.deploy.deploy.dir=${resource.repositories.root}/deploy
```

Set the directory where auto deployed WARs are copied to. The application server or servlet container must know to listen on that directory.

Different containers have different hot deploy paths. For example, Tomcat listens on *${catalina.base}/webapps* whereas JBoss listens on *${jboss.server.home.dir}/deploy*. Set a blank directory to automatically use the application server specific directory.

Examples:

```
auto.deploy.dest.dir=
```

```
auto.deploy.default.dest.dir=../webapps
auto.deploy.geronimo.dest.dir=${org.apache.geronimo.base.dir}/deploy
auto.deploy.geronimo-jetty.dest.dir=${org.apache.geronimo.base.dir}/deploy
auto.deploy.geronimo-tomcat.dest.dir=${org.apache.geronimo.base.dir}/deploy
auto.deploy.glassfish.dest.dir=${com.sun.aas.instanceRoot}/autodeploy
auto.deploy.glassfish-tomcat.dest.dir=${com.sun.aas.instanceRoot}/autodeploy
auto.deploy.jboss-jetty.dest.dir=${jboss.server.home.dir}/deploy
auto.deploy.jboss-tomcat.dest.dir=${jboss.server.home.dir}/deploy
auto.deploy.jetty.dest.dir=${jetty.home}/webapps
auto.deploy.jonas-jetty.dest.dir=${jonas.base}/webapps/autoload
auto.deploy.jonas-tomcat.dest.dir=${jonas.base}/webapps/autoload
auto.deploy.tomcat.dest.dir=${catalina.base}/webapps
auto.deploy.weblogic.dest.dir=${env.DOMAIN_HOME}/autodeploy
```

Set the interval in milliseconds on how often to scan the directory for changes.

```
auto.deploy.interval=10000
```

Set the number of attempts to deploy a file before blacklisting it.

```
auto.deploy.blacklist.threshold=10
```

Set the following to true if deployed WARs are unpacked. Set this to false if your application server has concurrency issues with deploying large WARs.

```
auto.deploy.unpack.war=true
```

Set the following to true if you want the deployer to rename portlet.xml to portlet-custom.xml. This is only needed when deploying the portal on WebSphere 6.1.x with a version before 6.1.0.7 because WebSphere's portlet container will try to process a portlet at the same time that Liferay is trying to process a portlet.

Note that according to IBM, on versions *after* 6.1.0.9, you need to add a context parameter to the web.xml descriptor in your portlet application called *com.ibm.websphere.portletcontainer.PortletDeploymentEnabled* and set it to *false*. This parameter causes WebSphere's built-in portlet container to ignore your portlet application when it is deployed, enabling Liferay to pick it up.

```
auto.deploy.custom.portlet.xml=false
```

Set this to 1 if you are using JBoss' PrefixDeploymentSorter. This will append a 1 in front of your WAR name. For example, if you are deploying a portlet called test-portlet.war, it will deploy it to 1test-portlet.war. JBoss now knows to load this portlet after the other WARs have loaded; however, it will remove the 1 from the context path.

Modify */server/default/conf/jboss-service.xml*.

See *org.jboss.deployment.scanner.PrefixDeploymentSorter*.

```
auto.deploy.jboss.prefix=1
```

Set the path to Tomcat's configuration directory. This property is used to auto deploy exploded WARs. Tomcat context XML files found in the auto deploy directory will be copied to Tomcat's configuration directory. The context XML file must have a docBase attribute that points to a valid WAR directory.

```
auto.deploy.tomcat.conf.dir=../conf/Catalina/localhost
```

Set the path to Tomcat's global class loader. This property is only used by Tomcat in a standalone environment.

```
auto.deploy.tomcat.lib.dir=../common/lib/ext
```

Set the URLs of Libraries that might be needed to download during the auto deploy process

```
library.download.url.quercus.jar=http://lportal.svn.sourceforge.net/viewvc/*
checkout*/lportal/portal/trunk/lib/development/quercus.jar
library.download.url.resin-util.jar=http://lpor-
tal.svn.sourceforge.net/viewvc/*checkout*/lportal/portal/trunk/lib/develop-
ment/resin-util.jar
library.download.url.script-10.jar=http://lportal.svn.sourceforge.net/viewvc
/*checkout*/lportal/portal/trunk/lib/development/script-10.jar
```

Hot Deploy

Input a list of comma delimited class names that implement *com.liferay.portal.kernel.deploy.hot.HotDeployListener*. These classes are used to process the deployment and undeployment of WARs at runtime.

Note: PluginPackageHotDeployListener must always be first.

```
hot.deploy.listeners=\
    com.liferay.portal.deploy.hot.PluginPackageHotDeployListener,\
    com.liferay.portal.deploy.hot.HookHotDeployListener,\
    com.liferay.portal.deploy.hot.LayoutTemplateHotDeployListener,\
    com.liferay.portal.deploy.hot.PortletHotDeployListener,\
    com.liferay.portal.deploy.hot.ThemeHotDeployListener,\
    com.liferay.portal.deploy.hot.ThemeLoaderHotDeployListener
```

Hot Undeploy

Set the following to true to enable undeploying plugins.

```
hot.undeploy.enabled=true
```

Set the undeploy interval in milliseconds on how long to wait for the undeploy process to finish.

```
hot.undeploy.interval=0
```

Set the following to true to undeploy a plugin before deploying a new version. This property will only be used if the property *hot.undeploy.enabled* is set to true.

```
hot.undeploy.on.redeploy=false
```

Plugin

Input a list of comma delimited supported plugin types.

```
plugin.types=portlet,theme,layout-template,web
```

Input a list of Liferay plugin repositories separated by \n characters.

```
plugin.repositories.trusted=http://plugins.liferay.com/official
plugin.repositories.untrusted=http://plugins.liferay.com/community
```

Set this property to false to avoid receiving on screen notifications when there is a new version of an installed plugin.

```
plugin.notifications.enabled=true
```

Input a list of plugin packages ids separated by \n characters. Administrators won't be notified when a new version of these plugins are available. The ids are of the form groupId/artifactId. You can also end the id with an asterisk to match any id that start with the previous character.

```
plugin.notifications.packages.ignored=liferay/sample-jsp-portlet
```

Portlet

Set this property for the portlet container implementation to use. The default implementation is the internal implementation and provides for the best backwards compatibility. The Sun implementation provides more features and will be the recommended implementation in the future.

```
portlet.container.impl=internal
#portlet.container.impl=sun
```

Set this property to define the default virtual path for all hot deployed portlets. See liferay-portlet-app_4_3_0.dtd and the virtual-path element for more information.

```
portlet.virtual.path=
```

Theme

Set this property to true to load the theme's merged CSS files for faster loading for production.

Set this property to false for easier debugging for development. You can also disable fast loading by setting the URL parameter *css_fast_load* to *0*.

```
theme.css.fast.load=true
```

Set the theme's shorcut icon.

```
theme.shortcut.icon=liferay.ico
```

Set this property to set the default virtual path for all hot deployed themes. See liferay-look-and-feel_4_3_0.dtd and the virtual-path element for more information.

```
theme.virtual.path=
```

Set this with an absolute path to specify where imported theme files from a LAR will be stored. This path will override the file-storage path specified in liferay-theme-loader.xml.

```
theme.loader.storage.path=
```

Themes can be imported via LAR files. Set this to true if imported themes should use a new theme id on every import. This will ensure that a copy of the old theme is preserved in the theme loader storage path. However, this also means that a lot of themes that are no longer used remain in the file system. It is recommended that you set this to false.

```
theme.loader.new.theme.id.on.import=false
```

Set this to true to decorate portlets by default.

```
theme.portlet.decorate.default=true
```

Resource Actions

Input a list of comma delimited resource action configurations that will be read from the class path.

```
resource.actions.configs=resource-actions/default.xml
```

Model Hints

Input a list of comma delimited model hints configurations.

```
model.hints.configs=\
    META-INF/portal-model-hints.xml,\
    META-INF/workflow-model-hints.xml,\
    META-INF/ext-model-hints.xml,\
    META-INF/portlet-model-hints.xml
```

Spring

Input a list of comma delimited Spring configurations. These will be loaded after the bean definitions specified in the *contextConfigLocation* parameter in *web.xml*.

```
spring.configs=\
    META-INF/data-source-spring.xml,\
    META-INF/misc-spring.xml,\
    META-INF/counter-spring.xml,\
    META-INF/documentlibrary-spring.xml,\
    META-INF/lock-spring.xml,\
    META-INF/mail-spring.xml,\
    META-INF/portal-spring.xml,\
    META-INF/portal-spring-jcr.xml,\
    META-INF/ext-spring.xml
```

Set the bean name for the Liferay data source.

```
spring.hibernate.data.source=liferayDataSource
```

Set the bean name for the Liferay session factory.

```
spring.hibernate.session.factory=&liferaySessionFactory
```

Hibernate

Many of the following properties should only be customized if you have advanced knowledge of Hibernate. They map to various Hibernate configuration options which themselves have detailed documentation. Please see http://www.hibernate.org for more information.

Input a list of comma delimited Hibernate configurations.

```
hibernate.configs=\
    META-INF/counter-hbm.xml,\
    META-INF/mail-hbm.xml,\
    META-INF/portal-hbm.xml,\
    META-INF/ext-hbm.xml
```

Use the Liferay SQL dialect because it will automatically detect the proper SQL dialect based on your connection URL.

```
hibernate.dialect=com.liferay.portal.dao.orm.hibernate.DynamicDialect
```

Set the Hibernate connection release mode. You should not modify this unless you know what you're doing. The default setting works best for Spring managed transactions. See the method buildSessionFactory in class *org.springframework.orm.hibernate3.LocalSessionFactoryBean* and search for the phrase "on_close" to understand how this works.

```
hibernate.connection.release_mode=on_close
```

Set the Hibernate cache provider. Ehcache is recommended in a clustered environment. See the property *net.sf.ehcache.configurationResourceName* for detailed configuration.

Examples:

```
hibernate.cache.provider_class=com.liferay.portal.dao.orm.hibernate.EhCache-
Provider
hibernate.cache.provider_class=net.sf.hibernate.cache.HashtableCacheProvider
hibernate.cache.provider_class=com.liferay.portal.dao.orm.hibernate.OSCache-
Provider
```

This property is used if Hibernate is configured to use Ehcache's cache provider.

```
net.sf.ehcache.configurationResourceName=/ehcache/hibernate.xml
```

Use the following ehcache configuration in a clustered environment.

```
net.sf.ehcache.configurationResourceName=/ehcache/hibernate-clustered.xml
```

Set other Hibernate cache settings.

```
hibernate.cache.use_query_cache=true
hibernate.cache.use_second_level_cache=true
hibernate.cache.use_minimal_puts=true
hibernate.cache.use_structured_entries=false
```

Use these properties to disable Hibernate caching. This may be a performance hit; you may only want to use these properties for diagnostic purposes.

```
hibernate.cache.provider_class=org.hibernate.cache.NoCacheProvider
hibernate.cache.use_query_cache=false
hibernate.cache.use_second_level_cache=false
```

Set the JDBC batch size to improve performance. If you're using Oracle 9i, however, you must set the batch size to 0 as a workaround for a hanging bug in the Oracle driver. See http://support.liferay.com/browse/LEP-1234 for more information.

Examples:

```
hibernate.jdbc.batch_size=20
hibernate.jdbc.batch_size=0
```

Set other miscellaneous Hibernate properties.

```
hibernate.jdbc.use_scrollable_resultset=true
hibernate.bytecode.use_reflection_optimizer=true
hibernate.show_sql=false
```

Use the classic query factory until WebLogic and Hibernate 3 can get along. See http://www.hibernate.org/250.html#A23 for more information.

```
hibernate.query.factory_class=org.hibernate.hql.classic.ClassicQueryTransla-
torFactory
```

Custom SQL

Input a list of comma delimited custom SQL configurations. Liferay Administrators should never need to customize this; this is more of an option for developers who are customizing Liferay's behavior.

```
custom.sql.configs=custom-sql/default.xml
```

Some databases do not recognize a NULL IS NULL check. Set the *custom.sql.function.isnull* and *custom.sql.function.isnotnull* properties for your specific database.

There is no need to manually set these properties because *com.liferay.portal.dao.orm.hibernate.DynamicDialect* already sets it. These properties are set, however, so that you can see how you can override it for a database that DynamicDialect does not yet know how to auto configure.

DB2

```
custom.sql.function.isnull=CAST(? AS VARCHAR(32672)) IS NULL
custom.sql.function.isnotnull=CAST(? AS VARCHAR(32672)) IS NOT NULL
```

MySQL (for testing only)

```
custom.sql.function.isnull=IFNULL(?, '1') = '1'
custom.sql.function.isnotnull=IFNULL(?, '1') = '0'
```

Sybase

```
custom.sql.function.isnull=ISNULL(?, '1') = '1'
```

```
custom.sql.function.isnotnull=ISNULL(?, '1') = '0'
```

Ehcache

Set the classpath to the location of the Ehcache config file for internal caches. Edit the file specified in the property *ehcache.multi-vm.config.location* to enable clustered cache.

```
ehcache.single.vm.config.location=/ehcache/liferay-single-vm.xml
ehcache.multi.vm.config.location=/ehcache/liferay-multi-vm.xml
```

Use the following in a clustered environment.

```
ehcache.multi.vm.config.location=/ehcache/liferay-multi-vm-clustered.xml
```

Commons Pool

Commons Pool is used to pool and recycle objects that are used very often. This can help lower memory usage. There is some debate over the synchronization issues related to Commons Pool. Set this to false to disable object pooling.

```
commons.pool.enabled=false
```

JavaScript

Set a list of JavaScript files that will be loaded programmatically in */html/common/themes/top_js.jsp*.

There are two lists of files specified in the properties *javascript.barebone.files* and *javascript.everything.files*.

As the name suggests, the barebone list is a trimmed down version of the everything list whereas the everything list is a list of all loaded JavaScript files.

The two lists of files exist for performance reasons because unauthenticated users usually do not utilize all the JavaScript that is available. See the property *javascript.barebone.enabled* for more information on the logic of when the barebone list is used and when the everything list is used and how to customize that logic.

The list of files are also merged and packed for further performance improvements. See the property *javascript.fast.load* for more details.

Specify the list of barebone files.

The ordering of the JavaScript files is important. Specifically, all JQuery scripts should go first.

The Liferay scripts are grouped in such a way that the first grouping denotes utility scripts that are used by the second and third groups. The second grouping denotes utility classes that rely on the first group, but does not rely on the second or third group. The third grouping denotes modules that rely on the first and second group.

```
javascript.barebone.files=\
```

```
    \
    #
    # JQuery scripts
    #
    \
    jquery/jquery.js,\
    jquery/cookie.js,\
    jquery/hover_intent.js,\
    jquery/j2browse.js,\
    jquery/livequery.js,\
    jquery/ui.core.js,\
    jquery/ui.datepicker.js,\
    jquery/ui.dialog.js,\
    \
    #
    # Miscellaneous scripts
    #
    \
    misc/class.js,\
    misc/swfobject.js,\
    \
    #
    # Liferay base utility scripts
    #
    \
    liferay/liferay.js,\
    liferay/browser.js,\
    liferay/util.js,\
    \
    #
    # Liferay utility scripts
    #
    \
    liferay/events.js,\
    liferay/popup.js,\
    liferay/portal.js,\
    liferay/portlet.js,\
    \
    #
    # Liferay modules
    #
    \
    liferay/dock.js,\
    liferay/menu.js

#
# Specify the list of everything files.
#
```

```
javascript.everything.files=\
    \
    #
    # JQuery scripts
    #
    \
    jquery/jquery.js,\
    jquery/cookie.js,\
    jquery/form.js,\
    jquery/hover_intent.js,\
    jquery/j2browse.js,\
    jquery/jeditable.js,\
    jquery/json.js,\
    jquery/livequery.js,\
    jquery/media.js,\
    jquery/ui.core.js,\
    jquery/ui.accordion.js,\
    jquery/ui.dialog.js,\
    jquery/ui.draggable.js,\
    jquery/ui.droppable.js,\
    jquery/ui.resizable.js,\
    jquery/ui.selectable.js,\
    jquery/ui.slider.js,\
    jquery/ui.sortable.js,\
    jquery/ui.tabs.js,\
    jquery/effects.core.js,\
    jquery/effects.blind.js,\
    jquery/effects.bounce.js,\
    jquery/effects.clip.js,\
    jquery/effects.drop.js,\
    jquery/effects.explode.js,\
    jquery/effects.fold.js,\
    jquery/effects.highlight.js,\
    jquery/effects.pulsate.js,\
    jquery/effects.scale.js,\
    jquery/effects.shake.js,\
    jquery/effects.slide.js,\
    jquery/effects.transfer.js,\
    jquery/ui.color_picker.js,\
    jquery/ui.autocomplete.js,\
    \
    #
    # Miscellaneous scripts
    #
    \
    misc/class.js,\
    misc/swfobject.js,\
    \
```

```
#
# Liferay base utility scripts
#
\
liferay/liferay.js,\
liferay/browser.js,\
liferay/util.js,\
liferay/language.js,\
liferay/layout.js,\
\
#
# Liferay utility scripts
#
\
liferay/events.js,\
liferay/popup.js,\
liferay/portal.js,\
liferay/portlet.js,\
\
#
# Liferay modules
#
\
liferay/auto_fields.js,\
liferay/color_picker.js,\
liferay/dock.js,\
liferay/dynamic_select.js,\
liferay/layout_configuration.js,\
liferay/layout_exporter.js,\
liferay/menu.js,\
liferay/notice.js,\
liferay/navigation.js,\
liferay/session.js,\
liferay/tags_selector.js,\
liferay/upload.js
```

Set this property to false to always load JavaScript files listed in the property *javascript.everything.files*. Set this to true to sometimes load *javascript.barebone.files* and sometimes load *javascript.everything.files*.

The default logic is coded in *com.liferay.portal.events.ServicePreAction* in such a way that unauthenticated users get the barebone list of JavaScript files whereas authenticated users get the everything list of JavaScript files.

```
javascript.barebone.enabled=true
```

Set this property to true to load the packed version of files listed in the properties *javascript.barebone.files* or *javascript.everything.files*.

Set this property to false for easier debugging for development. You can also disable fast loading by setting the URL parameter *js_fast_load* to *0*.

```
javascript.fast.load=true
```

Set the following to true to enable the display of JavaScript logging.

```
javascript.log.enabled=false
```

SQL Data

Set the default SQL IDs for common objects.

```
sql.data.com.liferay.portal.model.Country.country.id=19
sql.data.com.liferay.portal.model.Region.region.id=5
sql.data.com.liferay.portal.model.ListType.account.address=10000
sql.data.com.liferay.portal.model.ListType.account.email.address=10004
sql.data.com.liferay.portal.model.ListType.contact.email.address=11003
sql.data.com.liferay.portal.model.ListType.organization.status=12017
```

Company

This sets the default web id. Omni admin users must belong to the company with this web id.

```
company.default.web.id=liferay.com
```

The portal can authenticate users based on their email address, screen name, or user id.

```
company.security.auth.type=emailAddress
company.security.auth.type=screenName
company.security.auth.type=userId
```

Set this to true to ensure users login with https.

```
company.security.auth.requires.https=false
```

Set the following to true to allow users to select the *remember me* feature to automatically login to the portal.

```
company.security.auto.login=true
```

Set the following to the maximum age (in number of seconds) of the browser cookie that enables the *remember me* feature. A value of 31536000 signifies a lifespan of one year. A value of -1 signifies a lifespan of a browser session.

Rather than setting this to 0, set the property *company.security.auto.login* to false to disable the *remember me* feature.

```
company.security.auto.login.max.age=31536000
```

Set the following to true to allow users to ask the portal to send them their password.

```
company.security.send.password=true
```

Set the following to true to allow strangers to create accounts and register themselves on the portal.

```
company.security.strangers=true
```

Set the following to true if strangers can create accounts with email addresses that match the company mail suffix. This property is not used unless *company.security.strangers* is also set to true.

```
company.security.strangers.with.mx=true
```

Set the following to true if strangers who create accounts need to be verified via email.

```
company.security.strangers.verify=false
```

Set the following to true to allow community administrators to use their own logo instead of the enterprise logo.

```
company.security.community.logo=true
```

Users

Set the following to false if users cannot be deleted.

```
users.delete=true
```

Set the following to true to always autogenerate user screen names even if the user gives a specific user screen name.

```
users.screen.name.always.autogenerate=false
```

Input a class name that extends *com.liferay.portal.security.auth.ScreenNameGenerator*. This class will be called to generate user screen names.

```
users.screen.name.generator=com.liferay.portal.security.auth.ScreenNameGen-
erator
```

Input a class name that extends *com.liferay.portal.security.auth.ScreenNameValidator*. This class will be called to validate user ids.

Examples:

```
users.screen.name.validator=com.liferay.portal.security.auth.ScreenNameVal-
idator
users.screen.name.validator=com.liferay.portal.security.auth.LiberalScreen-
NameValidator
```

Set the maximum file size for user portraits. A value of 0 for the maximum file size can be used to indicate unlimited file size. However, the maximum file size allowed is set in property *com.liferay.portal.upload.UploadServletRequestImpl.max.size* found in system.properties.

```
users.image.max.size=307200
```

Groups and Roles

Input a list of comma delimited system group names that will exist in addition to the standard system groups. When the server starts, the portal checks to ensure all system groups exist. Any missing system group will be created by the portal.

```
system.groups=
```

Input a list of comma delimited system role names that will exist in addition to the standard system roles. When the server starts, the portal checks to ensure all system roles exist. Any missing system role will be created by the portal.

The standard system roles are: Administrator, Guest, Power User, and User. These roles cannot be removed or renamed.

```
system.roles=
```

Set the description of the Administrator system role.

```
system.role.Administrator.description=Administrators are super users who can
do anything.
```

Set the description of the Guest system role.

```
system.role.Guest.description=Unauthenticated users always have this role.
```

Set the description of the Power User system role.

```
system.role.Power.User.description=Power Users have their own public and
private pages.
```

Set the description of the User system role.

```
system.role.User.description=Authenticated users should be assigned this
role.
```

Input a list of comma delimited system community role names that will exist in addition to the standard system community roles. When the server starts, the portal checks to ensure all system community roles exist. Any missing system community role will be created by the portal.

The standard system community roles are: Community Administrator, Community Member, and Community Owner. These roles cannot be removed or renamed.

```
  system.community.roles=
```

Set the description of the Community Administrator system community role.

```
system.community.role.Community.Administrator.description=Community Adminis-
trators are super users of their community but cannot make other users into
Community Administrators.
```

Set the description of the Community Member system community role.

```
system.community.role.Community.Member.description=All users who belong to a
community have this role within that community.
```

Set the description of the Community Owner system community role.

```
system.community.role.Community.Owner.description=Community Owners are super
users of their community and can assign community roles to users.
```

Input a list of comma delimited system organization role names that will exist in addition to the standard system organization roles. When the server starts, the portal checks to ensure all system organization roles exist. Any missing system organization role will be created by the portal.

The standard system organization roles are: Organization Administrator, Organization Member, and Organization Owner. These roles cannot be removed or renamed.

```
system.organization.roles=
```

Set the description of the Organization Administrator system organization role.

```
system.organization.role.Organization.Administrator.description=Organization
Administrators are super users of their organization but cannot make other
users into Organization Administrators.
```

Set the description of the Organization Member system organization role.

```
system.organization.role.Organization.Member.description=All users who be-
long to a organization have this role within that organization.
```

Set the description of the Organization Owner system organization role.

```
system.organization.role.Organization.Owner.description=Organization Owners
are super users of their organization and can assign organization roles to
users.
```

Omni admin users can administer the portal's core functionality: gc, shutdown, etc. Omni admin users must belong to the default company.

Multiple portal instances might be deployed on one application server, and not all of the administrators should have access to this core functionality. Input the ids of users who are omniadmin users.

Leave this field blank if users who belong to the right company and have the Administrator role are allowed to administer the portal's core functionality.

```
omniadmin.users=
```

Set the following to true if all users are required to agree to the terms of use.

```
terms.of.use.required=true
```

Organizations

Set the following to true if organizations must have an associated country.

```
organizations.country.required=true
```

Languages and Time Zones

Specify the available locales. Messages corresponding to a specific language are specified in properties files with file names matching that of *content/Language_*.properties*. These values can also be overridden in properties files with file names matching that of *content/Language-ext_*.properties*. Use a comma to separate each entry.

All locales must use UTF-8 encoding.

See the following links to specify language and country codes:

http://ftp.ics.uci.edu/pub/ietf/http/related/iso639.txt

http://userpage.chemie.fu-berlin.de/diverse/doc/ISO_3166.html

```
locales=ar_SA,ca_AD,ca_ES,zh_CN,zh_TW,cs_CZ,nl_NL,en_US,fi_FI,fr_FR,de_DE,el
_GR,hu_HU,it_IT,ja_JP,ko_KR,fa_IR,pt_BR,ru_RU,es_ES,sv_SE,tr_TR,vi_VN
```

Set the following to true if unauthenticated users get their preferred language from the Accept-Language header. Set the following to false if unauthenticated users get their preferred language from their company.

```
locale.default.request=false
```

Specify the available time zones. The specified ids must match those from the class *java.util.TimeZone.*

```
time.zones=\
        Pacific/Midway,\
        Pacific/Honolulu,\
        America/Anchorage,\
        America/Los_Angeles,\
        America/Denver,\
        America/Chicago,\
        America/New_York,\
        America/Puerto_Rico,\
        America/St_Johns,\
        America/Sao_Paulo,\
        America/Noronha,\
        Atlantic/Azores,\
        UTC,\
        Europe/Lisbon,\
        Europe/Paris,\
        Europe/Istanbul,\
        Asia/Jerusalem,\
        Asia/Baghdad,\
        Asia/Tehran,\
        Asia/Dubai,\
        Asia/Kabul,\
        Asia/Karachi,\
        Asia/Calcutta,\
        Asia/Katmandu,\
        Asia/Dhaka,\
        Asia/Rangoon,\
        Asia/Saigon,\
        Asia/Shanghai,\
        Asia/Tokyo,\
        Asia/Seoul,\
        Australia/Darwin,\
        Australia/Sydney,\
        Pacific/Guadalcanal,\
        Pacific/Auckland,\
        Pacific/Enderbury,\
        Pacific/Kiritimati
```

Look and Feel

Set the following to false if the system does not allow users to modify the look and feel.

```
look.and.feel.modifiable=true
```

Set the default layout template id.

```
default.layout.template.id=2_columns_ii
```

Set the default theme id for regular themes.

```
default.regular.theme.id=classic
```

Set the default color scheme id for regular themes.

```
default.regular.color.scheme.id=01
```

Set the default theme id for wap themes.

```
default.wap.theme.id=mobile
```

Set the default color scheme id for wap themes.

```
default.wap.color.scheme.id=01
```

Set the following to true if you want a change in the theme selection of the public or private group to automatically be applied to the other (i.e. if public and private group themes should always be the same).

```
theme.sync.on.group=false
```

Request

Portlets that have been configured to use private request attributes in *liferay-portlet.xml* may still want to share some request attributes. This property allows you to configure which request attributes will be shared.

Set a comma delimited list of attribute names that will be shared when the attribute name starts with one of the specified attribute names. For example, if you set the value to *hello_,world_*, then all attribute names that start with *hello_* or *world_* will be shared.

```
request.shared.attributes=LIFERAY_SHARED_
```

Session

Specify the number of minutes before a session expires. This value is always overridden by the value set in *web.xml*.

```
session.timeout=30
```

Specify the number of minutes before a warning is sent to the user informing the user of the session expiration. Specify 0 to disable any warnings.

```
session.timeout.warning=1
```

Set the auto-extend mode to true to avoid having to ask the user whether to extend the session or not. Instead it will be automatically extended. The purpose of this mode is to keep the session open as long as the user browser is open and with a portal page loaded. It is recommended to use this setting along with a smaller *session.timeout*, such as 5 minutes for better performance.

```
session.timeout.auto.extend=false
```

Set this to true if the user is redirected to the default page when the session expires.

```
session.timeout.redirect.on.expire=false
```

Portlets that have been configured to use private session attributes in *liferay-portlet.xml* may still want to share some session attributes. This property allows you to configure which session attributes will be shared. Set a comma delimited list of attribute names that will be shared when the attribute name starts with one of the specified attribute names. For example, if you set the value to *hello_,world_*, then all attribute names that start with *hello_* or *world_* will be shared.

Note that this property is used to specify the sharing of session attributes from the portal to the portlet. This is not used to specify session sharing between portlet WARs or from the portlet to the portal.

```
session.shared.attributes=org.apache.struts.action.LOCALE,COMPANY_,USER_,LIF
ERAY_SHARED_
```

Set this to false to disable all persistent cookies. Features like automatically logging in will not work.

```
session.enable.persistent.cookies=true
```

The login process sets several cookies if persistent cookies are enabled. Set this property to set the domain of those cookies.

```
session.cookie.domain=
```

Set the following to true to invalidate the session when a user logs into the portal. This helps prevents phishing. Set this to false if you need the guest user and the authenticated user to have the same session.

```
session.enable.phishing.protection=true
```

Set the following to true to test whether users have cookie support before allowing them to sign in. This test will always fail if *tck.url* is set to true because that property disables session cookies.

```
session.test.cookie.support=true
```

Set the following to true to disable sessions. Doing this will use cookies to remember the user across requests. This is useful if you want to scale very large sites where the user may be sent to a different server for each request. The drawback to this approach is that you must not rely on the API for sessions provided by the servlet and portlet specs.

This feature is only available for Tomcat and requires that you set Tomcat's Manager class to *com.liferay.support.tomcat.session.SessionLessManagerBase*.

```
session.disabled=false
```

Input a list of comma delimited class names that extend *com.liferay.portal.struts.SessionAction*. These classes will run at the specified event.

```
    #
    # Servlet session create event
    #
    servlet.session.create.events=com.liferay.portal.events.SessionCreateAc-
tion

    #
    # Servlet session destroy event
    #
    servlet.session.destroy.events=com.liferay.portal.events.SessionDestroy-
Action
```

Set the following to true to track user clicks in memory for the duration of a user's session. Setting this to true allows you to view all live sessions in the Admin portlet.

```
session.tracker.memory.enabled=true
```

Set the following to true to track user clicks in the database after a user's session is invalidated. Setting this to true allows you to generate usage reports from the database. Use this cautiously because this will store a lot of usage data.

```
session.tracker.persistence.enabled=false
```

Set the following to true to convert the tracked paths to friendly URLs.

```
session.tracker.friendly.paths.enabled=false
```

Enter a list of comma delimited paths that should not be tracked.

```
session.tracker.ignore.paths=\
    /portal/css_cached,\
        /portal/javascript_cached,\
        /portal/render_portlet,\
        \
        /document_library/get_file
```

JAAS

Set the following to false to disable JAAS security checks. Disabling JAAS speeds up login. JAAS must be disabled if administrators are to be able to impersonate other users.

```
portal.jaas.enable=false
```

By default, *com.liferay.portal.security.jaas.PortalLoginModule* loads the correct JAAS login module based on what application server or servlet container the portal is deployed on. Set a JAAS implementation class to override this behavior.

```
portal.jaas.impl=
```

The JAAS process may pass in an encrypted password and the authentication will only succeed if there is an exact match. Set this property to false to relax that behavior so the user can input an unencrypted password.

```
portal.jaas.strict.password=false
```

Set the following to true to enable administrators to impersonate other users. JAAS must also be disabled for this feature to work.

```
portal.impersonation.enable=true
```

LDAP

Set the values used to connect to a LDAP store.

```
ldap.factory.initial=com.sun.jndi.ldap.LdapCtxFactory
ldap.base.provider.url=ldap://localhost:10389
ldap.base.dn=dc=example,dc=com
ldap.security.principal=uid=admin,ou=system
ldap.security.credentials=secret
ldap.referral=follow
```

Settings for *com.liferay.portal.security.auth.LDAPAuth* can be configured from the Admin portlet. It provides out of the box support for Apache Directory Server, Microsoft Active Directory Server, Novell eDirectory, and OpenLDAP. The default settings are for Apache Directory Server.

The LDAPAuth class must be specified in the property *auth.pipeline.pre* to be executed.

Encryption is implemented by *com.liferay.util.Encryptor.provider.class* in *system.properties*.

```
ldap.auth.enabled=false
ldap.auth.required=false
```

Set either bind or password-compare for the LDAP authentication method. Bind is preferred by most vendors so that you don't have to worry about encryption strategies.

```
ldap.auth.method=bind
ldap.auth.method=password-compare
```

Set the password encryption to used to compare passwords if the property *ldap.auth.method* is set to password-compare.

```
ldap.auth.password.encryption.algorithm=
ldap.auth.password.encryption.algorithm.types=MD5,SHA
```

Active Directory stores information about the user account as a series of bit fields in the UserAccountControl attribute.

If you want to prevent disabled accounts from logging into the portal you need to use a search filter similiar to the following:

```
(&(objectclass=person)(userprincipalname=@email_address@)(!(UserAccountCon-
trol:1.2.840.113556.1.4.803:=2)))
```

See the following links:

http://support.microsoft.com/kb/305144/

http://support.microsoft.com/?kbid=269181

```
ldap.auth.search.filter=(mail=@email_address@)
```

You can write your own class that extends *com.liferay.portal.security.ldap.AttributesTransformer* to transform the LDAP attributes before a user or group is imported to the LDAP store.

```
ldap.attrs.transformer.impl=com.liferay.portal.security.ldap.Attributes-
Transformer
```

You can write your own class that extends *com.liferay.portal.security.ldap.LDAPUser* to customize the behavior for exporting portal users to the LDAP store.

```
ldap.user.impl=com.liferay.portal.security.ldap.LDAPUser
```

When a user is exported to LDAP and the user does not exist, the user will be created with the following default object classes.

```
ldap.user.default.object.classes=top,person,inetOrgPerson,organizationalPer-
son
```

When importing and exporting users, the portal will use this mapping to connect LDAP user attributes and portal user variables.

```
ldap.user.mappings=screenName=cn\npassword=userPassword\nemailAddress=mail\n
firstName=givenName\nlastName=sn\njobTitle=title\ngroup=groupMembership
```

When importing groups, the portal will use this mapping to connect LDAP group attributes and portal user group variables.

```
ldap.group.mappings=groupName=cn\ndescription=description\nuser=uniqueMember
```

Settings for importing users and groups from LDAP to the portal.

```
ldap.import.enabled=false
ldap.import.on.startup=false
ldap.import.interval=10
ldap.import.user.search.filter=(objectClass=inetOrgPerson)
ldap.import.group.search.filter=(objectClass=groupOfUniqueNames)
```

Set either user or group for import method. If set to user, portal will import all users and the groups associated with those users. If set to group, the portal import all groups and the users associated those groups.

This value should be set based on how your LDAP server stores group membership information.

```
ldap.import.method=user
ldap.import.method=group
```

Settings for exporting users from the portal to LDAP. This allows a user to modify his first name, last name, etc. in the portal and have that change get pushed to the LDAP server. This will only be active if the property *ldap.auth.enabled* is also set to true. New users and groups will be created at the specified DN.

```
ldap.export.enabled=true
ldap.users.dn=ou=users,dc=example,dc=com
```

```
ldap.groups.dn=ou=groups,dc=example,dc=com
```

Set this to true to use the LDAP's password policy instead of the portal password policy.

```
ldap.password.policy.enabled=false
```

Set these values to be a portion of the error message returned by the appropriate directory server to allow the portal to recognize messages from the LDAP server. The default values will work for Fedora DS.

```
ldap.error.password.age=age
ldap.error.password.expired=expired
ldap.error.password.history=history
ldap.error.password.not.changeable=not allowed to change
ldap.error.password.syntax=syntax
ldap.error.password.trivial=trivial
ldap.error.user.lockout=retry limit
```

CAS

Set this to true to enable CAS single sign on. NTLM will work only if LDAP authentication is also enabled and the authentication is made by screen name. If set to true, then the property *auto.login.hooks* must contain a reference to the class *com.liferay.portal.security.auth.CASAutoLogin* and the filter *com.liferay.portal.servlet.filters.sso.cas.CASFilter* must be referenced in web.xml.

```
cas.auth.enabled=false
```

A user may be authenticated from CAS and not yet exist in the portal. Set this to true to automatically import users from LDAP if they do not exist in the portal.

```
cas.import.from.ldap=false
```

Set the default values for the required CAS URLs. Set either *cas.server.name* or *cas.service.url*. Setting *cas.server.name* allows deep linking. See LEP-4423.

```
cas.login.url=https://localhost:8443/cas-web/login
cas.logout.url=https://localhost:8443/cas-web/logout
cas.server.name=localhost:8080
cas.service.url=
#cas.service.url=http://localhost:8080/c/portal/login
cas.service.url=http://localhost:8080/c/portal/login
cas.validate.url=https://localhost:8443/cas-web/proxyValidate
```

NTLM

Set this to true to enable NTLM single sign on. NTLM will work only if LDAP authentication is also enabled and the authentication is made by screen name. If set to true, then the property "auto.login.hooks" must contain a reference to the class *com.liferay.portal.security.auth.NtlmAutoLogin* and the filter *com.liferay.portal.servlet.filters.sso.ntlm.NtlmFilter* must be referenced in web.xml.

```
ntlm.auth.enabled=false
```

```
ntlm.auth.domain.controller=127.0.0.1
ntlm.auth.domain=EXAMPLE
```

OpenID

Set this to true to enable OpenId authentication. If set to true, then the property *auto.login.hooks* must contain a reference to the class *com.liferay.portal.security.auth.OpenIdAutoLogin*.

```
open.id.auth.enabled=true
```

OpenSSO

These properties control Liferay's integration with OpenSSO.

Set this to true to enable OpenSSO authentication.

```
open.sso.auth.enabled=false
```

Set the log in URL and log out URL. The first URL is the link to your OpenSSO server (which can be the same server as the one running Liferay); the second URL is the link to your Liferay Portal.

```
open.sso.login.url=http://openssohost.example.com:8080/opensso/UI/Login?
goto=http://portalhost.example.com:8080/c/portal/login
open.sso.logout.url=http://openssohost.example.com:8080/opensso/UI/Logout?
goto=http://portalhost.example.com:8080/web/guest/home
```

Set the URL to the OpenSSO service.

```
open.sso.service.url=http://openssohost.example.com:8080/opensso
```

Set the HTTP attribute name for the user's screen name.

```
open.sso.screen.name.attr=uid
```

Set the HTTP attribute name for the user's email address.

```
open.sso.email.address.attr=mail
```

Set the HTTP attribute name for the user's Common Name.

```
open.sso.first.name.attr=cn
```

Set the HTTP attribute name for the user's Surname.

```
open.sso.last.name.attr=sn
```

Authentication Pipeline

Input a list of comma delimited class names that implement *com.liferay.portal.security.auth.Authenticator*. These classes will run before or after the portal authentication begins.

The Authenticator class defines the constant values that should be used as return codes from the classes implementing the interface. If# authentication is successful, return SUCCESS; if the user exists but the passwords do not match, return FAILURE;

and if the user does not exist on the system, return DNE.

Constants in Authenticator:

```
public static final int SUCCESS = 1;
public static final int FAILURE = -1;
public static final int DNE = 0;
```

In case you have several classes in the authentication pipeline, all of them have to return SUCCESS if you want the user to be able to login. If one of the authenticators returns FAILURE or DNE, the login fails.

Under certain circumstances, you might want to keep the information in the portal database in sync with an external database or an LDAP server. This can easily be achieved by implementing a class via LDAPAuth that updates the information stored in the portal user database whenever a user signs in.

Each portal instance can be configured at run time to either authenticate based on user ids or email addresses. See the Admin portlet for more information.

Available authenticators are:

com.liferay.portal.security.auth.LDAPAuth

See the LDAP properties to configure the behavior of the LDAPAuth class.

```
auth.pipeline.pre=com.liferay.portal.security.auth.LDAPAuth
auth.pipeline.post=
```

Set this to true to enable password checking by the internal portal authentication. If set to false, you're essentially delegating password checking is delegated to the authenticators configured in *auth.pipeline.pre* and *auth.pipeline.post* settings.

```
auth.pipeline.enable.liferay.check=true
```

Input a list of comma delimited class names that implement *com.liferay.portal.security.auth.AuthFailure*. These classes will run when a user has a failed login or when a user has reached the maximum number of failed logins.

```
auth.failure=com.liferay.portal.security.auth.LoginFailure
auth.max.failures=com.liferay.portal.security.auth.LoginMaxFailures
auth.max.failures.limit=5
```

Set the following to true if users are forwarded to the last visited path upon successful login. If set to false, users will be forwarded to their default layout page.

```
auth.forward.by.last.path=true
```

The login page reads a redirect by a parameter named *redirect*. If this property is set to true, then users will be redirected to the given redirect path upon successful login. If the user does not have permission to view that page, then the rule set by the property *auth.forward.by.last.path* will apply.

You can set the redirect manually from another application, by appending the *redirect* parameter in a url that looks like this: */c/portal/login?redirect=%2Fgroup%2Femployees%2Fcalendar*. This url will redirect the user to the path */group/employees/calendar* upon successful login.

```
auth.forward.by.redirect=true
```

Enter a list of comma delimited paths that can be considered part of the last visited path.

```
auth.forward.last.paths=/document_library/get_file
```

Enter a URL that will be used to login portal users whenever needed. By default, the portal's login page is used.

```
#auth.login.url=/web/guest/home
```

Enter a friendly URL of a page that will be used to login portal users whenever the user is navigating a community and authentication is needed. By default, the portal's login page or the URL set in the property *auth.login.url* is used.

```
auth.login.community.url=/login
```

Enter the name of the login portlet used in a page identified by the URL of the previous property (if one has been set). This will allow the portlet to have access to the redirect parameter and thus forward the user to the page where he was trying to access when necessary. You should leave the default value unless you have your own custom login portlet.

```
auth.login.portlet.name=58
```

Enter a list of comma delimited paths that do not require authentication.

```
auth.public.paths=\
        /blogs/find_entry,\
        /blogs/rss,\
        /blogs/trackback,\
        \
        /bookmarks/open_entry,\
        \
        /document_library/get_file,\
        \
        /journal/get_article,\
        /journal/get_articles,\
        /journal/get_latest_article_content,\
        /journal/get_structure,\
        /journal/get_template,\
        /journal/view_article_content,\
        /journal_articles/view_article_content,\
        \
        /layout_management/sitemap,\
        \
        /message_boards/find_category,\
        /message_boards/find_message,\
        /message_boards/find_thread,\
        /message_boards/get_message_attachment,\
        /message_boards/rss,\
        \
        /my_places/view,\
```

```
    \
    /polls/view_chart,\
    \
    /portal/expire_session,\
    /portal/extend_session,\
    /portal/extend_session_confirm,\
    /portal/json_service,\
    /portal/logout,\
    /portal/open_id_request,\
    /portal/open_id_response,\
    /portal/session_click,\
    /portal/session_tree_js_click,\
    /portal/status,\
    \
    /search/open_search,\
    /search/open_search_description.xml,\
    \
    /shopping/notify,\
    \
    /tags/rss,\
    \
    /wiki/get_page_attachment,\
    /wiki/rss
```

Auto Login

Input a list of comma delimited class names that implement *com.liferay.portal.security.auth.AutoLogin*. These classes will run in consecutive order for all unauthenticated users until one of them return a valid user id and password combination. If no valid combination is returned, then the request continues to process normally. If a valid combination is returned, then the portal will automatically login that user with the returned user id and password combination.

For example, *com.liferay.portal.security.auth.RememberMeAutoLogin* reads from a cookie to automatically log in a user who previously logged in while checking the *Remember Me* box.

This interface allows deployers to easily configure the portal to work with other SSO servers. See *com.liferay.portal.security.auth.CASAutoLogin* for an example of how to configure the portal with Yale's SSO server.

```
auto.login.hooks=com.liferay.portal.security.auth.CASAutoLogin,com.liferay.-
portal.security.auth.NtlmAutoLogin,com.liferay.portal.securi-
ty.auth.OpenIdAutoLogin,com.liferay.portal.security.auth.OpenSSOAutoLogin,co
m.liferay.portal.security.auth.RememberMeAutoLogin
```

Set the hosts that will be ignored for auto login.

```
auto.login.ignore.hosts=
```

Set the paths that will be ignored for auto login.

```
auto.login.ignore.paths=
```

SSO with MAC (Message Authentication Code)

To use SSO with MAC, post to an URL like:

http://localhost:8080/c/portal/login?cmd=already-registered&login=<userId|emailAddress>&password=<MAC>

Pass the MAC in the password field. Make sure the MAC gets URL encoded because it might contain characters not allowed in a URL.

SSO with MAC also requires that you set the following property in system.properties:

```
com.liferay.util.servlet.SessionParameters=false
```

See the following links:

http://support.liferay.com/browse/LEP-1288

http://en.wikipedia.org/wiki/Message_authentication_code

Set the following to true to enable SSO with MAC.

```
auth.mac.allow=false
```

Set the algorithm to use for MAC encryption.

```
auth.mac.algorithm=MD5
```

Set the shared key used to generate the MAC.

```
auth.mac.shared.key=
```

Passwords

Set the following encryption algorithm to encrypt passwords. The default algorithm is SHA (SHA-1). If set to NONE, passwords are stored in the database as plain text. The SHA-512 algorithm is currently unsupported.

Examples:

```
passwords.encryption.algorithm=CRYPT
passwords.encryption.algorithm=MD2
passwords.encryption.algorithm=MD5
passwords.encryption.algorithm=NONE
passwords.encryption.algorithm=SHA
passwords.encryption.algorithm=SHA-256
passwords.encryption.algorithm=SHA-384
passwords.encryption.algorithm=SSHA
```

Digested passwords are encoded via base64 or hex encoding. The default is base64.

```
passwords.digest.encoding=base64
#passwords.digest.encoding=hex
```

Input a class name that extends *com.liferay.portal.security.pwd.BasicToolkit*. This class will be called to generate and validate passwords.

Examples:

```
passwords.toolkit=com.liferay.portal.security.pwd.PasswordPolicyToolkit
passwords.toolkit=com.liferay.portal.security.pwd.RegExpToolkit
```

If you choose to use *com.liferay.portal.security.pwd.PasswordPolicyToolkit* as your password toolkit, you can choose either static or dynamic password generation. Static is set through the property *passwords.passwordpolicytoolkit.static* and dynamic uses the class *com.liferay.util.PwdGenerator* to generate the password. If you are using LDAP password syntax checking, you will also have to use the static generator so that you can guarantee that passwords obey its rules.

Examples:

```
passwords.passwordpolicytoolkit.generator=static
passwords.passwordpolicytoolkit.generator=dynamic
passwords.passwordpolicytoolkit.static=iheartliferay
```

If you choose to use *com.liferay.portal.security.pwd.RegExpToolkit* as your password toolkit, set the regular expression pattern that will be used to generate and validate passwords.

Note that \ is replaced with \\ to work in Java.

The first pattern ensures that passwords must have at least 4 valid characters consisting of digits or letters.

The second pattern ensures that passwords must have at least 8 valid characters consisting of digits or letters.

Examples:

```
passwords.regexptoolkit.pattern=(?=.{4})(?:[a-zA-Z0-9]*)
passwords.regexptoolkit.pattern=(?=.{8})(?:[a-zA-Z0-9]*)
```

Set the length and key for generating passwords.

Examples:

```
passwords.regexptoolkit.charset=0123456789
passwords.regexptoolkit.charset=0123456789ABCDEFGHIJKLMNOPQRSTUVWXYZabcde-
fghijklmnopqrstuvwxyz
```

Examples:

```
passwords.regexptoolkit.length=4
passwords.regexptoolkit.length=8
```

Set the name of the default password policy.

```
passwords.default.policy.name=Default Password Policy
```

Permissions

Set the default permission checker class used by *com.liferay.portal.security.permission.PermissionCheckerFactory* to check permissions for actions on objects. This class can be overridden with a custom class that extends *com.liferay.portal.security.permission.PermissionCheckerImpl*.

```
permissions.checker=com.liferay.portal.security.permission.PermissionCheck-
erImpl
```

Set the algorithm used to check permissions for a user. This is useful so that you can optimize the search for different databases. See *com.liferay.portal.service.impl.PermissionLocalServiceImpl*. The default is method two.

The first algorithm uses several *if* statements to query the database for these five things in order. If it finds any one of them, it returns *true:*

- Is the user connected to one of the permissions via group or organization roles?
- Is the user associated with groups or organizations that are directly connected to one of the permissions?
- Is the user connected to one of the permissions via user roles?
- Is the user connected to one of the permissions via user group roles?
- Is the user directly connected to one of the permissions?

```
permissions.user.check.algorithm=1
```

The second algorithm (the default) does a database join and checks the permissions in one step, by calling *countByGroupsRoles*, *countByGroupsPermissions*, *countByUsersRoles*, *countByUserGroupRole*, and *countByUsersPermissions* in one method.

```
permissions.user.check.algorithm=2
```

The third algorithm checks the permissions by checking for three things. It combines the role check into one step. If it finds any of the following items, it returns *true:*

- Is the user associated with groups or organizations that are directly connected to one of the permissions?
- Is the user associated with a role that is directly connected to one of the permissions?
- Is the user directly connected to one of the permissions?

```
permissions.user.check.algorithm=3
```

The fourth algorithm does a database join and checks the permissions that algorithm three checks in one step, by calling *countByGroupsPermissions*, *countByRolesPermissions*, and *countByUsersPermissions* in one method.

```
permissions.user.check.algorithm=4
```

Set the default permissions list filter class. This class must implement *com.liferay.portal.kernel.security.permission.PermissionsListFilter*. This is used if you want to filter the list of permissions before it is actually persisted. For example, if you want to make sure that all users who create objects never have the UPDATE action, then you can filter that list and remove any permissions that have the UPDATE action before it is persisted.

```
permissions.list.filter=com.liferay.portal.security.permission.Permis-
sionsListFilterImpl
```

Captcha

Set the maximum number of captcha checks per portlet session. Set this value to

0 to always check. Set this value to a number less than 0 to never check. Unauthenticated users will always be checked on every request if captcha checks is enabled.

```
captcha.max.challenges=1
```

Set whether or not to use captcha checks for the following actions.

```
captcha.check.portal.create_account=true
captcha.check.portal.send_password=true
captcha.check.portlet.message_boards.edit_category=false
captcha.check.portlet.message_boards.edit_message=false
```

Startup Events

Input a list of comma delimited class names that extend *com.liferay.portal.struts.SimpleAction*. These classes will run at the specified event.

The following is a global startup event that runs once when the portal initializes.

```
global.startup.events=com.liferay.portal.events.GlobalStartupAction
```

The following is an application startup event that runs once for every web site instance of the portal that initializes.

```
application.startup.events=com.liferay.portal.events.AppStartupAction
#application.startup.events=com.liferay.portal.events.AppStartupAction,com.l
iferay.portal.events.SampleAppStartupAction
```

Shutdown Events

Input a list of comma delimited class names that extend *com.liferay.portal.struts.SimpleAction*. These classes will run at the specified event.

Global shutdown event that runs once when the portal shuts down.

```
global.shutdown.events=com.liferay.portal.events.GlobalShutdownAction
```

Application shutdown event that runs once for every web site instance of the portal that shuts down.

```
application.shutdown.events=com.liferay.portal.events.AppShutdownAction
```

Programmatically kill the Java process on shutdown. This is a workaround for a bug in Tomcat and Linux where the process hangs on forever.

See http://support.liferay.com/browse/LEP-2048 for more information.

```
shutdown.programmatically.exit=false
```

Portal Events

Input a list of comma delimited class names that extend *com.liferay.portal.struts.Action*. These classes will run before or after the specified event.

Servlet service event: the pre-service events have an associated error page and will forward to that page if an exception is thrown during excecution of the events. The pre-service events process before Struts processes the request.

Examples:

```
servlet.service.events.pre=com.liferay.portal.events.ServicePreAction

servlet.service.events.pre=com.liferay.portal.events.LogMemoryUsageAction,co
m.liferay.portal.events.LogThreadCountAction,com.liferay.portal.events.Ser-
vicePreAction

servlet.service.events.pre=com.liferay.portal.events.LogSessionIdAction,com.
liferay.portal.events.ServicePreAction

servlet.service.events.pre=com.liferay.portal.events.ServicePreAction,com.li
feray.portal.events.RandomLayoutAction

servlet.service.events.pre=com.liferay.portal.events.ServicePreAction,com.li
feray.portal.events.RandomLookAndFeelAction
```

Use the following to define the error page.

```
servlet.service.events.pre.error.page=/common/error.jsp
```

The post-service events process after Struts processes the request.

```
servlet.service.events.post=com.liferay.portal.events.ServicePostAction
```

Login event

Define events that can occur pre-login and post-login.

```
login.events.pre=com.liferay.portal.events.LoginPreAction

login.events.post=com.liferay.portal.events.LoginPostAction,com.liferay.por-
tal.events.DefaultLandingPageAction
```

Logout event

Similarly, events can be defined for the log out event.

```
logout.events.pre=com.liferay.portal.events.LogoutPreAction
```

Example post events:

```
logout.events.post=com.liferay.portal.events.LogoutPostAction

logout.events.post=com.liferay.portal.events.LogoutPostAction,com.liferay.-
portal.events.GarbageCollectorAction
```

Default Landing Page

Set the default landing page path for logged in users relative to the server path. This is the page users are automatically redirected to after logging in. For example, if you want the default landing page to be http://localhost:8080/web/guest/login, set this to /web/guest/login. To activate this feature, set auth.forward.by.last.path to true. To customize the behavior, see *com.liferay.portal.events.DefaultLandingPageAction* in the *login.events.post* property above.

```
#default.landing.page.path=/web/guest/login
```

Default Logout Page

Set the default logout page path for users relative to the server path. This is the page users are automatically redirected to after logging out. For example, if you want the default logout page to be http://localhost:8080/web/guest/logout, set this to */web/guest/logout*. To activate this feature, set *auth.forward.by.last.path* to true. To customize the behavior, see *com.liferay.portal.events.DefaultLogoutPageAction* in the *logout.events.post* property above.

```
#default.logout.page.path=/web/guest/logout
```

Default Guest Public Layouts

The Guest group must have at least one public page. The settings for the initial public page are specified in the following properties.

If you need to add more than one page, set the property *default.guest.public.layout.lar* to specify a LAR file instead.

For even more complex behavior, override the *addDefaultGuestPublicLayouts* method in *com.liferay.portal.service.impl.GroupLocalServiceImpl*.

Set the name of the public layout.

```
default.guest.public.layout.name=Welcome
```

Set the layout template id of the public layout.

```
default.guest.public.layout.template.id=2_columns_ii
```

Set the portlet ids for the columns specified in the layout template.

```
default.guest.public.layout.column-1=58
default.guest.public.layout.column-2=47
default.guest.public.layout.column-3=
default.guest.public.layout.column-4=
```

Set the friendly url of the public layout.

```
default.guest.public.layout.friendly.url=/home
```

Set the regular theme id for the public layout.

```
#default.guest.public.layout.regular.theme.id=classic
```

Set the regular color scheme id for the public layout.

```
#default.guest.public.layout.regular.color.scheme.id=01
```

Set the wap theme id for the public layout.

```
#default.guest.public.layout.wap.theme.id=mobile
```

Set the wap color scheme for the public layout.

```
#default.guest.public.layout.wap.color.scheme.id=01
```

Specify a LAR file that can be used to create the guest public layouts. If this property is set, the previous layout properties will be ignored.

```
#default.guest.public.layouts.lar=${resource.repositories.root}/deploy/de-
fault_guest_public.lar
```

Default User Private Layouts

If the properties *layout.user.private.layouts.enabled* and *layout.user.private.layouts.auto.create* are both set to true, then users will have private layouts and they will be automatically created. The settings below are used for the creation of for the initial private pages.

If you need to add more than one page, set the property *default.user.private.layout.lar* to specify a LAR file instead.

For even more complex behavior, override the *addDefaultUserPrivateLayouts* method in *com.liferay.portal.events.ServicePreAction*.

Set the name of the private layout.

```
default.user.private.layout.name=Welcome
```

Set the layout template id of the private layout.

```
default.user.private.layout.template.id=2_columns_ii
```

Set the portlet ids for the columns specified in the layout template.

```
default.user.private.layout.column-1=71_INSTANCE_OYOd,82,23,61
default.user.private.layout.column-2=11,29,8,19
default.user.private.layout.column-3=
default.user.private.layout.column-4=
```

Set the friendly url of the private layout.

```
default.user.private.layout.friendly.url=/home
```

Set the regular theme id for the private layout.

```
#default.user.private.layout.regular.theme.id=classic
```

Set the regular color scheme id for the private layout.

```
#default.user.private.layout.regular.color.scheme.id=01
```

Set the wap theme id for the private layout.

```
#default.user.private.layout.wap.theme.id=mobile
```

Set the wap color scheme for the private layout.

```
#default.user.private.layout.wap.color.scheme.id=01
```

Specify a LAR file that can be used to create the user private layouts. If this property is set, the previous layout properties will be ignored.

```
#default.user.private.layouts.lar=${resource.repositories.root}/deploy/de-
fault_user_private.lar
```

Default User Public Layouts

If the properties *layout.user.public.layouts.enabled* and *layout.user.public.layouts.auto.create* are both set to true, then users will have public layouts and they will be automatically created. The settings below are used for the creation of for the initial public pages.

If you need to add more than one page, set the property *default.user.public.layout.lar* to specify a LAR file instead.

For even more complex behavior, override the *addDefaultUserPublicLayouts* method in *com.liferay.portal.events.ServicePreAction*.

Set the name of the public layout.

```
default.user.public.layout.name=Welcome
```

Set the layout template id of the public layout.

```
default.user.public.layout.template.id=2_columns_ii
```

Set the portlet ids for the columns specified in the layout template.

```
default.user.public.layout.column-1=82,23
default.user.public.layout.column-2=8,19
default.user.public.layout.column-3=
default.user.public.layout.column-4=
```

Set the friendly url of the public layout.

```
default.user.public.layout.friendly.url=/home
```

Set the regular theme id for the public layout.

```
#default.user.public.layout.regular.theme.id=classic
```

Set the regular color scheme id for the public layout.

```
#default.user.public.layout.regular.color.scheme.id=01
```

Set the wap theme id for the public layout.

```
#default.user.public.layout.wap.theme.id=mobile
```

Set the wap color scheme for the public layout.

```
#default.user.public.layout.wap.color.scheme.id=01
```

Specify a LAR file that can be used to create the user public layouts. If this property is set, the previous layout properties will be ignored.

```
#default.user.public.layouts.lar=${resource.repositories.root}/deploy/de-
fault_user_public.lar
```

Default Admin

Set the default admin password.

```
default.admin.password=test
```

Set the default admin screen name prefix.

```
default.admin.screen.name=test
```

Set the default admin email address prefix.

```
default.admin.email.address.prefix=test
```

Set the default admin first name.

```
default.admin.first.name=Test
```

Set the default admin middle name.

```
default.admin.middle.name=
```

Set the default admin last name.

```
default.admin.last.name=Test
```

Layouts

Set the list of layout types. The display text of each of the layout types is set in *content/Language.properties* and prefixed with *layout.types*. You can create new layout types and specify custom settings for each layout type. End users input dynamic values as designed in the edit page. End users see the layout as designed in the view page. The generated URL can reference properties set in the edit page. Parentable layouts can contain child layouts. You can also specify a comma delimited list of configuration actions that will be called for your layout when it is updated or deleted.

```
layout.types=portlet,panel,embedded,article,url,link_to_layout
```

Set whether or not private layouts are enabled. Set whether or not private layouts are modifiable. Set whether or not private layouts should be auto created if a user has no private layouts. If private layouts are not enabled, the other two properties are assumed to be false.

```
layout.user.private.layouts.enabled=true
layout.user.private.layouts.modifiable=true
layout.user.private.layouts.auto.create=true
```

Set whether or not public layouts are enabled. Set whether or not public layouts are modifiable. Set whether or not public layouts should be auto created if a user has no public layouts. If public layouts are not enabled, the other two properties are assumed to be false.

```
layout.user.public.layouts.enabled=true
layout.user.public.layouts.modifiable=true
layout.user.public.layouts.auto.create=true
```

Default Settings Layouts

```
layout.edit.page=/portal/layout/edit/portlet.jsp
layout.view.page=/portal/layout/view/portlet.jsp
layout.url=${liferay:mainPath}/portal/layout?p_l_id=${liferay:plid}
layout.url.friendliable=true
layout.parentable=true
```

```
layout.sitemapable=true
layout.configuration.action.update=
layout.configuration.action.delete=
```

Settings for portlet layouts are inherited from the default settings.

```
layout.edit.page[portlet]=/portal/layout/edit/portlet.jsp
layout.view.page[portlet]=/portal/layout/view/portlet.jsp
layout.url[portlet]=${liferay:mainPath}/portal/layout?p_l_id=${liferay:plid}
layout.url.friendliable[portlet]=true
layout.parentable[portlet]=true
layout.configuration.action.update[portlet]=
layout.configuration.action.delete[portlet]=
```

Settings for panel layouts.

```
layout.edit.page[panel]=/portal/layout/edit/panel.jsp
layout.view.page[panel]=/portal/layout/view/panel.jsp
layout.url[panel]=${liferay:mainPath}/portal/layout?p_l_id=${liferay:plid}
layout.url.friendliable[panel]=true
layout.parentable[panel]=true
```

Settings for embedded layouts.

```
layout.edit.page[embedded]=/portal/layout/edit/embedded.jsp
layout.view.page[embedded]=/portal/layout/view/embedded.jsp
layout.url[embedded]=${liferay:mainPath}/portal/layout?p_l_id=${lifer-
ay:plid}
layout.url.friendliable[embedded]=true
layout.parentable[embedded]=false
layout.sitemapable[embedded]=true
layout.configuration.action.update[embedded]=
layout.configuration.action.delete[embedded]=
```

Settings for article layouts.

```
layout.edit.page[article]=/portal/layout/edit/article.jsp
layout.view.page[article]=/portal/layout/view/article.jsp
layout.url.friendliable[article]=true
layout.url[article]=${liferay:mainPath}/portal/layout?p_l_id=${liferay:plid}
layout.parentable[article]=false
layout.sitemapable[article]=true
layout.configuration.action.update[article]=com.liferay.portal.model.Layout-
TypeArticleConfigurationUpdateAction
layout.configuration.action.delete[article]=com.liferay.portal.model.Layout-
TypeArticleConfigurationDeleteAction
```

Settings for URL layouts.

```
layout.edit.page[url]=/portal/layout/edit/url.jsp
layout.view.page[url]=
layout.url[url]=${url}
layout.url.friendliable[url]=true
layout.parentable[url]=false
layout.sitemapable[url]=false
```

```
layout.configuration.action.update[url]=
layout.configuration.action.delete[url]=
```

Settings for page layouts.

```
layout.edit.page[link_to_layout]=/portal/layout/edit/link_to_layout.jsp
layout.view.page[link_to_layout]=
layout.url[link_to_layout]=${liferay:mainPath}/portal/layout?p_l_id=${link-
ToPlid}
layout.url.friendliable[link_to_layout]=true
layout.parentable[link_to_layout]=true
layout.sitemapable[link_to_layout]=false
layout.configuration.action.update[link_to_layout]=
layout.configuration.action.delete[link_to_layout]=
```

Specify static portlets that cannot be moved and will always appear on every layout. Static portlets will take precedence over portlets that may have been dynamically configured for the layout.

For example, if you want the Hello World portlet to always appear at the start of the iteration of the first column for user layouts, set the property *layout.static.portlets.start.column-1[user]* to *47*. If you want the Hello World portlet to always appear at the end of the second column for user layouts, set the property *layout.static.portlets.end.column-2[user]* to *47*. You can input a list of comma delimited portlet ids to specify more than one portlet. If the portlet is instanceable, add the suffix *_INSTANCE_abcd* to the portlet id, where *abcd* is any random alphanumeric string.

The static portlets are fetched based on the properties controlled by custom filters using EasyConf. By default, the available filters are user, community, and organization.

```
layout.static.portlets.start.column-1[user]=3,6
layout.static.portlets.end.column-1[user]=14
layout.static.portlets.start.column-2[user]=71_INSTANCE_abcd,7
layout.static.portlets.end.column-2[user]=34,70
layout.static.portlets.start.column-3[user]=
layout.static.portlets.end.column-3[user]=
```

It is also possible to set static portlets based on the layout's friendly URL.

```
layout.static.portlets.start.column-1[user][/home]=3,6
layout.static.portlets.end.column-2[community][/home]=14
```

Set the static layouts for community layouts.

```
layout.static.portlets.start.column-1[community]=
layout.static.portlets.end.column-1[community]=
layout.static.portlets.start.column-2[community]=
layout.static.portlets.end.column-2[community]=
layout.static.portlets.start.column-3[community]=
layout.static.portlets.end.column-3[community]=
```

Set the static layouts for organization layouts.

```
layout.static.portlets.start.column-1[organization]=
layout.static.portlets.end.column-1[organization]=
layout.static.portlets.start.column-2[organization]=
layout.static.portlets.end.column-2[organization]=
layout.static.portlets.start.column-3[organization]=
layout.static.portlets.end.column-3[organization]=
```

Set the private group, private user, and public servlet mapping for *com.liferay.-portal.servlet.FriendlyURLServlet*. This value must match the servlet mapping set in we-b.xml.

For example, if the private group pages are mapped to */group* and the group's friendly URL is set to */guest* and the layout's friendly URL is set to */company/community*, then the friendly URL for the page will be *http://www.liferay.com/group/guest/company/community*. Private group pages map to a community's private pages and are only available to authenticated users with the proper permissions.

For example, if the public pages are mapped to */web* and the group or user's friendly URL is set to */guest* and the layout's friendly URL is set to */company/community*, then the friendly URL for the page will be *http://www.liferay.com/web/guest/company/community*. Public pages are available to unauthenticated users.

The friendly URLs for users, groups, and layouts can be set during runtime.

```
layout.friendly.url.private.group.servlet.mapping=/group
layout.friendly.url.private.user.servlet.mapping=/user
layout.friendly.url.public.servlet.mapping=/web
```

Redirect to this resource if the user requested a friendly URL that does not exist. Leave it blank to display nothing.

Note: For backward compatibility, this overrides the property *layout.show.http.status* for the 404 status code.

```
layout.friendly.url.page.not.found=/html/portal/404.html
```

Set the reserved keywords that cannot be used in a friendly URL.

```
layout.friendly.url.keywords=c,group,web,image,wsrp,page,public,private,rss,
tags
```

Set the following to true if layouts should remember (across requests) that a window state was set to maximized.

```
layout.remember.request.window.state.maximized=false
```

Set the following to true if guest users should see the maximize window icon.

```
layout.guest.show.max.icon=false
```

Set the following to true if guest users should see the minimize window icon.

```
layout.guest.show.min.icon=false
```

Set the following to true if users are shown that they do not have access to a portlet. The portlet init parameter *show-portlet-access-denied* will override this setting.

```
layout.show.portlet.access.denied=true
```

Set the following to true if users are shown that a portlet is inactive. The portlet init parameter *show-portlet-inactive* will override this setting.

```
layout.show.portlet.inactive=true
```

Set the following to true if the portal should show HTTP status codes like 404 if the requested page is not found.

```
layout.show.http.status=true
```

Set the default layout template id used when creating layouts.

```
layout.default.template.id=2_columns_ii
```

Set the following to false to disable parallel rendering. You can also disable it on a per request basis by setting the attribute key *com.liferay.portal.util.WebKeys.PORTLET_PARALLEL_RENDER* to the *Boolean.FALSE* in a pre service event or by setting the URL parameter *p_p_parallel* to *0*.

```
layout.parallel.render.enable=true
```

Set the name of a class that implements *com.liferay.portal.util.LayoutClone*. This class is used to remember maximized and minimized states on shared pages. The default implementation persists the state in the browser session.

```
layout.clone.impl=com.liferay.portal.util.SessionLayoutClone
```

Set the following to true to cache the content of layout templates. This is recommended because it improves performance for production servers. Setting it to false is useful during development if you need to make a lot of changes.

```
layout.template.cache.enabled=true
```

Set the default value for the *p_l_reset* parameter. If set to true, then render parameters are cleared when different pages are hit. This is not the behavior promoted by the portlet specification, but is the one that most end users seem to prefer.

```
layout.default.p_l_reset=true
```

Portlet URL

Set the following to true if calling setParameter on a portlet URL appends the parameter value versus replacing it. There is some disagreement in the interpretation of the JSR 168 spec among portlet developers over this specific behavior. Liferay Portal successfully passes the portlet TCK tests whether this value is set to true or false.

See http://support.liferay.com/browse/LEP-426 for more information.

```
portlet.url.append.parameters=false
```

Set the following to true to allow portlet URLs to generate with an anchor tag.

```
portlet.url.anchor.enable=false
```

JSR 286 specifies that portlet URLs are escaped by default. Set this to false to provide for better backwards compatibility.

If this is set to true, but a specific portlet application requires that its portlet URLs not be escaped by default, then modify portlet.xml and set the container runtime option *javax.portlet.escapeXml* to false.

```
portlet.url.escape.xml=false
```

Preferences

Set the following to true to validate portlet preferences on startup.

```
preference.validate.on.startup=false
```

Struts

Input the custom Struts request processor that will be used by Struts based portlets. The custom class must extend *com.liferay.portal.struts.PortletRequestProcessor* and have the same constructor.

```
struts.portlet.request.processor=com.liferay.portal.struts.PortletRequest-
Processor
```

Images

Set the location of the default spacer image that is used for missing images. This image must be found in the class path.

```
image.default.spacer=com/liferay/portal/dependencies/spacer.gif
```

Set the location of the default company logo image that is used for missing company logo images. This image must be found in the class path.

```
image.default.company.logo=com/liferay/portal/dependencies/company_logo.png
```

Set the locations of the default user portrait images that are used for missing user portrait images. This image must be found in the class path.

```
image.default.user.female.portrait=com/liferay/portal/dependencies/user_fe-
male_portrait.gif
image.default.user.male.portrait=com/liferay/portal/dependencies/user_male_p
ortrait.gif
```

Editors

You can configure individual JSP pages to use a specific implementation of the available WYSIWYG editors: liferay, fckeditor, simple, tinymce, or tinymcesimple.

```
editor.wysiwyg.default=fckeditor
editor.wysiwyg.portal-web.docroot.html.portlet.blogs.edit_entry.jsp=fckedi-
tor
editor.wysiwyg.portal-web.docroot.html.portlet.calendar.edit_configura-
tion.jsp=fckeditor
editor.wysiwyg.portal-web.docroot.html.portlet.enterprise_ad-
min.view.jsp=fckeditor
editor.wysiwyg.portal-web.docroot.html.portlet.invitation.edit_configura-
tion.jsp=fckeditor
editor.wysiwyg.portal-web.docroot.html.portlet.journal.edit_article_con-
tent.jsp=fckeditor
```

```
editor.wysiwyg.portal-web.docroot.html.portlet.jour-
nal.edit_article_content_xsd_el.jsp=fckeditor
editor.wysiwyg.portal-web.docroot.html.portlet.journal.edit_configura-
tion.jsp=fckeditor
editor.wysiwyg.portal-web.docroot.html.portlet.mail.edit.jsp=fckeditor
editor.wysiwyg.portal-web.docroot.html.portlet.mail.edit_message.jsp=fckedi-
tor
editor.wysiwyg.portal-web.docroot.html.portlet.message_boards.edit_configu-
ration.jsp=fckeditor
editor.wysiwyg.portal-web.docroot.html.portlet.shopping.edit_configura-
tion.jsp=fckeditor
editor.wysiwyg.portal-web.docroot.html.portlet.wiki.edit_html.jsp=fckeditor
```

Fields

Set the following fields to false so users cannot see them. Some company policies require gender and birthday information to always be hidden.

```
field.enable.com.liferay.portal.model.Contact.male=true
field.enable.com.liferay.portal.model.Contact.birthday=true
field.enable.com.liferay.portal.model.Organization.status=false
```

Mime Types

Input a list of comma delimited mime types that are not available by default from *javax.activation.MimetypesFileTypeMap*.

```
mime.types=\
    application/pdf pdf,\
    application/vnd.ms-excel xls,\
    application/vnd.ms-powerpoint ppt,\
    application/msword doc
```

Amazon License Keys

Enter a list of valid Amazon license keys. Configure additional keys by incrementing the last number. The keys are used following a Round-Robin algorithm. This is made available only for personal use. Please see the Amazon license at http://www.amazon.com for more information.

```
amazon.license.0=
amazon.license.1=
amazon.license.2=
amazon.license.3=
```

Instant Messenger

Set the AIM login and password which the system will use to communicate with users.

```
aim.login=
```

```
aim.password=
```

Due to a bug in JOscarLib 0.3b1, you must set the full path to the ICQ jar.

See the following posts:

http://sourceforge.net/forum/message.php?msg_id=1972697

http://sourceforge.net/forum/message.php?msg_id=1990487

```
icq.jar=C:/Java/orion-2.0.7/lib/icq.jar
```

Set the ICQ login and password which the system will use to communicate with users.

```
icq.login=
icq.password=
```

Set the MSN login and password which the system will use to communicate with users.

```
msn.login=
msn.password=
```

Set the YM login and password which the system will use to communicate with users.

```
ym.login=
ym.password=
```

Lucene Search

Set the following to true if you want to avoid any writes to the index. This is useful in some clustering environments where there is a shared index and only one node of the cluster updates it.

```
index.read.only=false
```

Set the following to true if you want to index your entire library of files on startup.

```
index.on.startup=false
```

Set the following to true if you want the indexing on startup to be executed on a separate thread to speed up execution.

```
index.with.thread=true
```

Designate whether Lucene stores indexes in a database via JDBC, file system, or in RAM.

Examples:

```
lucene.store.type=jdbc
lucene.store.type=file
lucene.store.type=ram
```

Lucene's storage of indexes via JDBC has a bug where temp files are not removed. This can eat up disk space over time. Set the following property to true to automatically clean up the temporary files once a day. See LEP-2180.

```
lucene.store.jdbc.auto.clean.up=true
```

Set the JDBC dialect that Lucene uses to store indexes in the database. This is only referenced if Lucene stores indexes in the database. Liferay will attempt to load the proper dialect based on the URL of the JDBC connection. For example, the property *lucene.store.jdbc.dialect.mysql* is read for the JDBC connection URL *jdbc:mysql://localhost/lportal*.

```
lucene.store.jdbc.dialect.db2=org.apache.lucene.store.jdbc.dialect.DB2Dialect
lucene.store.jdbc.dialect.derby=org.apache.lucene.store.jdbc.dialect.DerbyDialect
lucene.store.jdbc.dialect.hsqldb=org.apache.lucene.store.jdbc.dialect.HSQLDialect
lucene.store.jdbc.dialect.jtds=org.apache.lucene.store.jdbc.dialect.SQLServerDialect
lucene.store.jdbc.dialect.microsoft=org.apache.lucene.store.jdbc.dialect.SQLServerDialect
lucene.store.jdbc.dialect.mysql=org.apache.lucene.store.jdbc.dialect.MySQLDialect
#lucene.store.jdbc.dialect.mysql=org.apache.lucene.store.jdbc.dialect.MySQLInnoDBDialect
#lucene.store.jdbc.dialect.mysql=org.apache.lucene.store.jdbc.dialect.MySQLMyISAMDialect
lucene.store.jdbc.dialect.oracle=org.apache.lucene.store.jdbc.dialect.OracleDialect
lucene.store.jdbc.dialect.postgresql=org.apache.lucene.store.jdbc.dialect.PostgreSQLDialect
```

Set the directory where Lucene indexes are stored. This is only referenced if Lucene stores indexes in the file system.

```
lucene.dir=${resource.repositories.root}/lucene/
```

Input a class name that extends *com.liferay.portal.search.lucene.LuceneFileExtractor*. This class is called by Lucene to extract text from complex files so that they can be properly indexed.

```
lucene.file.extractor=com.liferay.portal.search.lucene.LuceneFileExtractor
```

The file extractor can sometimes return text that is not valid for Lucene. This property expects a regular expression. Any character that does not match the regular expression will be replaced with a blank space. Set an empty regular expression to disable this feature.

Examples:

```
lucene.file.extractor.regexp.strip=
lucene.file.extractor.regexp.strip=[\\d\\w]
```

Set the default analyzer used for indexing and retrieval.

Examples:

```
lucene.analyzer=org.apache.lucene.analysis.br.BrazilianAnalyzer
lucene.analyzer=org.apache.lucene.analysis.cn.ChineseAnalyzer
```

```
lucene.analyzer=org.apache.lucene.analysis.cjk.CJKAnalyzer
lucene.analyzer=org.apache.lucene.analysis.cz.CzechAnalyzer
lucene.analyzer=org.apache.lucene.analysis.nl.DutchAnalyzer
lucene.analyzer=org.apache.lucene.analysis.fr.FrenchAnalyzer
lucene.analyzer=org.apache.lucene.analysis.de.GermanAnalyzer
lucene.analyzer=org.apache.lucene.analysis.KeywordAnalyzer
lucene.analyzer=org.apache.lucene.index.memory.PatternAnalyzer
lucene.analyzer=org.apache.lucene.analysis.PerFieldAnalyzerWrapper
lucene.analyzer=org.apache.lucene.analysis.ru.RussianAnalyzer
lucene.analyzer=org.apache.lucene.analysis.SimpleAnalyzer
lucene.analyzer=org.apache.lucene.analysis.snowball.SnowballAnalyzer
lucene.analyzer=org.apache.lucene.analysis.standard.StandardAnalyzer
lucene.analyzer=org.apache.lucene.analysis.StopAnalyzer
lucene.analyzer=org.apache.lucene.analysis.WhitespaceAnalyzer
```

Set Lucene's merge factor. Higher numbers mean indexing goes faster but uses more memory. The default value from Lucene is 10. This should never be set to a number lower than 2.

```
lucene.merge.factor=10
```

Set how often to run Lucene's optimize method. Optimization speeds up searching but slows down writing. Set this property to 0 to always optimize. Set this property to an integer greater than 0 to optimize every X writes.

```
lucene.optimize.interval=1
```

SourceForge

```
    source.forge.mirrors=\
        http://downloads.sourceforge.net,\       # Redirect
        http://internap.dl.sourceforge.net,\     # San Jose, CA
        http://superb-east.dl.sourceforge.net,\ # McLean, Virginia
        http://superb-west.dl.sourceforge.net,\ # Seattle, Washington
        http://easynews.dl.sourceforge.net,\     # Phoenix, AZ
        http://kent.dl.sourceforge.net,\         # Kent, UK
        http://ufpr.dl.sourceforge.net,\         # Curitiba, Brazil
        http://belnet.dl.sourceforge.net,\       # Brussels, Belgium
        http://switch.dl.sourceforge.net,\       # Lausanne, Switzerland
        http://mesh.dl.sourceforge.net,\         # Duesseldorf, Germany
        http://ovh.dl.sourceforge.net,\          # Paris, France
        http://dfn.dl.sourceforge.net,\          # Berlin, Germany
        http://heanet.dl.sourceforge.net,\       # Dublin, Ireland
        http://garr.dl.sourceforge.net,\         # Bologna, Italy
        http://surfnet.dl.sourceforge.net        # Amsterdam, The Netherlands
        http://jaist.dl.sourceforge.net,\        # Ishikawa, Japan
        http://nchc.dl.sourceforge.net,\         # Tainan, Taiwan
        http://optusnet.dl.sourceforge.net       # Sydney, Australia
```

Value Object

You can add a listener for a specific class by setting the property *value.object.listener* with a list of comma delimited class names that implement *com.liferay.portal.model.ModelListener*. These classes are pooled and reused and must be thread safe.

```
value.object.listener.com.liferay.portal.model.Contact=com.liferay.portal.model.ContactListener
value.object.listener.com.liferay.portal.model.Layout=com.liferay.portal.model.LayoutListener
value.object.listener.com.liferay.portal.model.LayoutSet=com.liferay.portal.model.LayoutSetListener
value.object.listener.com.liferay.portal.model.PortletPreferences=com.liferay.portal.model.PortletPreferencesListener
value.object.listener.com.liferay.portal.model.User=com.liferay.portal.model.UserListener
value.object.listener.com.liferay.portlet.journal.model.JournalArticle=com.liferay.portlet.journal.model.JournalArticleListener
value.object.listener.com.liferay.portlet.journal.model.JournalTemplate=com.liferay.portlet.journal.model.JournalTemplateListener
```

Value objects are cached by default. You can disable caching for all objects or per object.

For mapping tables, the key is the mapping table itself.

```
value.object.finder.cache.enabled=true
value.object.finder.cache.enabled.com.liferay.portal.model.Layout=true
value.object.finder.cache.enabled.com.liferay.portal.model.User=true
value.object.finder.cache.enabled.Users_Roles=true
```

Last Modified

Set the following to true to check last modified date on server side CSS and JavaScript.

```
last.modified.check=true
```

Enter a list of comma delimited paths that will only be executed when newer than the last modified date. These paths must extend *com.liferay.portal.lastmodified.LastModifiedAction*.

```
    last.modified.paths=\
        /portal/css_cached,\
        /portal/javascript_cached
```

XSS (Cross Site Scripting)

Set the following to false to ensure that all persisted data is stripped of XSS hacks.

```
xss.allow=false
```

You can override the *xss.allow* setting for a specific class by setting the property *xss.allow* plus the class name.

```
xss.allow.com.liferay.portal.model.Portlet=true
xss.allow.com.liferay.portal.model.PortletPreferences=true
```

You can override the *xss.allow* setting for a specific field in a class by setting the property *xss.allow* plus the class and field name.

```
xss.allow.com.liferay.portlet.journal.model.JournalArticle.content=true
xss.allow.com.liferay.portlet.journal.model.JournalStructure.xsd=true
xss.allow.com.liferay.portlet.journal.model.JournalTemplate.xsl=true
```

Communication Link

Set the JGroups properties used by the portal to communicate with other instances of the portal. This is only needed if the portal is running in a clustered environment. The JGroups settings provide a mechanism for the portal to broadcast messages to the other instances of the portal. The specified multi-cast address should be unique for internal portal messaging only. You will still need to set the Hibernate and Ehcache settings for database clustering.

```
comm.link.properties=UDP(bind_addr=127.0.0.1;mcast_addr=231.12.21.102;mcast_
port=45566;ip_ttl=32;mcast_send_buf_size=150000;mcast_recv_buf_size=80000):P
ING(timeout=2000;num_initial_members=3):MERGE2(min_interval=5000;max_inter-
val=10000):FD_SOCK:VERIFY_SUSPECT(timeout=1500):pbcast.NAKACK(gc_lag=50;re-
transmit_timeout=300,600,1200,2400,4800;max_xmit_size=8192):UNICAST(timeout=
300,600,1200,2400):pbcast.STABLE(desired_avg_gossip=20000):FRAG(frag_size=80
96;down_thread=false;up_thread=false):pbcast.GMS(join_timeout=5000;join_retr
y_timeout=2000;shun=false;print_local_addr=true)
```

Content Delivery Network

Set the hostname that will be used to serve static content via a CDN. This property can be overridden dynamically at runtime by setting the HTTP parameter *cdn_host*.

```
cdn.host=
```

Counter

Set the number of increments between database updates to the Counter table. Set this value to a higher number for better performance.

```
counter.increment=100
```

Lock

Set the lock expiration time for each class.

Example: 1 Day

```
lock.expiration.time.com.liferay.portlet.documentlibrary.model.DLFileEntry=8
6400000
```

Example: 20 Minutes

```
lock.expiration.time.com.liferay.portlet.wiki.model.WikiPage=1200000
```

JBI

Connect to either Mule or ServiceMix as your ESB.

Examples:

```
jbi.workflow.url=http://localhost:8080/mule-web/workflow
jbi.workflow.url=http://localhost:8080/servicemix-web/workflow
```

JCR

Liferay includes Jackrabbit (http://jackrabbit.apache.org) by default as its JSR-170 Java Content Repository.

```
jcr.initialize.on.startup=false
jcr.workspace.name=liferay
jcr.node.documentlibrary=documentlibrary
jcr.jackrabbit.repository.root=${resource.repositories.root}/jackrabbit
jcr.jackrabbit.config.file.path=${jcr.jackrabbit.repository.root}/reposito-
ry.xml
jcr.jackrabbit.repository.home=${jcr.jackrabbit.repository.root}/home
jcr.jackrabbit.credentials.username=none
jcr.jackrabbit.credentials.password=none
```

OpenOffice

Enabling OpenOffice integration allows the Document Library portlet to provide document conversion functionality. To start OpenOffice as a service, run the command:

```
soffice -headless -accept="socket,host=127.0.0.1,port=8100;urp;" -nofirst-
startwizard
```

This is tested with OpenOffice 2.3.x.

```
openoffice.server.enabled=false
openoffice.server.host=127.0.0.1
openoffice.server.port=8100
```

POP

Set this to true to enable polling of email notifications from a POP server. The user credentials are the same used for SMTP authentication and is specified in the *mail/MailSession* configuration for each application server.

```
pop.server.notifications.enabled=false
```

Set the interval on which the POPNotificationsJob will run. The value is set in one minute increments.

```
pop.server.notifications.interval=1
pop.server.subdomain=events
```

Quartz

These properties define the connection to the built-in Quartz job scheduling engine.

```
org.quartz.dataSource.ds.connectionProvider.class=com.liferay.portal.sched-
uler.quartz.QuartzConnectionProviderImpl
org.quartz.jobStore.class=org.quartz.impl.jdbcjobstore.JobStoreTX
org.quartz.jobStore.dataSource=ds
org.quartz.jobStore.driverDelegateClass=com.liferay.portal.sched-
uler.quartz.DynamicDriverDelegate
org.quartz.jobStore.isClustered=false
org.quartz.jobStore.misfireThreshold=60000
org.quartz.jobStore.tablePrefix=QUARTZ_
org.quartz.jobStore.useProperties=true
org.quartz.scheduler.instanceId=AUTO
org.quartz.threadPool.class=org.quartz.simpl.SimpleThreadPool
org.quartz.threadPool.threadCount=5
org.quartz.threadPool.threadPriority=5
```

Scheduler

Set this to false to disable all scheduler classes defined in *liferay-portlet.xml* and in the property *scheduler.classes*.

```
scheduler.enabled=true
```

Input a list of comma delimited class names that implement *com.liferay.portal.kernel.job.Scheduler*. These classes allow jobs to be scheduled on startup. These classes are not associated to any one portlet.

```
scheduler.classes=
```

Social Bookmarks

The Blogs portlet allows for the posting of entries to various popular social bookmarking sites. The example ones are the defaults; to configure more, just add the site in the format below.

```
social.bookmark.types=blinklist,delicious,digg,furl,newsvine,reddit,techno-
rati
social.bookmark.post.url[blinklist]=http://blinklist.com/index.php?
Action=Blink/addblink.php&url=${liferay:social-bookmark:url}&Title=${lifer-
ay:social-bookmark:title}
social.bookmark.post.url[delicious]=http://del.icio.us/post?url=${lifer-
ay:social-bookmark:url}&title=${liferay:social-bookmark:title}
social.bookmark.post.url[digg]=http://digg.com/submit?phase=2&url=${lifer-
ay:social-bookmark:url}
social.bookmark.post.url[furl]=http://furl.net/storeIt.jsp?u=${liferay:so-
cial-bookmark:url}&t=${liferay:social-bookmark:title}
social.bookmark.post.url[newsvine]=http://www.newsvine.com/_tools/seed&save?
u=${liferay:social-bookmark:url}&h=${liferay:social-bookmark:title}
social.bookmark.post.url[reddit]=http://reddit.com/submit?url=${liferay:so-
```

```
cial-bookmark:url}&title=${liferay:social-bookmark:title}
social.bookmark.post.url[technorati]=http://technorati.com/cosmos/search.htm
l?url=${liferay:social-bookmark:url}
```

Velocity Engine

Input a list of comma delimited class names that extend *com.liferay.util.velocity.VelocityResourceListener*. These classes will run in sequence to allow you to find the applicable ResourceLoader to load a Velocity template.

```
velocity.engine.resource.listeners=com.liferay.portal.velocity.ServletVeloc-
ityResourceListener,com.liferay.portal.velocity.JournalTemplateVelocityRe-
sourceListener,com.liferay.portal.velocity.ThemeLoaderVelocityResourceLis-
tener,com.liferay.portal.velocity.ClassLoaderVelocityResourceListener
```

Set the Velocity resource managers. We extend the Velocity's default resource managers for better scalability.

Note that the modification check interval is not respected because the resource loader implementation does not know the last modified date of a resource. This means you will need to turn off caching if you want to be able to modify VM templates in themes and see the changes right away.

```
velocity.engine.resource.manager=com.liferay.portal.velocity.LiferayRe-
sourceManager
velocity.engine.resource.manager.cache=com.liferay.portal.velocity.Lifer-
ayResourceCache
velocity.engine.resource.manager.cache.enabled=true
#velocity.engine.resource.manager.modification.check.interval=0
```

Input a list of comma delimited macros that will be loaded. These files must exist in the class path.

```
velocity.engine.velocimacro.library=VM_global_library.vm,VM_liferay.vm
```

Set the Velocity logging configuration.

```
velocity.engine.logger=org.apache.velocity.runtime.log.SimpleLog4JLogSystem
velocity.engine.logger.category=org.apache.velocity
```

Virtual Hosts

Set the hosts that will be ignored for virtual hosts.

```
    virtual.hosts.ignore.hosts=\
        127.0.0.1,\
        localhost
```

Set the paths that will be ignored for virtual hosts.

```
virtual.hosts.ignore.paths=\
        /c,\
        \
        /c/portal/change_password,\
        /c/portal/css_cached,\
        /c/portal/extend_session,\
```

```
        /c/portal/extend_session_confirm,\
        /c/portal/javascript_cached,\
        /c/portal/json_service,\
        /c/portal/layout,\
        /c/portal/login,\
        /c/portal/logout,\
        /c/portal/render_portlet,\
        /c/portal/reverse_ajax,\
        /c/portal/session_tree_js_click,\
        /c/portal/status,\
        /c/portal/update_layout,\
        /c/portal/update_terms_of_use,\
        /c/portal/upload_progress_poller,\
        \
        /c/layout_configuration/templates,\
        /c/layout_management/update_page
```

HTTP

See *system.properties* for more HTTP settings.

Set the maximum number of connections.

```
#com.liferay.portal.util.HttpImpl.max.connections.per.host=2
#com.liferay.portal.util.HttpImpl.max.total.connections=20
```

Set the proxy authentication type.

```
#com.liferay.portal.util.HttpImpl.proxy.auth.type=username-password
#com.liferay.portal.util.HttpImpl.proxy.auth.type=ntlm
```

Set user name and password used for HTTP proxy authentication.

```
#com.liferay.portal.util.HttpImpl.proxy.username=
#com.liferay.portal.util.HttpImpl.proxy.password=
```

Set additional properties for NTLM authentication.

```
#com.liferay.portal.util.HttpImpl.proxy.ntlm.domain=
#com.liferay.portal.util.HttpImpl.proxy.ntlm.host=
```

Set the connection timeout when fetching HTTP content.

```
com.liferay.portal.util.HttpImpl.timeout=10000
```

Servlet Filters

If the user can unzip compressed HTTP content, the compression filter will zip up the HTTP content before sending it to the user. This will speed up page rendering for users that are on dial up.

```
com.liferay.portal.servlet.filters.compression.CompressionFilter=true
```

This double click filter will prevent double clicks at the server side. Prevention of double clicks is already in place on the client side. However, some sites require a more robust solution. This is turned off by default since most sites will not need it.

```
com.liferay.portal.servlet.filters.doubleclick.DoubleClickFilter=false
```

The header filter is used to set request headers.

```
com.liferay.portal.servlet.filters.header.HeaderFilter=true
```

The strip filter will remove blank lines from the outputted content. This will speed up page rendering for users that are on dial up.

```
com.liferay.portal.servlet.filters.strip.StripFilter=true
```

The layout cache filter will cache pages to speed up page rendering for guest users. See *ehcache.xml* to modify the cache expiration time to live.

```
com.liferay.portal.servlet.filters.layoutcache.LayoutCacheFilter=true
```

The session id filter ensure that only one session is created between http and https sessions. This is useful if you want users to login via https but have them view the rest of the site via http. This is disabled by default. Do not enable this unless you thoroughly understand how cookies, http, and https work.

```
com.liferay.portal.servlet.filters.sessionid.SessionIdFilter=false
```

The Velocity filter will process */css/main.css as a Velocity template.

```
com.liferay.portal.servlet.filters.velocity.VelocityFilter=false
```

The virtual host filter maps hosts to public and private pages. For example, if the public virtual host is www.helloworld.com and the friendly URL is /helloworld, then http://www.helloworld.com is mapped to http://localhost:8080/web/helloworld.

```
    com.liferay.portal.servlet.filters.virtualhost.VirtualHostFilter=true
```

Upload Servlet Request

Set the maximum file size. Default is 1024 * 1024 * 100.

```
com.liferay.portal.upload.UploadServletRequestImpl.max.size=104857600
```

Set the temp directory for uploaded files.

```
#com.liferay.portal.upload.UploadServletRequestImpl.temp.dir=C:/Temp
```

Set the threshold size to prevent extraneous serialization of uploaded data.

```
com.liferay.portal.upload.LiferayFileItem.threshold.size=262144
```

Set the threshold size to prevent out of memory exceptions caused by caching excessively large uploaded data. Default is 1024 * 1024 * 10.

```
com.liferay.portal.upload.LiferayInputStream.threshold.size=10485760
```

Web Server

Set the HTTP and HTTPs ports when running the portal in a J2EE server that is sitting behind another web server like Apache. Set the values to -1 if the portal is not running behind another web server like Apache.

```
web.server.http.port=-1
web.server.https.port=-1
```

Set the hostname that will be used when the portlet generates URLs. Leaving this blank will mean the host is derived from the servlet container.

```
web.server.host=
```

Set the preferred protocol.

```
web.server.protocol=https
```

Set this to true to display the server name at the bottom of every page. This is useful when testing clustering configurations so that you can know which node you are accessing.

```
web.server.display.node=false
```

WebDAV

Set the following to true to enable programmatic configuration to let the WebDAV be configured for litmus testing. This should never be set to true unless you are running the litmus tests.

```
webdav.litmus=false
```

Set a list of files for the WebDAV servlet to ignore processing.

```
webdav.ignore=.DS_Store,.metadata_index_homes_only,.metadata_never_index,.Sp
otlight-V100,.TemporaryItems,.Trashes
```

Set the tokens for supported WebDAV storage paths.

```
webdav.storage.tokens=document_library,image_gallery,journal
```

Set the class names for supported WebDAV storage classes.

```
webdav.storage.class[document_library]=com.liferay.portlet.documentli-
brary.webdav.DLWebDAVStorageImpl
webdav.storage.class[image_gallery]=com.liferay.portlet.imagegallery.web-
dav.IGWebDAVStorageImpl
webdav.storage.class[journal]=com.liferay.portlet.journal.webdav.JournalWeb-
DAVStorageImpl
```

Main Servlet

Servlets can be protected by *com.liferay.portal.servlet.filters.secure.SecureFilter*.

Input a list of comma delimited IPs that can access this servlet. Input a blank list to allow any IP to access this servlet. SERVER_IP will be replaced with the IP of the host server.

```
main.servlet.hosts.allowed=
```

Set the following to true if this servlet can only be accessed via https.

```
main.servlet.https.required=false
```

Axis Servlet

See Main Servlet on how to protect this servlet.

```
axis.servlet.hosts.allowed=127.0.0.1,SERVER_IP
axis.servlet.https.required=false
```

JSON Tunnel Servlet

See Main Servlet on how to protect this servlet.

```
json.servlet.hosts.allowed=
json.servlet.https.required=false
```

Liferay Tunnel Servlet

See Main Servlet on how to protect this servlet.

```
tunnel.servlet.hosts.allowed=127.0.0.1,SERVER_IP
tunnel.servlet.https.required=false
```

Spring Remoting Servlet

See Main Servlet on how to protect this servlet.

```
spring.remoting.servlet.hosts.allowed=127.0.0.1,SERVER_IP
spring.remoting.servlet.https.required=false
```

WebDAV Servlet

See Main Servlet on how to protect this servlet.

```
webdav.servlet.hosts.allowed=
webdav.servlet.https.required=false
```

Admin Portlet

You can set some administrative defaults by using these properties. The first time you bring up your portal, these values will then already be set in the Admin portlet. All values should be separated by \n characters.

Set up default group names.

```
admin.default.group.names=
```

Set up default role names.

```
admin.default.role.names=Power User\nUser
```

Set up default user group names.

```
admin.default.user.group.names=
```

The rest of these properties map to their values in the Admin portlet.

```
admin.mail.host.names=
admin.reserved.screen.names=
admin.reserved.email.addresses=
admin.email.from.name=Joe Bloggs
admin.email.from.address=test@liferay.com
admin.email.user.added.enabled=true
admin.email.user.added.subject=com/liferay/portlet/admin/dependencies/email_
user_added_subject.tmpl
admin.email.user.added.body=com/liferay/portlet/admin/dependencies/email_use
r_added_body.tmpl
admin.email.password.sent.enabled=true
admin.email.password.sent.subject=com/liferay/portlet/admin/dependencies/ema
il_password_sent_subject.tmpl
admin.email.password.sent.body=com/liferay/portlet/admin/dependencies/email_
password_sent_body.tmpl
```

Announcements Portlet

Configure email notification settings.

```
announcements.email.from.name=Joe Bloggs
announcements.email.from.address=test@liferay.com
announcements.email.to.name=
announcements.email.to.address=noreply@liferay.com
announcements.email.subject=com/liferay/portlet/announcements/dependencies/e
mail_subject.tmpl
announcements.email.body=com/liferay/portlet/announcements/dependencies/emai
l_body.tmpl
```

Set the list of announcement types. The display text of each of the announcement types is set in content/Language.properties.

```
announcements.entry.types=general,news,test
```

Set the interval on which the CheckEntryJob will run. The value is set in one minute increments.

```
announcements.entry.check.interval=15
```

Blogs Portlet

The following properties affect the Blogs portlet.

```
blogs.email.comments.added.enabled=true
blogs.email.comments.added.subject=com/liferay/portlet/blogs/dependencies/em
ail_comments_added_subject.tmpl
blogs.email.comments.added.body=com/liferay/portlet/blogs/dependencies/email
_comments_added_body.tmpl
blogs.page.abstract.length=400
blogs.rss.abstract.length=200
blogs.trackback.excerpt.length=50
```

Set the interval on which the TrackbackVerifierJob will run. The value is set in one minute increments.

```
blogs.trackback.verifier.job.interval=5
```

Calendar Portlet

Set the list of event types. The display text of each of the event types is set in *content/Language.properties.*

```
calendar.event.types=anniversary,appointment,bill-payment,birthday,break-
fast,call,chat,class,club-event,concert,dinner,event,graduation,happy-
hour,holiday,interview,lunch,meeting,movie,net-event,other,party,perfor-
mance,press-release,reunion,sports-event,training,travel,tv-
show,vacation,wedding
```

Set the interval on which the CheckEventJob will run. The value is set in one minute increments.

```
calendar.event.check.interval=15
```

Configure email notification settings.

```
calendar.email.from.name=Joe Bloggs
calendar.email.from.address=test@liferay.com
calendar.email.event.reminder.enabled=true
calendar.email.event.reminder.subject=com/liferay/portlet/calendar/dependen-
cies/email_event_reminder_subject.tmpl
calendar.email.event.reminder.body=com/liferay/portlet/calendar/dependen-
cies/email_event_reminder_body.tmpl
```

Communities Portlet

Configure email notification settings.

```
communities.email.from.name=Joe Bloggs
communities.email.from.address=test@liferay.com
communities.email.membership.reply.subject=com/liferay/portlet/communities/d
ependencies/email_membership_reply_subject.tmpl
communities.email.membership.reply.body=com/liferay/portlet/communities/de-
pendencies/email_membership_reply_body.tmpl
communities.email.membership.request.subject=com/liferay/portlet/communities
/dependencies/email_membership_request_subject.tmpl
communities.email.membership.request.body=com/liferay/portlet/communities/de
pendencies/email_membership_request_body.tmpl
```

Document Library Portlet

Set the name of a class that implements *com.liferay.documentlibrary.util.Hook*. The document library server will use this to persist documents.

Available hooks are:

- com.liferay.documentlibrary.util.FileSystemHook
- com.liferay.documentlibrary.util.JCRHook
- com.liferay.documentlibrary.util.S3Hook

Examples:

```
dl.hook.impl=com.liferay.documentlibrary.util.FileSystemHook
dl.hook.impl=com.liferay.documentlibrary.util.JCRHook
dl.hook.impl=com.liferay.documentlibrary.util.S3Hook
```

FileSystemHook

```
dl.hook.file.system.root.dir=${resource.repositories.root}/document_library
```

S3Hook

```
dl.hook.s3.access.key=
dl.hook.s3.secret.key=
dl.hook.s3.bucket.name=
```

Set the maximum file size and valid file extensions for documents. A value of 0 for the maximum file size can be used to indicate unlimited file size. However, the maximum file size allowed is set in the property *com.liferay.portal.upload.UploadServletRequestImpl.max.size*.

Examples:

```
#dl.file.max.size=307200
#dl.file.max.size=1024000
dl.file.max.size=3072000
```

A file extension of * will permit all file extensions.

You can map a GIF for the extension by adding the image to the theme's image display and document library folder. The wildcard extension of * will be ignored. For example, the default image for the DOC extension would be found in: */html/themes/_unstyled/images/document_library/doc.gif.*

Example File Extensions:

```
dl.file.extensions=.bmp,.css,.doc,.dot,.gif,.gz,.htm,.html,.jpg,.js,.lar,.od
b,.odf,.odg,.odp,.ods,.odt,.pdf,.png,.ppt,.rtf,.swf,.sxc,.sxi,.sxw,.tar,.tif
f,.tgz,.txt,.vsd,.xls,.xml,.zip
```

Set which files extensions are comparable by the diff tool. If OpenOffice integration is enabled, then it is also possible to compare some binary files that are can be converted to text.

```
dl.comparable.file.extensions=.css,.js,.htm,.html,.txt,.xml
#dl.comparable.file.extensions=.css,.doc,.js,.htm,.html,.odt,.rtf,.sxw,.txt,
.xml
```

Set folder names that will be used to synchronize with a community's set of private and public layouts. This will allow users to manage layouts using the Document Library portlet, and ultimately, via WebDAV. This feature is experimental.

```
dl.layouts.sync.enabled=false
dl.layouts.sync.private.folder=Pages - Private
dl.layouts.sync.public.folder=Pages - Public
```

Image Gallery Portlet

Set the maximum file size and valid file extensions for images. A value of 0 for the maximum file size can be used to indicate unlimited file size. However, the maximum file size allowed is set in the property *com.liferay.portal.upload.UploadServletRequestImpl.max.size*.

```
ig.image.max.size=10240000
```

A file extension of * will permit all file extensions.

```
ig.image.extensions=.bmp,.gif,.jpeg,.jpg,.png,.tif,.tiff
```

Set the maximum thumbnail height and width in pixels. Set dimension of the custom images to 0 to disable creating a scaled image of that size.

```
ig.image.thumbnail.max.dimension=150
#ig.image.custom1.max.dimension=100
#ig.image.custom2.max.dimension=0
```

Invitation Portlet

```
invitation.email.max.recipients=20
invitation.email.message.body=com/liferay/portlet/invitation/dependencies/em
ail_message_body.tmpl
invitation.email.message.subject=com/liferay/portlet/invitation/dependen-
cies/email_message_subject.tmpl
```

Journal Portlet

Set this to true if article ids should always be autogenerated.

```
journal.article.force.autogenerate.id=true
```

Set this to true so that only the latest version of an article that is also not approved can be saved without incrementing version.

```
journal.article.force.increment.version=false
```

Set the list of article types. The display text of each of the article types is set in content/Language.properties.

```
journal.article.types=announcements,blogs,general,news,press-release,test
```

Set the token used when inserting simple page breaks in articles.

```
journal.article.token.page.break=@page_break@
```

Set the interval on which the CheckArticleJob will run. The value is set in one minute increments.

```
journal.article.check.interval=15
```

Set this to true if feed ids should always be autogenerated.

```
journal.feed.force.autogenerate.id=false
```

Set this to true if structure ids should always be autogenerated.

```
journal.structure.force.autogenerate.id=false
```

Set this to true if template ids should always be autogenerated.

```
journal.template.force.autogenerate.id=false
```

Input a comma delimited list of variables which are restricted from the context in Velocity based Journal templates.

```
journal.template.velocity.restricted.variables=serviceLocator
```

Set the maximum file size and valid file extensions for images. A value of 0 for the maximum file size can be used to indicate unlimited file size. However, the maximum file size allowed is set in the property *com.liferay.portal.upload.UploadServletRequestImpl.max.size*.

```
journal.image.small.max.size=51200
```

A file extension of * will permit all file extensions.

```
journal.image.extensions=.gif,.jpeg,.jpg,.png
```

Input a list of comma delimited class names that extend *com.liferay.portlet.journal.util.TransformerListener*. These classes will run in sequence to allow you to modify the XML and XSL before it's transformed and allow you to modify the final output.

```
journal.transformer.listener=\
    com.liferay.portlet.journal.util.TokensTransformerListener,\
    #com.liferay.portlet.journal.util.PropertiesTransformerListener,\
    com.liferay.portlet.journal.util.ContentTransformerListener,\
    com.liferay.portlet.journal.util.LocaleTransformerListener,\
    com.liferay.portlet.journal.util.RegexTransformerListener,\
    com.liferay.portlet.journal.util.ViewCounterTransformerListener
```

Enter a list of regular expression patterns and replacements that will be applied to outputted Journal content. The list of properties must end with a subsequent integer (0, 1, etc.) and it is assumed that the list has reached an end when the pattern or replacement is not set. See *com.liferay.portlet.journal.util.RegexTransformerListener* for implementation details.

```
#journal.transformer.regex.pattern.0=beta.sample.com
#journal.transformer.regex.replacement.0=production.sample.com
#journal.transformer.regex.pattern.1=staging.sample.com
#journal.transformer.regex.replacement.1=production.sample.com
```

Set whether to synchronize content searches when server starts.

```
journal.sync.content.search.on.startup=false
```

Configure mail notification settings.

```
journal.email.from.name=Joe Bloggs
journal.email.from.address=test@liferay.com
journal.email.article.approval.denied.enabled=false
journal.email.article.approval.denied.subject=com/liferay/portlet/journal/de
pendencies/email_article_approval_denied_subject.tmpl
```

```
journal.email.article.approval.denied.body=com/liferay/portlet/journal/de-
pendencies/email_article_approval_denied_body.tmpl
journal.email.article.approval.granted.enabled=false
journal.email.article.approval.granted.subject=com/liferay/portlet/journal/d
ependencies/email_article_approval_granted_subject.tmpl
journal.email.article.approval.granted.body=com/liferay/portlet/journal/de-
pendencies/email_article_approval_granted_body.tmpl
journal.email.article.approval.requested.enabled=false
journal.email.article.approval.requested.subject=com/liferay/portlet/journal
/dependencies/email_article_approval_requested_subject.tmpl
journal.email.article.approval.requested.body=com/liferay/portlet/journal/de
pendencies/email_article_approval_requested_body.tmpl
journal.email.article.review.enabled=false
journal.email.article.review.subject=com/liferay/portlet/journal/dependen-
cies/email_article_review_subject.tmpl
journal.email.article.review.body=com/liferay/portlet/journal/dependencies/e
mail_article_review_body.tmpl
```

Specify the strategy used when Journal content is imported using the LAR system.

```
journal.lar.creation.strategy=com.liferay.portlet.journal.lar.JournalCre-
ationStrategyImpl
```

Specify the path to the template used for providing error messages on Journal templates.

```
journal.error.template.velocity=com/liferay/portlet/journal/dependencies/er-
ror.vm
journal.error.template.xsl=com/liferay/portlet/journal/dependencies/er-
ror.xsl
```

Journal Articles Portlet

Set the available values for the number of articles to display per page.

```
journal.articles.page.delta.values=5,10,25,50,100
```

Mail Portlet

Set the following to false if administrator should not be allowed to change the mail domain via the Admin portlet.

```
mail.mx.update=true
```

Set the name of a class that implements *com.liferay.mail.util.Hook*. The mail server will use this class to ensure that the mail and portal servers are synchronized on user information. The portal will not know how to add, update, or delete users from the mail server except through this hook.

Available hooks are:

- com.liferay.mail.util.CyrusHook
- com.liferay.mail.util.DummyHook
- com.liferay.mail.util.FuseMailHook

- com.liferay.mail.util.SendmailHook
- com.liferay.mail.util.ShellHook

Example:

```
mail.hook.impl=com.liferay.mail.util.DummyHook
```

CyrusHook

Set the commands for adding, updating, and deleting a user where %1% is the user id. Replace the password with the password for the cyrus user.

Add Examples:

```
mail.hook.cyrus.add.user=cyrusadmin password create %1%
mail.hook.cyrus.add.user=cyrus_adduser password %1%
```

Delete Examples:

```
mail.hook.cyrus.delete.user=cyrusadmin password delete %1%
mail.hook.cyrus.delete.user=cyrus_userdel password %1%
```

Other properties:

```
mail.hook.cyrus.home=/home/cyrus
```

FuseMailHook

See http://www.fusemail.com/support/api.html for more information. You must also update the *mail.account.finder* property.

```
mail.hook.fusemail.url=https://www.fusemail.com/api/request.html
mail.hook.fusemail.username=
mail.hook.fusemail.password=
mail.hook.fusemail.account.type=group_subaccount
mail.hook.fusemail.group.parent=
```

SendmailHook

Set the commands for adding, updating, and deleting a user where %1% is the user id and %2% is the password. Set the home and virtual user table information.

```
mail.hook.sendmail.add.user=adduser %1% -s /bin/false
mail.hook.sendmail.change.password=autopasswd %1% %2%
mail.hook.sendmail.delete.user=userdel -r %1%
mail.hook.sendmail.home=/home
mail.hook.sendmail.virtusertable=/etc/mail/virtusertable
mail.hook.sendmail.virtusertable.refresh=bash -c "makemap hash
/etc/mail/virtusertable < /etc/mail/virtusertable"
```

ShellHook

Set the location of the shell script that will interface with any mail server.

```
mail.hook.shell.script=/usr/sbin/mailadmin.ksh
```

Set to true to enable SMTP debugging.

```
mail.smtp.debug=false
```

Input a list of comma delimited email addresses that will receive a BCC of every email sent through the mail server.

```
mail.audit.trail=
```

Message Boards Portlet

Configure mail notification settings.

```
message.boards.email.from.name=Joe Bloggs
message.boards.email.from.address=test@liferay.com
message.boards.email.html.format=true
message.boards.email.message.added.enabled=true
message.boards.email.message.added.subject.prefix=com/liferay/portlet/mes-
sageboards/dependencies/email_message_added_subject_prefix.tmpl
message.boards.email.message.added.body=com/liferay/portlet/messageboards/de
pendencies/email_message_added_body.tmpl
message.boards.email.message.added.signature=com/liferay/portlet/message-
boards/dependencies/email_message_added_signature.tmpl
message.boards.email.message.updated.enabled=true
message.boards.email.message.updated.subject.prefix=com/liferay/portlet/mes-
sageboards/dependencies/email_message_updated_subject_prefix.tmpl
message.boards.email.message.updated.body=com/liferay/portlet/messageboards/
dependencies/email_message_updated_body.tmpl
message.boards.email.message.updated.signature=com/liferay/portlet/message-
boards/dependencies/email_message_updated_signature.tmpl
```

Set this to true to allow anonymous posting.

```
message.boards.anonymous.posting.enabled=true
```

Enter time in minutes on how often this job is run. If a user's ban is set to expire at 12:05 PM and the job runs at 2 PM, the expire will occur during the 2 PM run.

```
message.boards.expire.ban.job.interval=120
```

Enter time in days to automatically expire bans on users. Set to 0 to disable auto expire.

Examples:

```
message.boards.expire.ban.interval=10
message.boards.expire.ban.interval=0
```

Enter rss feed abstract length. This value limits what goes in the RSS feed from the beginning of the message board post. The default is the first 200 characters.

```
message.boards.rss.abstract.length=200
```

My Places Portlet

Set this to true to show user public sites with no layouts.

```
my.places.show.user.public.sites.with.no.layouts=true
```

Set this to true to show user private sites with no layouts.

```
my.places.show.user.private.sites.with.no.layouts=true
```

Set this to true to show organization public sites with no layouts.

```
my.places.show.organization.public.sites.with.no.layouts=true
```

Set this to true to show organization private sites with no layouts.

```
my.places.show.organization.private.sites.with.no.layouts=true
```

Set this to true to show community public sites with no layouts.

```
my.places.show.community.public.sites.with.no.layouts=true
```

Set this to true to show community private sites with no layouts.

```
my.places.show.community.private.sites.with.no.layouts=true
```

Navigation Portlet

Specify the options that will be provided to the user in the edit configuration mode of the portlet.

```
navigation.display.style.options=1,2,3,4,5,6
```

Define each mode with 4 comma delimited strings that represent the form: headerType, rootLayoutType, rootLayoutLevel, and includedLayouts.

```
navigation.display.style[1]=breadcrumb,relative,0,auto
navigation.display.style[2]=root-layout,absolute,2,auto
navigation.display.style[3]=root-layout,absolute,1,auto
navigation.display.style[4]=none,absolute,1,auto
navigation.display.style[5]=none,absolute,1,all
navigation.display.style[6]=none,absolute,0,auto
```

Nested Portlets Portlet

```
nested.portlets.layout.template.default=2_columns_i
```

Add a comma separated list of layout template ids that should not be allowed in the Nested Portlets Portlet.

```
nested.portlets.layout.template.unsupported=freeform,1_column
```

Portlet CSS Portlet

Set this to true to enable the ability to modify portlet CSS at runtime via the Look and Feel icon. Disabling it can speed up performance.

```
portlet.css.enabled=true
```

Shopping Portlet

Set the following to true if cart quantities must be a multiple of the item's minimum quantity.

```
shopping.cart.min.qty.multiple=true
```

Set the following to true to forward to the cart page when adding an item from the category page. The item must not have dynamic fields. All items with dynamic fields will forward to the item's details page regardless of the following setting.

```
shopping.category.forward.to.cart=false
```

Set the following to true to show special items when browsing a category.

```
shopping.category.show.special.items=false
```

Set the following to true to show availability when viewing an item.

```
shopping.item.show.availability=true
```

Set the maximum file size and valid file extensions for images. A value of 0 for the maximum file size can be used to indicate unlimited file size. However, the maximum file size allowed is set in the property *com.liferay.portal.upload.UploadServletRequestImpl.max.size*.

```
shopping.image.small.max.size=51200
shopping.image.medium.max.size=153600
shopping.image.large.max.size=307200
```

A file extension of * will permit all file extensions.

```
shopping.image.extensions=.gif,.jpeg,.jpg,.png
```

Configure email notification settings.

```
shopping.email.from.name=Joe Bloggs
shopping.email.from.address=test@liferay.com
shopping.email.order.confirmation.enabled=true
shopping.email.order.confirmation.subject=com/liferay/portlet/shopping/de-
pendencies/email_order_confirmation_subject.tmpl
shopping.email.order.confirmation.body=com/liferay/portlet/shopping/depen-
dencies/email_order_confirmation_body.tmpl
shopping.email.order.shipping.enabled=true
shopping.email.order.shipping.subject=com/liferay/portlet/shopping/dependen-
cies/email_order_shipping_subject.tmpl
shopping.email.order.shipping.body=com/liferay/portlet/shopping/dependen-
cies/email_order_shipping_body.tmpl
```

Software Catalog Portlet

Set the maximum file size and max file dimensions for thumbnnails. A value of 0 for the maximum file size can be used to indicate unlimited file size. However, the maximum file size allowed is set in the property *com.liferay.portal.upload.UploadServletRequestImpl.max.size*.

```
sc.image.max.size=307200
sc.image.thumbnail.max.height=200
sc.image.thumbnail.max.width=160
```

Tags Compiler Portlet

Set this to true to enable the ability to compile tags from the URL. Disabling it can speed up performance.

```
tags.compiler.enabled=true
```

Tags Portlet

Input a class name that implements *com.liferay.portlet.tags.util.TagsAssetValidator*. This class will be called to validate assets. The DefaultTagsAssetValidator class is just an empty class that doesn't actually do any validation.

The MinimalTagsAssetValidator requires all assets to have at least one tag entry.

Examples:

```
tags.asset.validator=com.liferay.portlet.tags.util.DefaultTagsAssetValidator
#tags.asset.validator=com.liferay.portlet.tags.util.MinimalTagsAssetValida-
tor
```

Tasks Portlet

Specify the default number of approval stages.

```
tasks.default.stages=2
```

Specify the default role name for each stage of approval ordered from lowest level of approval to highest. These Roles must have the APPROVE_PROPOSAL permission.

```
tasks.default.role.names=Community Administrator,Community Owner
```

Translator Portlet

Set the default languages to translate a given text.

```
translator.default.languages=en_es
```

Web Form Portlet

Set the maximum number of dynamic fields to process.

```
web.form.portlet.max.fields=50
```

Wiki Portlet

Set the URL of a page that contains more information about the classic syntax of the wiki. It will be shown to the user when editing a page.

```
wiki.classic.syntax.help.url=http://wiki.liferay.com/index.php/Wiki_Portlet
```

Set the name of the default page for a wiki node. The name for the default page must be a valid wiki word. A wiki word follows the format of having an upper case letter followed by a series of lower case letters followed by another upper case letter and another series of lower case letters. See http://www.usemod.com/cgi-bin/wiki.pl?WhatIsaWiki for more information on wiki naming conventions.

```
wiki.front.page.name=FrontPage
```

Set the name of the default node that will be automatically created when the Wiki portlet is first used in a community.

```
wiki.initial.node.name=Main
```

Set the following property to specify the requirments for the names of wiki pages. By default only a few characters are forbidden. Uncomment the regular expression below to allow only CamelCase titles.

```
wiki.page.titles.regexp=([^/\\[\\]%&?@]+)
#wiki.page.titles.regexp=(((\\p{Lu}\\p{Ll}+)_?)+)
```

Set the following property to specify the characters that will be automatically removed from the titles when importing wiki pages. This regexp should remove any characters that are forbidden in the regexp specified in wiki.page.titles.regexp.

```
wiki.page.titles.remove.regexp=([/\\[\\]%&?@]+)
```

Set the list of supported wiki formats and the default wiki format.

```
wiki.formats=creole,html
wiki.formats.default=creole
```

Configure settings for each of the wiki formats.

```
wiki.formats.engine[classic_wiki]=com.liferay.portlet.wiki.engines.frik-
i.FrikiEngine
wiki.formats.configuration.main[classic_wiki]=wiki.transform
wiki.formats.configuration.interwiki[classic_wiki]=intermap.txt
wiki.formats.edit.page[classic_wiki]=/html/portlet/wiki/edit/wiki.jsp
wiki.formats.help.page[classic_wiki]=/html/portlet/wiki/help/classic_wi-
ki.jsp
wiki.formats.help.url[classic_wiki]=http://wiki.liferay.com/index.php/Wiki_P
ortlet
```

```
wiki.formats.engine[creole]=com.liferay.portlet.wiki.engines.jspwiki.JSP-
WikiEngine
wiki.formats.configuration.main[creole]=jspwiki.properties
wiki.formats.edit.page[creole]=/html/portlet/wiki/edit/wiki.jsp
wiki.formats.help.page[creole]=/html/portlet/wiki/help/creole.jsp
wiki.formats.help.url[creole]=http://www.wikicreole.org/wiki/Creole1.0
```

```
wiki.formats.engine[html]=com.liferay.portlet.wiki.engines.HtmlEngine
wiki.formats.edit.page[html]=/html/portlet/wiki/edit/html.jsp
```

```
wiki.formats.engine[plain_text]=com.liferay.portlet.wiki.engines.TextEngine
wiki.formats.edit.page[plain_text]=/html/portlet/wiki/edit/plain_text.jsp
```

Set the list of supported wiki importers.

```
wiki.importers=MediaWiki
```

Configure settings for each of the wiki importers.

```
wiki.importers.page[MediaWiki]=/html/portlet/wiki/import/mediawiki.jsp
wiki.importers.class[MediaWiki]=com.liferay.portlet.wiki.importers.mediawi-
ki.MediaWikiImporter
```

Configure email notification settings.

```
wiki.email.from.name=Joe Bloggs
wiki.email.from.address=test@liferay.com

wiki.email.page.added.enabled=true
wiki.email.page.added.subject.prefix=com/liferay/portlet/wiki/dependencies/e
mail_page_added_subject_prefix.tmpl
wiki.email.page.added.body=com/liferay/portlet/wiki/dependencies/email_page_
added_body.tmpl
wiki.email.page.added.signature=com/liferay/portlet/wiki/dependencies/email_
page_added_signature.tmpl

wiki.email.page.updated.enabled=true
wiki.email.page.updated.subject.prefix=com/liferay/portlet/wiki/dependen-
cies/email_page_updated_subject_prefix.tmpl
wiki.email.page.updated.body=com/liferay/portlet/wiki/dependencies/email_pag
e_updated_body.tmpl
wiki.email.page.updated.signature=com/liferay/portlet/wiki/dependencies/emai
l_page_updated_signature.tmpl
wiki.rss.abstract.length=200
```

Plugin Management

One of the primary ways of extending the functionality of Liferay Portal is by the use of *plugins*. Plugins are an umbrella term for installable *portlet*, *theme*, *layout template*, and *web module* Java EE .war files. Though Liferay comes bundled with a number of functional portlets, themes, layout templates, and web modules, plugins provide a means of extending Liferay to be able to do almost anything.

Portlets

Portlets are small web applications that run in a portion of a web page. The heart of any portal implementation is its portlets, because all of the functionality of a portal resides in its portlets. Liferay's core is a portlet container. The container's job is to manage the portal's pages and to aggregate the set of portlets that are to appear on any particular page. This means that all of the features and functionality of a portal application must be in its portlets.

Portlet applications, like servlet applications, have become a Java standard which various portal server vendors have implemented. The JSR-168 standard defines the portlet 1.0 specification, and the JSR-286 standard defines the portlet 2.0 specification. A Java standard portlet should be deployable on any portlet container which supports the standard. Portlets are placed on the page in a certain order by the end user and are served up dynamically by the portal server. This means that certain "givens" that apply to servlet-based projects, such as control over URLs or access to the *HttpServletRequest* object, don't apply in portlet projects, because the portal server generates these objects dynamically.

Tip: Liferay 4.4.2 and below support the Portlet 1.0 standard: JSR-168. Liferay 5.0 and above support the Portlet 2.0 standard: JSR-286. You cannot run Portlet 2.0 portlets in Liferay 4.4.2, but because the Portlet 2.0 standard is backwards-compatible, portlets written to the 1.0 standard will run in Liferay 5.x and above.

Portal applications come generally in two flavors: 1) portlets can be written to provide small amounts of functionality and then aggregated by the portal server into a larger application, or 2) whole applications can be written to reside in only one or a few portlet windows. The choice is up to those designing the application. The developer only has to worry about what happens inside of the portlet itself; the portal server handles building out the page as it is presented to the user.

Most developers nowadays like to use certain frameworks to develop their applications, because those frameworks provide both functionality and structure to a project. For example, Struts enforces the Model-View-Controller design pattern and provides lots of functionality—such as custom tags and form validation—that make it easier for a developer to implement certain standard features. With Liferay, developers are free to use all of the leading frameworks in the Java EE space, including Struts, Spring, and Java Server Faces. This allows developers familiar with those frameworks to more easily implement portlets, and also facilitates the quick porting of an application using those frameworks over to a portlet implementation.

Additionally, Liferay supports "portlets" written in other programming languages. This allows you to take advantage of existing expertise in your organization with PHP, Ruby, or Python. Your developers can find sample portlets written in these environments in Liferay's plugin repository.

Does your organization make use of any Enterprise Planning (ERP) software that exposes its data via web services? You could write a portlet plugin for Liferay that can consume that data and display it as part of a dashboard page for your users. Do you subscribe to a stock service? You could pull stock quotes from that service and display them on your page, instead of using Liferay's built-in Stocks portlet. Do you have a need to combine the functionality of two or more servlet-based applications on one page? You could make them into portlet plugins and have Liferay display them in whatever layout you want. Do you have existing Struts, Spring MVC, or JSF applications that you want to integrate with your portal? It is a straightforward task to migrate these applications into Liferay, and then they can take advantage of the layout, security, and administration infrastructure that Liferay provides.

Themes

Themes are hot deployable plugins which can completely transform the look and feel of the portal. Most organizations have their own look and feel standards which go across all of the web sites and web applications in the infrastructure. Liferay makes it possible for a site designer to create a theme plugin which can then be installed, allowing for the complete transformation of the portal to whatever look and feel is needed. There are lots of available theme plugins on Liferay's web site, and more are being added every day. This makes it easier for those who wish to develop themes for Liferay, as you can now choose a theme which most closely resembles what you want to do and then customize it. This is much easier than starting a theme from scratch. There is more about theme development in the *Liferay Developer's Guide*.

Layout Templates

Layout Templates are ways of choosing how your portlets will be arranged on a page. They make up the body of your page, the large area where you drag and drop your portlets to create your pages. Liferay Portal comes with several built-in layout templates, but if you have a complex page layout (especially for your home page), you may wish to create a custom layout template of your own. This is covered in the *Liferay Developer's Guide*.

Web Plugins

Web plugins are regular Java EE web modules that are designed to work with Liferay. Liferay supports integration with various Enterprise Service Bus (ESB) implementations, as well as Single Sign-On implementations, workflow engines and so on. These are implemented as web modules that are used by Liferay portlets to provide functionality.

Installing Plugins from Liferay's Official and Community Repositories

Liferay Portal comes with two portlets which can handle plugin installation: the **Plugin Installer** and the **Update Manager**. Both portlets have similar functionality; the only difference between them is that the Update Manager can go out to the repositories and determine if you are running the most recent version of a plugin. For this reason, we will use the Update Manager portlet to install plugins.

From an appropriate private page on either a personal or public community, go up to the Dock and select *Add Content*. From the *Admin* category, click the *Add* button next to *Update Manager*. Then close the Add Content window.

You should now see the Update Manager on your page. Move it to an appropriate area of the page.

The default look of the Update Manager shows which plugins are already installed on the system, what their version numbers are, and whether an update is available.

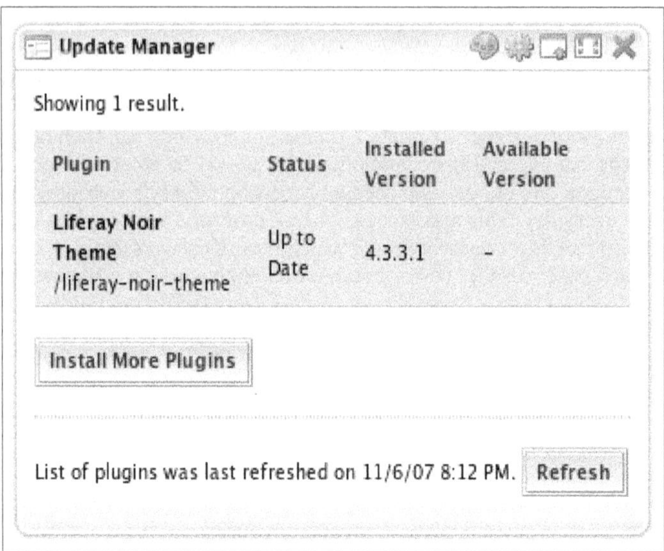

Illustration 66: Update Manager

If you would like to see what plugins are available, you can do so by clicking the *Install More Plugins* button. Please note that the machine upon which Liferay is running must have access to the Internet in order to be able to read the Official and Community repositories. If the machine does not have access to the Internet, you will need to download the plugins from the site and install them manually. We will discuss how to do this later in this chapter.

From the initial page you can also refresh the list of plugins. This causes the portlet to access the repository on the Internet and update the list of plugins that are available. When the refresh is complete, a status message is displayed which shows whether the refresh was successful.

After the *Install More Plugins* button is clicked, a new view of the portlet appears. This view has multiple tabs, and by default, displays the *Portlet Plugins* tab. Note that the list displayed is a list of all of the plugins that are available across all of the repositories to which the server is subscribed. Above this is a search mechanism which allows you to search for plugins by their name, by whether they are installed, by tag, or by which repository they are in.

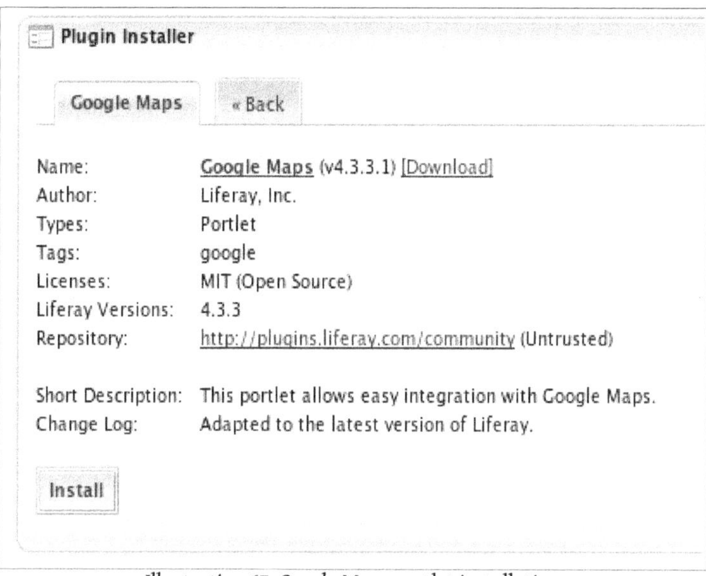

Illustration 67: Google Maps portlet installation

To install a plugin, choose the plugin by clicking on its name. For example, if your web site is for an organization to which visitors are likely to travel, you might want to install the Google Maps plugin. This plugin provides a handy interface to Google Maps from inside of Liferay, and therefore from inside of your web site.

Find the Google Maps plugin in the list by searching for it or browsing to it. Once you have found it, click on its name. Another page will be displayed which describes the portlet plugin in more detail. Below the description is an *Install* button. Click this button to install your plugin.

The plugin chosen will be automatically downloaded and installed on your instance of Liferay. If you have the Liferay console open, you can view the deployment as it happens. When it is finished, you should be able to go back to the Add Content window and add your new plugin to a page in your portal.

The same procedure is used for installing new Liferay Themes, Layout Templates, and web modules. Instead of the *Portlet Plugins* tab, you would use the appropriate tab for the type of plugin you wish to install to view the list of plugins of that type. For themes, convenient thumbnails (plus a larger version when you click on the details of a particular theme) are shown in the list.

After clicking on the *Install* button for a theme, the theme becomes available on the *Look and Feel* tab of any page.

Illustration 68: Portlet Plugins in the Plugin Installer

Installing Plugins Manually

Installing plugins manually is almost as easy as installing plugins via the Plugin Installer. There are several scenarios in which you would need to install plugins manually rather than from Liferay's repositories:

- Your server is firewalled without access to the Internet. This makes it impossible for your instance of Liferay to connect to the plugin repositories.
- You are installing portlets which you have either purchased from a vendor, downloaded separately, or developed yourself.
- For security reasons, you do not want to allow portal administrators to install plugins from the Internet before they are evaluated.

You can still use the Update Manager / Plugin Installer portlets to install plugins that are not available from the on line repositories. This is by far the easiest way to install plugins.

If your server is firewalled, you will not see any plugins displayed in the *Portlet Plugins* tab or in the *Theme Plugins* tab. Instead, you will need to click the *Upload File* tab. This gives you a simple interface for uploading a .war file containing a plugin to your Liferay Portal.

Click the *Browse* button and navigate your file system to find the portlet or theme .war you have downloaded. The other field on the page is optional: you can specify your own context for deployment. If you leave this field blank, the default context defined in the plugin (or the .war file name itself) will be used.

That's all the information the Plugin Installer needs in order to deploy your portlet, theme, layout template or web module. Click the *Install* button, and your plugin will be uploaded to the server and deployed. If it is a portlet, you should see it in the

Add Content window. If it is a theme, it will be available on the *Look and Feel* tab in the page definition.

If you do not wish to use the Update Manager or Plugin Installer to deploy plugins, you can also deploy them at the operating system level. The first time Liferay starts, it creates a *hot deploy* folder which is by default created inside the home folder of the user who launched Liferay. For example, say that on a Linux system, the user *lportal* was created in order to run Liferay. The first time Liferay is launched, it will create a folder structure in */home/lportal/liferay* to house various configuration and administrative data. One of the folders it creates is called *deploy*. If you copy a portlet or theme plugin into this folder, Liferay will deploy it and make it available for use just as though you'd installed it via the Update Manager or Plugin Installer. In fact, this is what the Update Manager and Plugin Installer portlets are doing behind the scenes.

You can change the defaults for this directory structure so that it is stored anywhere you like by modifying the appropriate properties in your *portal-ext.properties* file. Please see the above section on the *portal-ext..properties* file for more information.

To have Liferay hot deploy a portlet or theme plugin, copy the plugin into your hot deploy folder, which by default is in *<User Home>/liferay/deploy*. If you are watching the Liferay console, you should see messages like the following:

```
19:54:15,339 INFO  [AutoDeployDir:76] Processing westminstercatechism-port-
let-5.1.0.1.war
19:54:15,340 INFO  [PortletAutoDeployListener:77] Copying portlets for
/home/liferay/liferay/deploy/westminstercatechism-portlet-5.1.0.1.war
19:54:15,345 INFO  [BaseDeployer:532] Deploying westminstercatechism-port-
let-5.1.0.1.war
  Expanding: /home/liferay/liferay/deploy/westminstercatechism-port-
let-5.1.0.1.war into /home/liferay/Documents/Liferay/code/portal/bun-
dles/liferay-portal-5.1-tomcat-5.5/temp/20080804195415349
  Copying 1 file to /home/liferay/Documents/Liferay/code/portal/bundles/lif-
eray-portal-5.1-tomcat-5.5/temp/20080804195415349/WEB-INF
  Copying 1 file to /home/liferay/Documents/Liferay/code/portal/bundles/lif-
eray-portal-5.1-tomcat-5.5/temp/20080804195415349/WEB-INF/classes
  Copying 1 file to /home/liferay/Documents/Liferay/code/portal/bundles/lif-
eray-portal-5.1-tomcat-5.5/temp/20080804195415349/WEB-INF/classes
  Copying 1 file to /home/liferay/Documents/Liferay/code/portal/bundles/lif-
eray-portal-5.1-tomcat-5.5/temp/20080804195415349/META-INF
19:54:16,727 INFO  [BaseDeployer:1248] Modifying Servlet 2.3 /home/lifer-
ay/Documents/Liferay/code/portal/bundles/liferay-portal-5.1-tomcat-5.5/temp/
20080804195415349/WEB-INF/web.xml
  Copying 31 files to /home/liferay/Documents/Liferay/code/portal/bun-
dles/liferay-portal-5.1-tomcat-5.5/webapps/westminstercatechism-portlet
  Copying 1 file to /home/liferay/Documents/Liferay/code/portal/bundles/lif-
eray-portal-5.1-tomcat-5.5/webapps/westminstercatechism-portlet
  Deleting directory /home/liferay/Documents/Liferay/code/portal/bun-
dles/liferay-portal-5.1-tomcat-5.5/temp/20080804195415349
19:54:17,082 INFO  [PortletAutoDeployListener:87] Portlets for /home/lifer-
ay/liferay/deploy/westminstercatechism-portlet-5.1.0.1.war copied success-
fully
19:54:23,170 INFO  [PortletHotDeployListener:201] Registering portlets for
westminstercatechism-portlet
19:54:23,192 INFO  [PortletHotDeployListener:208] 1 portlets for westmin-
```

```
stercatechism-portlet are ready for registration
19:54:23,261 INFO  [PortletHotDeployListener:284] 1 portlets for westmin
stercatechism-portlet registered successfully
```

As long as you see the *registered successfully* message, your plugin was installed correctly, and will be available for use in the portal.

Plugin Troubleshooting

Sometimes for various reasons plugins fail to install. There are different reasons for this based on several factors, including

- Liferay configuration
- The container upon which Liferay is running
- Changing the configuration options in multiple places
- How Liferay is being launched

You will often be able to tell if you have a plugin deployment problem by looking at the Liferay server console. If you see the plugin get recognized by the hot deploy listener, you will see a *plugin copied successfully* message. If this message is not followed up by a *plugin registered successfully* message, you have an issue with your plugin deployment configuration, and it is likely one of the factors above.

We will look at each of these factors.

Liferay Configuration Issues

Tip: This applies to Liferay versions prior to version 4.3.5. Liferay versions above 4.3.5 are able to auto detect the type of server it is running on, which makes things a lot easier.

Liferay by default comes as a bundle or as a .war file. Though every effort has been made to make the .war file as generic as possible, sometimes the default settings are inappropriate for the container upon which Liferay is running. Most of these problems have been resolved in Liferay 4.3.5 with the addition of code that allows Liferay to determine which application server it is running on and adjust the way it deploys plugins as a result.

In versions of Liferay prior to 4.3.5, there is a property called *auto.deploy.dest.dir* that defines the folder where plugins are deployed after the hot deploy utilities have finished preparing them. This folder maps to a folder that the container defines as an auto-deploy or a hot deploy folder. By default, this property is set to *../webapps*. This default value works for Tomcat containers (if Tomcat has been launched from its *bin* folder), but will not work for other containers that define their hot deploy folders in a different place.

For example, Glassfish defines the hot deploy folder as a folder called *autodeploy* inside of the domain folder in which your server is running. By default, this is in *<Glassfish Home>/domains/domain1/autodeploy*. JBoss defines the hot deploy folder as a root folder inside of the particular server configuration you are using. By default, this is in *<JBoss Home>/server/default/deploy*. WebLogic defines this folder inside of the domain directory. By default, this is in *<Bea Home>/user_projects/domains/<domain name>/autodeploy*.

You will first need to determine where the hot deploy folder is for the container you are running. Consult your product documentation for this. Once you have this value, there are two places in which you can set it: the *portal-ext.properties* file and in the Plugin Installer portlet.

To change this setting in the *portal-ext.properties* file, browse to where Liferay was deployed in your application server. Inside of this folder should be a *WEB-INF/classes* folder. Here you will find the *portal-ext.properties* file. Open this file in a text editor and look for the property *auto.deploy.dest.dir*. If it does not appear in the file, you can add it. The safest way to set this property—as we will see later—is to define the property using an absolute path from the root of your file system to your application server's hot deploy folder. For example, if you are using Glassfish, and you have the server installed in */java/glassfish*, your *auto.deploy.dest.dir* property would look like the following:

```
auto.deploy.dest.dir=/java/glassfish/domains/domain1/autodeploy
```

Remember, if you are on a Windows system, use forward slashes instead of back slashes, like so:

```
auto.deploy.dest.dir=C:/java/glassfish/domains/domain1/autodeploy
```

Save the file and then restart your container. Now plugins should install correctly.

If you would rather change this setting via the Plugin Installer portlet (because you do not wish to restart your container), you can do that by clicking on the *Configuration* tab. On this page are a number of settings you can change, including the default folders for hot deploy, where Liferay should look for plugin repositories, and so on.

Destination Directory	../webapps

Illustration 69: Changing the hot deploy destination directory

The setting to change is the field marked *Destination Directory*. Change this to the full path to your container's auto deploy folder from the root of your file system. When you are finished, click the *Save* button at the bottom of the form. The setting will now take effect without your having to restart your container.

Note that the setting in the portlet overrides the setting in the properties file.

If you are having hot deploy trouble in Liferay versions 4.3.5 and greater, it is possible that the administrator of your application server has changed the default folder for auto deploy in your application server. In this case, you would want to set *auto.deploy.dest.dir* to the customized folder location as you would with older versions of Liferay. In Liferay 4.3.5 and greater, this setting still exists, but is blank. Add the property to your *portal-ext.properties* file and set its value to the fully qualified path to the auto deploy folder configured in your application server.

The Container Upon Which Liferay Is Running

There are some containers, such as Oracle Application Server and WebSphere®, which do not have a hot deploy feature. Unfortunately, these containers do not work with Liferay's hot deploy system. But this does not mean that you cannot install plugins on these containers. Some users have had success deploying plugins manually using the application server's deployment tools. On some containers, Liferay is able to pick up the portlet plugins once they get deployed to the container manually, especially if you add it to the same Enterprise Application project that was created for Liferay.

When Liferay hot deploys portlet and theme .war files, it sometimes makes modifications to those files right before deployment. In order to successfully deploy plugins using an application server vendor's tools, you will want to run your plugins through this process before you attempt to deploy them.

Using the **Plugin Installer** portlet, click the *Configuration* tab. The second-most field on the form is labeled **Destination Directory.** Place the path to which you would like plugin .war files copied after they are processed by Liferay's plugin installer process. You will use this as a staging directory for your plugins before you install them manually with your server's deployment tools. When you are finished, click *Save.*

Now you can deploy plugins using the Plugin Installer portlet or by dropping .war files into your auto deploy directory. Liferay will pick up the files, modify them, and then copy the result into the destination directory you have configured. You may then deploy them from here to your application server.

Changing the Configuration Options in Multiple Places

Sometimes, especially during development when several people have administrative access to the server at the same time, the auto deploy folder location can get customized in both the *portal-ext.properties* file and in the Plugin Installer portlet. If this happens, the value in the Plugin Installer takes precedence over the value in the properties file. If you go into the Plugin Installer and change the value to the correct setting, plugin deployment will start working again.

How Liferay Is Being Launched

Tip: This applies to Liferay versions prior to version 4.3.5. Liferay versions above 4.3.5 are able to auto detect the type of server it is running on, and this property is no longer detected via the relative path from the server launch location.

In versions of Liferay prior to 4.3.5, the default value of the hot deploy destination directory is a relative path (e.g., *../webapps* or *../server/default/deploy*). This path is relative to the folder from which the application server is normally launched. For example, Tomcat has the pictured directory structure.

The start up and shut down scripts are in the *bin* folder. So to start Tomcat, you would normally go into the *bin* folder to run the startup script which starts Liferay running in Tomcat.

Tomcat's hot deploy folder is the *webapps* folder. This folder is on the same level the *bin* folder is on. If you are at the command prompt inside of the *bin* folder (where you started Tomcat), to get to a file in the hot deploy folder you would reference it by using two dots to go back up one folder, and then the path separator (/), and then the name of the folder (*webapps*). So in the default configuration, the hot deploy destination directory is relative to the folder from which the application server was launched.

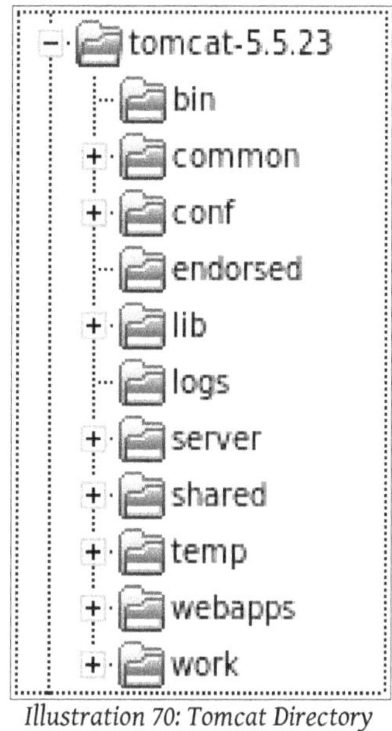

Illustration 70: Tomcat Directory Structure

If you are launching your application server from another script—perhaps as part of a cron job—and your script does not enter the folder the application server's startup scripts are in (in this case, *<Tomcat Home>/bin*), the relative path that is set by default will not work. Instead, the path will be relative to the path from which you launched the startup script. This will cause Liferay to create—in the Tomcat example—a *webapps* folder one folder up from where the startup script was launched. Since this is not the correct hot deploy folder for your application server, you will see the *copied successfully* message in the server console, but you will never see the *registered successfully* message.

To fix this, you can do one of two things: 1) Change the relative path to an absolute path as recommended above; or 2) Change the way you launch Liferay by making sure you go into the folder where the application server's startup scripts are before you launch them. Either one of these methods should fix your hot deploy problem and will result in the successful deployment of portlet and theme plugins.

Creating Your Own Plugin Repository

As your enterprise builds its own library of portlets for internal use, you can create your own plugin repository to make it easy to install and upgrade portlets. This will allow different departments who may be running different instances of Liferay to share portlets and install them as needed. If you are a software development house, you may wish to create a plugin repository for your own products. Liferay makes it easy for you to create your own plugin repository and make it available to others.

You can create your plugin repository in two ways:

1. Add the Software Catalog portlet to an instance of Liferay and create the repository by using its graphical interface and an HTTP server.
2. Create an XML file using the Liferay Plugin Repository DTD (http://www.liferay.com/dtd/liferay-plugin-repository_5_1_0.dtd) and an HTTP server.

Both methods have their benefits. The first method allows users to upload their plugins to an HTTP server to which they have access. They can then register their plugins with the repository by adding a link to it via the portlet's graphical user interface. Liferay will then generate the XML necessary to connect the repository to a Plugin Installer portlet running another instance of Liferay. This XML file can then be placed on an HTTP server, and the URL to it can be added to the Plugin Installer, making the portlets in this repository available to the server running Liferay.

The second method does not require an instance of Liferay to be running. You can upload plugins to an HTTP server of your choice, and then create an XML file called *liferay-plugin-repository.xml* manually. If you make this file available on an HTTP server (it can be the same one upon which the plugins are stored, or a different one altogether), you can connect the repository to a Plugin Installer portlet running on an instance of Liferay.

We will first look at creating a plugin repository using the Software Catalog portlet.

The Software Catalog Portlet

You will want to use the **Software Catalog** portlet if you will have multiple users submitting portlets into the repository, and if you don't want to worry about creating the *liferay-plugin-repository.xml* file yourself.

The Software Catalog portlet is not an *instanceable* portlet, which means that each community can have only one instance of the portlet. If you add the portlet to anoth-

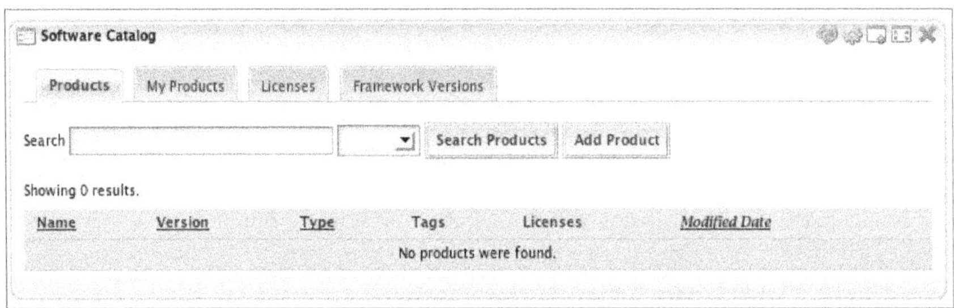

Illustration 71: Software Catalog with no products

er page in the community, it will hold the same data as the portlet that was first added. Different communities, however, can have different software repositories, so you can host several software repositories on the same instance of Liferay if you wish —they just have to be in different communities.

Choose the community that will host the plugin repository and add the Software Catalog portlet to the appropriate page in that community. You can do this by navigating to the page, selecting *Add Content* from the Dock, expanding the *Admin* category, and clicking the *Add* button next to the Software Catalog. Close the *Add Content* window and then drag the Software Catalog portlet to a wide column and drop it there.

The Software Catalog portlet has several tabs. The first tab is labeled *Products*. The default view of the portlet, when populated with software, displays what plugins are available for install or download. This can be seen in the version on Liferay's home page.

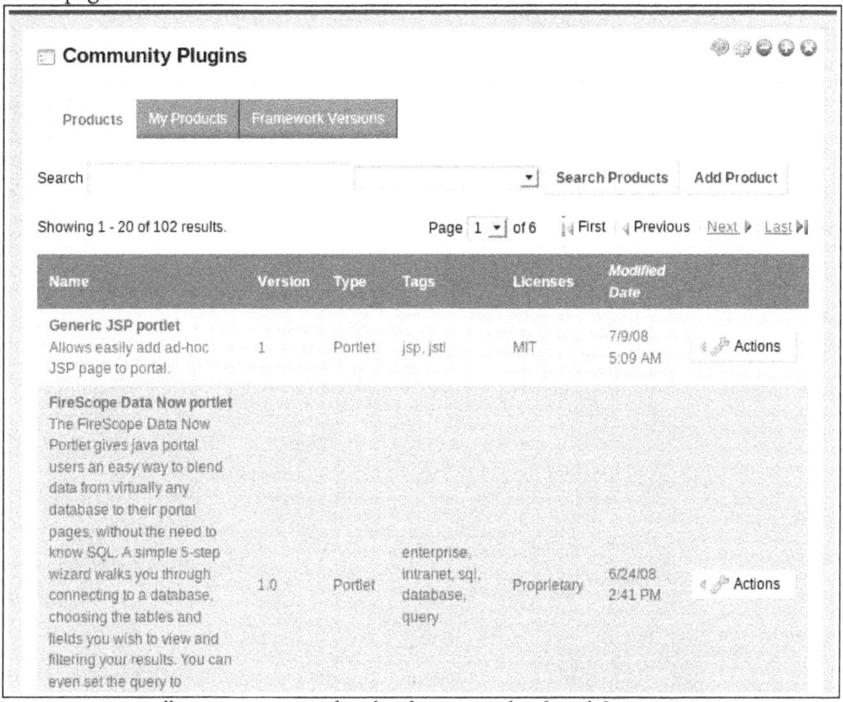

Illustration 72: Populated Software Catalog from liferay.com

We will use an example community in order to better illustrate how to use the Software Catalog portlet. Assume you, as the portal administrator, have created a community called *Old Computers*. This community will be a web site for users to collaborate on setting up and using old computers with obsolete hardware and operating systems. Users who participate in the site will eventually get upgraded to Power User status and get their own blog page. To implement this, you have created a My Summary portlet which displays the user's name, picture, and description from his or her user profile. Because this portlet is generic enough that it could be useful to anyone using Liferay, you have decided to make it available in your own software catalog.

In your *Old Computers* community, you have created a page called *Software*. This is where you have added your Software Catalog portlet.

The first step in adding a plugin to your software repository is to add a *license* for your product. A license communicates to users the terms upon which you are allowing them to download and use your software. Click the *Licenses* tab and then click the *Add License* button that appears. You will then see a form which allows you to enter the title of your license, a URL pointing to the actual license document, and check boxes denoting whether the license is open source, active, or recommended.

When you have finished filling out the form, click the *Save* button. Your license will be saved. Once you have at least one license in the system, you can begin adding software products to your software catalog. Click the *Products* tab, and then click the *Add Product* button.

Your next step will be to create the product record in the software catalog portlet. This will register the product in the software catalog and allow you to start adding versions of your software for users to download and / or install directly from their instances of Liferay. You will first need to put the .war file containing your software on a web server that is accessible without authentication to the users who will be installing your software. In the example above, the *Old Computers* site is on the Internet, so you would place the file on a web server that is accessible to anyone on the Internet. If you are creating a software catalog for an internal Intranet, you would place the file on a web server that is available to anyone inside of your organization's firewall.

To create the product record in the Software Catalog portlet, click the *Products* tab, and then click the *Add Product* button. Fill out the form with information about your product.

Software Catalog

Product « Back

Name: My Summary
Type: Portlet
Licenses: **Recommended Licenses** MIT License **Other Licenses**
Author: Computerman
Page URL: http://localhost/web/old-computers/home
Tags: blogs, mysummary (Comma delimited list)
Short Description: This portlet displays a summary of information about the user who owns a particular page.
Long Description: This portlet displays a summary of information about the user who owns a particular page. This information is taken from the user's profile.
Permissions: Configure »

Illustration 73: Adding a product to the Software Catalog (partial view)

Name: The name of your software product.

Type: Select whether this is a portlet or a theme plugin.

Licenses: Select the license(s) under which you are releasing this software.

Author: Enter the name of the author of the software.

Page URL: If the software has a home page, enter its url here.

Tags: Enter any tags you would like added to this software.

Short Description: Enter a short description. This will be displayed in the summary table of your software catalog.

Long Description: Enter a longer description. This will be displayed on the details page for this software product.

Permissions: Click the *Configure* link to set permissions for this software product.

Group ID: Enter a group ID. A group ID is a name space which usually identifies the company or organization that made the software. For our example, we will use *old-computers.*

Artifact ID: Enter an Artifact ID. The artifact ID is a unique name within the name space for your product. For our example, we will use *my-summary-portlet.*

Screenshot: Click the *Add Screenshot* button to add a screen shot of your product for users to view.

When you have finished filling out the form, click the *Save* button. You will be brought back to the product summary page, and you will see that your product has been added to the repository.

Illustration 74: Product has been added to the Software Catalog

Notice that in the version column, *N/A* is being displayed. This is because there are not yet any released *versions* of your product. To make your product downloadable, you need to create a version of your product and point it to the file you uploaded to your HTTP server earlier.

Before you do that, however, you need to add a *Framework Version* to your software catalog. A Framework version denotes what version of Liferay your plugin is designed for and works on. You cannot add a version of your product without linking it to a version of the framework for which it is designed.

Why is this so important? Because as Liferay gains more and more features, you may wish to take advantage of those features in future versions of your product, while still keeping older versions of your product available for those who are using older versions of Liferay. This is perfectly illustrated in the example My Summary portlet we are using. Liferay had a My Summary portlet of its own, which does exactly what we have described here. For version 5.1, however, this portlet has been replaced by the *World of Liferay* (WOL) portlet, which makes use of the many social networking features which have been added to Liferay. So rather than just displaying a summary of your information, the WOL portlet adds features such as status updates, a "wall" for each user in his or her profile that other users can "write" on, the ability to become "friends" with other users—thereby granting them access to their profiles—and more.

None of this would work in older versions of Liferay, because the core engine that enables developers to create features like this is not there. So in this case, you would want to keep the older My Summary portlet available for users who have not yet upgraded, but also make the WOL portlet available to those who are using the latest version of Liferay. This is what *Framework Versions* does for you. If you connect to Liferay's software repositories with a Liferay 4.4.2 version, you will see the My Summary portlet. If you connect to Liferay's software repositories with a Liferay 5.1 version, you will see the WOL portlet.

So click the *Framework Versions* tab and then click the *Add Framework Version* button.

Give the framework a name, a URL, and leave the *Active* check box checked. For our example, we have entered *4.3.4* for the name, because our portlet should work on that version and higher, and http://www.liferay.com for the URL. Click *Save.*

Now go back to the *Products* tab and click on your product. You will notice that a message is displayed stating that the product does not have any released versions. Click the *Add Product Version* button.

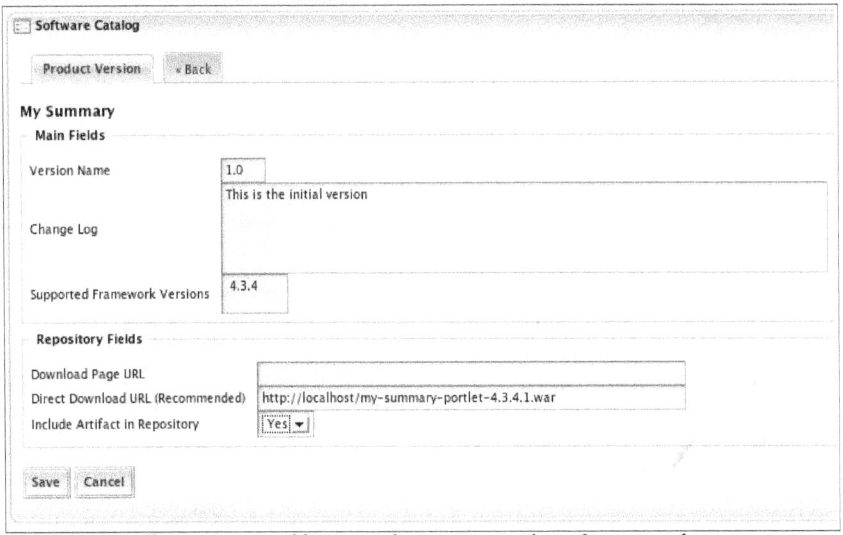

Software Catalog

Product Version | « Back

My Summary

Main Fields

Version Name: 1.0

Change Log: This is the initial version

Supported Framework Versions: 4.3.4

Repository Fields

Download Page URL

Direct Download URL (Recommended): http://localhost/my-summary-portlet-4.3.4.1.war

Include Artifact in Repository: Yes

Save | Cancel

Illustration 75: Adding a product version to the Software Catalog

Version Name: Enter the version of your product.

Change Log: Enter some comments regarding what changed between this version and any previous versions.

Supported Framework Versions: Select the framework version for which your software product is intended. Enter a + at the end of the version number if you want to specify a version plus any future versions.

Download Page URL: If your product has a descriptive web page, enter its URL here.

Direct Download URL (Recommended): Enter a direct download link to your software product here. The Plugin Installer portlet will follow this link in order to download your software product.

Include Artifact in Repository: To enable others to use the Plugin Installer portlet to connect to your repository and download your plugin, select *yes* here.

When you are finished filling out the form, click the *Save* button. Your product version will be saved, and your product will now be available in the software repository.

Generating The Software Catalog

The Software Catalog works by generating an XML document which the Plugin Installer reads. Using the data from this XML document, the Plugin Installer knows where it can download the plugins from, what version of Liferay the plugins are designed for, and all other data about the plugins that have been entered into the Software Catalog portlet.

In order to get your Software Catalog to generate this XML data, you will need to access a particular URL. If you have created a friendly URL for your community (for example, the default community, which is called *guest*, has a friendly URL of */guest* already configured for it), you can use the friendly URL. If not, you will first need to know the Group ID of the community in which your Software Catalog portlet resides. You can do this by accessing the Manage Pages interface and looking at the URLs for any of the pages. The URL will look something like this: *http://localhost:8080/web/10148/1*.

Obviously, it is much easier if you are using Friendly URLs, and we highly recommend that you do.

Next, go to your browser and go to the following URL:

```
http://<server name>:<port number>/software_catalog?<Friendly URL name or
Group ID>
```

For example, if you are on the same machine as your Liferay instance, and that instance is running on port 8080, and your group ID from the database is 10148, you would use the following URL:

```
http://localhost:8080/software_catalog?10148
```

If you have also created a friendly URL called *old-computers* for this organization or community, you would use the following URL:

```
http://localhost:8080/software_catalog?old-computers
```

If you have configured everything properly, an XML document should be returned:

```
<plugin-repository>
<settings/>
        <plugin-package>
<name>My Summary</name>
<module-id>oldcomputers/download-portlet/4.3.4.1/war</module-id>
<modified-date>Fri, 23 Nov 2007 17:07:33 -0500</modified-date>
```

```
        <types>
<type>portlet</type>
</types>
        <tags>
<tag>documentlibrary</tag>
<tag>4.2</tag>
</tags>
<short-description>My Summary portlet</short-description>
<long-description>My Summary portlet</long-description>
<change-log>Initial Version</change-log>
<download-url>http://localhost/my-summary-portlet-4.3.4.1.war</download-url>
<author>Rich Sezov</author>
<screenshots/>
        <licenses>
<license osi-approved="true">MIT License</license>
</licenses>
        <liferay-versions>
<liferay-version>4.3.4</liferay-version>
</liferay-versions>
</plugin-package>
</plugin-repository>
```

Save this document to a file called *liferay-plugin-package.xml* and put this file on your HTTP server where you uploaded your portlet .war file. You can then give out the URL to the directory which holds this file on your web site, and anyone with an instance of Liferay will be able to point their Plugin Installer portlets to it.

Benefits of the Software Catalog Portlet

As you can see, the Software Catalog portlet makes it easy for you to create a repository of your software. Users of Liferay can configure their Plugin Installer portlets to attach to your repository, and the proper versions of your software will be automatically made available to them by a single click. This is by far the easiest way for you to keep track of your software, and for your users to obtain your software.

Another benefit of the Software Catalog portlet is that by using it, you make available to your users a standard interface for manually downloading your software. For those who prefer to manually download plugins, your Software Catalog gives them an interface to go in, find your software either by browsing or by searching, preview screen shots, and download your software—and you don't have to build any of those pages yourself. Simply configure your software in the portlet, and all of that is done for you.

Manually Creating A Software Catalog

If you do not wish to use the Software Catalog portlet to create your software catalog, you can create it manually by manually typing out the XML file that the Software Catalog portlet would normally generate. Note that if you do this, you will not have a graphical user interface to your software that end users can use to download your software manually: you will have to build this yourself. Keep in mind that many instances of Liferay Portal sit behind a firewall without access to the Internet. Because of this, if you are making your software available to Internet users, some of them will have to download it manually. In this case, the Software Catalog portlet is the easiest way to provide a user interface for downloading your software.

To manually create a software catalog, obtain the DTD for the XML file from Liferay's source code. You will find this DTD in the *definitions* folder in the Liferay source. It is a file called *liferay-plugin-package_5_1_0.dtd*. Use this DTD with a validating XML editor (a good, free choice is JEdit with all the XML plugins) to create your software catalog manually.

Connecting to a Software Catalog

If there is a software catalog of plugins that you would like to point your instance of Liferay to, all you need is the URL to the catalog. Once you have the URL, go to your Plugin Installer portlet and click the *Configuration* tab. You will see that there are two fields in which you can enter URLs to plugin repositories: *Trusted Plugin Repositories* and *Untrusted Plugin Repositories*. Currently, the only difference between the two is to provide a visual cue for administrators as to which repositories are trusted and untrusted.

Enter the URL to the repository to which you wish to connect in one of the fields and click *Save*. The portlet will connect to the repository, and items from this repository will be shown in the list.

Liferay Services Oriented Architecture

Liferay includes a utility called the *Service Builder* which is used to generate all of the low level code for accessing resources from the portal database. This utility is further explained in the *Liferay Developer's Guide*, but it is mentioned here because of its feature which generates interfaces not only for Java code, but also for web services and JavaScript. This means that the method calls for storing and retrieving portal objects are all the same, and are generated in the same step.

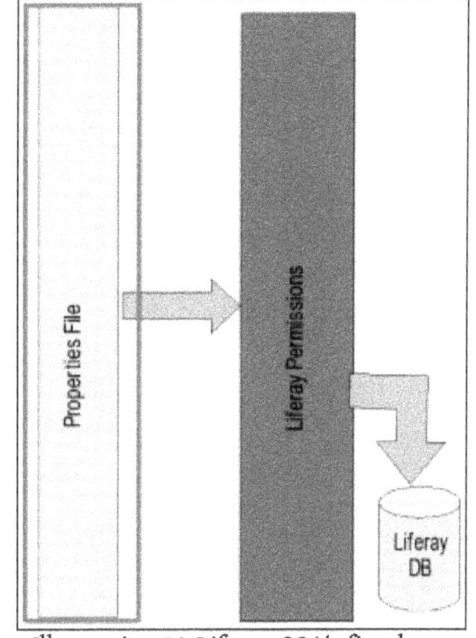

Illustration 76: Liferay SOA's first layer of security.

Because the actual method calls for retrieving data are the same regardless of how one gets access to those methods (i.e., locally or through web services), Liferay provides a consistent interface for accessing portal data that few other products can match. The actual interfaces for the various services will be covered in the *Liferay Developer's Guide*, but before they can be used there are steps that need to be taken to enable users to access those services remotely.

In the default *portal.properties* file, there

is a section called **Main Servlet**. This section defines the security settings for all of the remote services provided by Liferay. Copy this section and paste it into your custom *portal-ext.properties* file, and you can configure security settings for the Axis Servlet, the Liferay Tunnel Servlet, the Spring Remoting Servlet, the JSON Tunnel Servlet, and the WebDAV servlet.

By default, a user connecting from the same machine Liferay is running on can access remote services so long as that user has the permission to use those services in Liferay's permissions system. Of course, you are not really "remote" unless you are accessing services from a different machine. Liferay has two layers of security when it comes to accessing its services remotely. Without explicit rights to both layers, a remote exception will be thrown and access to those services will not be granted.

The first layer of security that a user needs to get through in order to call a method from the service layer is servlet security. The *Main Servlet* section of the *portal-ext.properties* file is used to enable or disable access to Liferay's remote services. In that section of the properties file, there are properties for each of Liferay's remote services.

You can set each service individually with the security settings that you require. For example, you may have a batch job which runs on another machine in your network. This job looks in a particular shared folder on your network and uploads documents to your community's document library portlet on a regular basis, using Liferay's web services. To enable this batch job to get through the first layer of security, you would modify the *portal-ext.properties* file and put the IP address of the machine on which the batch job is running in the list for that particular service. For example, if the batch job uses the Axis web services to upload the documents, you would enter the IP address of the machine on which the batch job is running to the *axis.servlet.hosts.allowed* property. A typical entry might look like this:

```
axis.servlet.hosts.allowed=192.168.100.100, 127.0.0.1, SERVER_IP
```

If the machine on which the batch job is running has the IP address 192.168.100.100, this configuration will allow that machine to connect to Liferay's web services and pass in user credentials to be used to upload the documents.

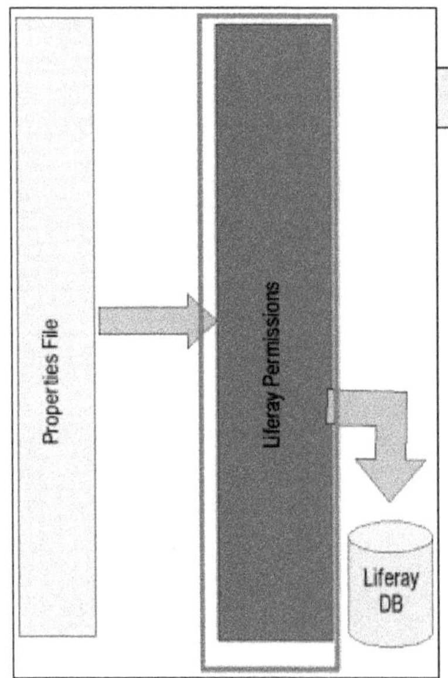

Illustration 77: Liferay SOA's second layer of security.

The second layer of security is Liferay's security model that it uses for every object in the portal. The user ID that accesses the services remotely must have the proper permission to operate on the objects it will be accessing. Otherwise, a remote exception will be thrown. The Portal Administrator will need to make use of Liferay's usual means of granting access to these resources to the user ID that will be operating on them remotely.

For example, say that a Document Library folder called *Documents* has been set up in a community. A group has been created called *Document Uploaders* which has the rights to add documents to this folder. Your batch job will be accessing Liferay's web services in order to upload documents into this folder. In order for this to work, you will have to call the web service using a user ID that is a member of this group (or that has individual rights to add documents to this folder). Otherwise, you will be prevented from using the Web Service.

To call the web service using credentials, you would use the following URL syntax:

```
http://" + userIdAsString + ":" + password + "@<server.com>:<port>/tunnel-
web/secure/axis/" + serviceName
```

The user ID is the user's ID from the Liferay database. This may be obtained by logging in as the user and clicking *My Account* from the Dock. In the top left corner of the portlet that appears is the user ID.

For example, to get Organization data using a user that has the ID of *2* with a password of *test*, you would use the following URL:

```
http://2:test@localhost:8080/tunnel-web/secure/axis/Portal_OrganizationSer-
vice
```

Tip: In older versions of Liferay (4.2.x and below), this password had to be the encrypted version from Liferay's database.

It is important to note here how *Password Policies* (covered in Chapter 3) can be used in combination with this feature. If you are enforcing password policies on your users (requiring them to change their passwords on a periodic basis, etc.), any administrative ID which accesses Liferay's web services in a batch job will have its password expire too.

To prevent this from happening, you can add a new password policy which does not enforce the password expiration and add your administrative user ID to it. Then your batch job can run as many times as you need it to, and the administrative ID's password will never expire.

In summary, accessing Liferay remotely requires the successful passing of two security checks:

1. The IP address must be pre-configured in the server's *portal-ext.properties* file.

2. The user ID being used must have permission to access the resources it is attempting to access.

Accessing Liferay's WSDL

After configuring the security settings properly, your first step in obtaining access to remote web services is to access the WSDL. If you are on a browser on the same machine Liferay is running on, you can do this by accessing the following URL:

```
http://localhost:<port number>/tunnel-web/axis
```

If, for example, you are running on Tomcat on port 8080, you would specify this URL:

```
http://localhost:8080/tunnel-web/axis
```

If you are on a different machine from the Liferay server, you will need to pass in your user credentials on the URL to access the WSDL:

```
http://<user ID>:<password>@<server name>:<port number>/tunnel-web/axis
```

In any case, once you successfully browse to this URL, you will see the list of web services.

WSDL for each service is available by clicking on the *WSDL* link next to the name of the service. There are many services; one for each of the services available from the Liferay API.

Once you click on one of the *WSDL* links, the Web Service Definition Language document will be displayed. This document can be used to generate client code in any language that supports it. You can either save the document to your local machine and then generate the client code that way, or use your tool to trigger Liferay to generate the document dynamically by using one of the URLs above.

For further information about developing applications that take advantage of Liferay's remote services, please see the *Liferay Developer's Guide*.

5. Enterprise Configuration

Liferay Portal is a robust, enterprise-ready portal solution. As such, it is fully ready to support mission-critical, enterprise applications in an environment configured for multiple redundancy and 24/7 up times. The product, however, like other products of its kind, does not come configured this way out of the box, and so there are some steps that need to be taken in order to configure it this way.

This chapter will cover these topics in detail. Because Liferay runs on so many different Java EE application servers, it will be impossible to cover all of the differences between these application servers. For this reason, we will cover the configuration of Liferay only. As an example, we will cover how to configure Liferay to work in a clustered environment, but we will not cover how to create the cluster in your application server. Please consult the documentation for your particular application server to see how you can configure your application server of choice to work as a cluster.

We will, however, cover the configuration of Liferay for a number of advanced scenarios, such as

- Clustering and Distributed Caching
- Liferay Workflow
- Deploying Customized versions of Liferay
- Performance Testing and Tuning

During this discussion, we will mention a number of other open source products upon which Liferay relies for much of this functionality. These products all have their own documentation which should be consulted for a fuller view of what these products can do. For example, Liferay uses Ehcache for its caching mechanism. We will cover how to configure Ehcache to enable various caching functionality in Liferay, but will refer you to that product's documentation for further information about that product.

Sometimes Liferay supports multiple products which perform the same function. There are, for example, multiple implementations of Enterprise Service Buses for use with workflow, and Liferay supports several of them. We will leave it up to you to select which product best fits the needs of your project without recommending one product over another.

With all of that said, let's get started configuring Liferay for the enterprise.

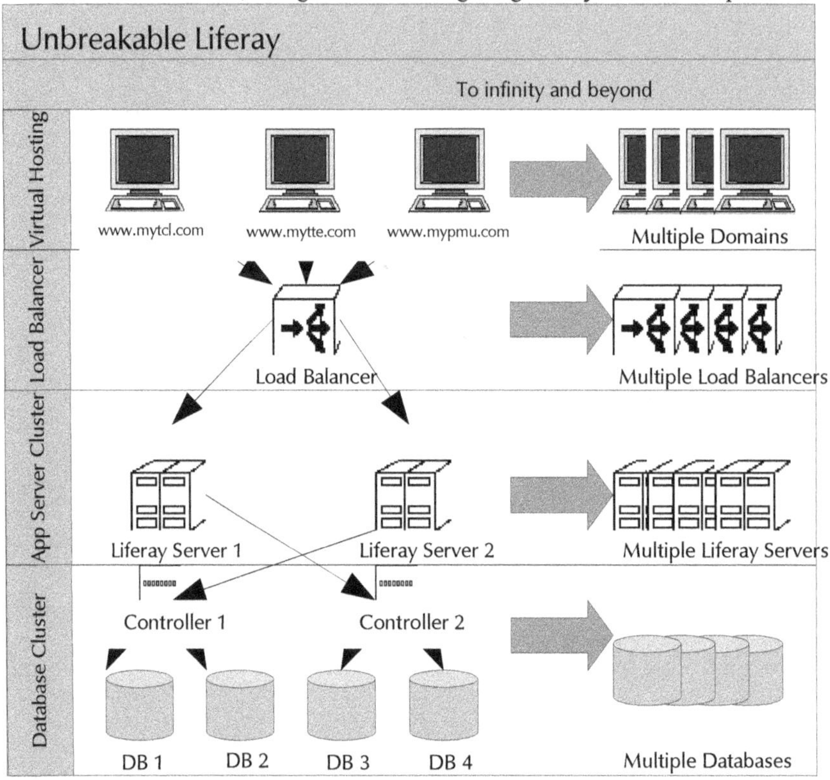

Illustration 78: "Unbreakable" Liferay architectecture

Liferay Clustering

Once you have Liferay installed in more than one node on your application server, there are several optimizations that need to be made. At a minimum, Liferay should be configured in the following way for a clustered environment:

- All nodes should be pointing to the same Liferay database
- Jackrabbit, the JSR-170 content repository, should be:
  - On a shared file system available to all the nodes (not really recommended, though), or
  - In a database that is shared by all the nodes
- Similarly, Lucene, the full text search indexer, should be:

  - On a shared file system available to all the nodes (not really recommended, though), or
  - In a database that is shared by all the nodes, or
  - On separate file systems for all of the nodes, or
  - Disabled, and a separate pluggable enterprise search server configured.
- If you have not configured your application server to use farms for deployment, the hot deploy folder should be a separate folder for all the nodes, and plugins will have to be deployed to all of the nodes individually. This can be done via a script.

Many of these configuration changes can be made by adding or modifying properties in your *portal-ext.properties* file. Remember that this file overrides the defaults that are in the *portal.properties* file. The original version of this file can be found in the Liferay source code or can be extracted from the *portal-impl.jar* file in your Liferay installation. It is a best practice to copy the relevant section that you want to modify from *portal.properties* into your *portal-ext.properties* file, and then modify the values there.

All Nodes Should Be Pointing to the Same Liferay Database

This is pretty self-explanatory. Each node should be configured with a data source that points to one Liferay database (or a database cluster) that all of the nodes will share. This ensures that all of the nodes operate from the same basic data set. This means, of course, that Liferay cannot (and should not) use the embedded HSQL database that is shipped with the bundles. It is also best if the database server is a separate physical box from the server which is running Liferay.

Jackrabbit Sharing

Liferay uses Jackrabbit—which is a project from Apache—as its JSR-170 compliant document repository. By default, Jackrabbit is configured to store the documents on the local file system upon which Liferay is installed, in the *$HOME/liferay/jackrabbit* folder. Inside this folder is Jackrabbit's configuration file, called *repository.xml*.

To simply move the default repository location to a shared folder, you do not need to edit Jackrabbit's configuration file. Instead, find the section in *portal.properties* labeled **JCR** and copy/paste that section into your *portal-ext.properties* file. One of the properties, by default, is the following:

```
jcr.jackrabbit.repository.root=${resource.repositories.root}/jackrabbit
```

Change this property to point to a shared folder that all of the nodes can see. A new Jackrabbit configuration file will be generated in that location.

Note that because of file locking issues, this is not the best way to share Jackrabbit resources. If you have two people logged in at the same time uploading content, you could encounter data corruption using this method, and because of this, we do not recommend it for a production system. Instead, to enable better data protection, you should redirect Jackrabbit into your database of choice. You can use the Liferay database or another database for this purpose. This will require editing Jackrabbit's configuration file.

The default Jackrabbit configuration file has sections commented out for moving the Jackrabbit configuration into the database. This has been done to make it as easy as possible to enable this configuration. To move the Jackrabbit configuration into the database, simply comment out the sections relating to the file system and comment in the sections relating to the database. These by default are configured for a MySQL database. If you are using another database, you will likely need to modify the configuration, as there are changes to the configuration file that are necessary for specific databases. For example, the default configuration uses Jackrabbit's *DbFileSystem* class to mimic a file system in the database. While this works well in MySQL, it does not work for all databases. For example, if you are using an Oracle database, you will need to modify this to use *OracleFileSystem*. Please see the Jackrabbit documentation at http://jackrabbit.apache.org for further information.

You will also likely need to modify the JDBC database URLs so that they point your database. Don't forget to create the database first, and grant the user ID you are specifying in the configuration file access to create, modify, and drop tables.

Once you have configured Jackrabbit to store its repository in a database, the next time you bring up Liferay, the necessary database tables will be created automatically. Jackrabbit, however, does not create indexes on these tables, and so over time this can be a performance penalty. To fix this, you will need to manually go into your database and index the primary key columns for all of the Jackrabbit tables.

All of your Liferay nodes should be configured to use the same Jackrabbit repository in the database. Once that is working, you can create a Jackrabbit cluster (please see the section below).

Search Configuration

You can configure search in one of two ways: use pluggable enterprise search (recommended for a cluster configuration) or configure Lucene in such a way that either the index is stored on each node's file system or is shared in a database.

Pluggable Enterprise Search

As an alternative to using Lucene, Liferay 5.1 now supports pluggable search engines. The first implementation of this uses the open source search engine *Solr*, but in the future there will be many such plugins for your search engine of choice. This allows you to use a completely separate product from Liferay which can be installed on any application server in your environment. Your search engine then operates completely independently of your Liferay Portal nodes in a clustered environment, acting as a search service for all of the nodes simultaneously.

What this does is solve the problem below with sharing Lucene indexes. You can now share one search index among all of the nodes of your cluster without having to worry about putting it in a database (if you wish, you can still do this if you configure Solr or another search engine that way) or maintaining separate search indexes on all of your nodes. Each Liferay node will send requests to the search engine to update the search index when needed, and these updates are then queued and handled automatically by the search engine.

Since at the time of this writing there is only one implementation of the pluggable enterprise search, we will cover how to implement this using Solr.

Since Solr is a standalone search engine, you will need to download it and install it first according to the instructions on the Solr web site (http://lucene.apache.org/solr). Once you have Solr up and running, integrating it with Liferay is easy, but it will require a restart of your application server.

The first thing you will need to define is the location of your search index. Assuming you are running a Linux server and you have mounted a file system for the index at */solr*, create an environment variable that points to this folder. This environment variable needs to be called *$SOLR_HOME*. So for our example, we would define:

```
$SOLR_HOME=/solr
```

This environment variable can be defined anywhere you need: in your operating system's start up sequence, in the environment for the user who is logged in, or in the start up script for your application server. If you are going to use Tomcat to host Solr, you would modify *catalina.sh* or *catalina.bat* and add the environment variable there.

Once you have created the environment variable, you then can use it in your application server's start up configuration as a parameter to your JVM. This is configured differently per application server, but again, if you are using Tomcat, you would edit *catalina.sh* or *catalina.bat* and append the following to the *$JAVA_OPTS* variable:

```
-Dsolr.solr.home=$SOLR_HOME
```

This takes care of telling Solr where to store its search index.

Next, you have a choice. If you have installed Solr on the same system upon which Liferay is running, you can simply go to a **Plugin Installer** portlet and install the *solr-web* plugin. Of course, if you are doing this for a clustered environment, it is likely that you are not running Liferay and your search engine on the same box, so you will have to make a change to a configuration file in the plugin before you install it. In this case, go to the Liferay web site (http://www.liferay.com) and download the plugin manually.

Open or extract the plugin. Inside the plugin, you will find a file called *solr-spring.xml* in the *WEB-INF/classes/META-INF* folder. Open this file in a text editor and you will see that there are two entries which define where the Solr server can be found by Liferay:

```
<bean id="indexSearcher" class="com.liferay.portal.search.solr.-
SolrIndexSearcherImpl">
	<property name="serverURL" value="http://localhost:8080/solr/se-
lect" />
</bean>
<bean id="indexWriter" class="com.liferay.portal.search.solr.SolrIndexWri-
terImpl">
	<property name="serverURL" value="http://localhost:8080/solr/up-
date" />
</bean>
```

Modify these values so that they point to the server upon which you are running Solr. Then save the file and put it back into the plugin archive in the same place it was before.

Next, extract the file *schema.xml* from the plugin. It should be in the *docroot/WEB-INF/conf* folder. Copy this file to *$SOLR_HOME/conf* (you may have to create the *conf* directory). Now go ahead and start the application server upon which you are going to install Solr. This can be the same server Liferay is running on or a completely different box (a separate box for your search server will give you better performance). Install the Solr .war file to this application server.

You can now hot deploy the *solr-web* plugin to all of your nodes. See the next section for instructions on hot deploying to a cluster.

Once the plugin is hot deployed, your Liferay search is automatically upgraded to use Solr. It is likely, however, that initial searches will come up with nothing: this is because you will need to reindex everything using Solr.

Go to the **Admin Portlet**. Click the *Server* tab and then click the *Execute* button next to *Reindex all search indexes*. It may take a while, but Liferay will begin sending indexing requests to Solr for execution. When the process is complete, Solr will have a complete search index of your site, and will be running independently of all of your Liferay nodes.

Installing the plugin to your nodes has the effect of overriding any calls to Lucene for searching. All of Liferay's search boxes will now use Solr as the search index. This is ideal for a clustered environment, as it allows all of your nodes to share one search server and one search index, and this search server operates independently of all of your nodes.

Lucene Configuration

Lucene, the search indexer which Liferay uses, can be in a shared configuration for a clustered environment, or an index can be created on each node of the cluster. If you wish to have a shared index, you will need to either share the index on the file system or in the database.

The Lucene configuration can be changed by modifying values in your *portal-ext.properties* file. Open your *portal.properties* file and search for the text *Lucene*. Copy that section and then paste it into your *portal-ext.properties* file.

If you wish to store the Lucene search index on a file system that is shared by all of the Liferay nodes, you can modify the location of the search index by changing the *lucene.dir* property. By default, this property points to the */liferay/lucene* folder inside the home folder of the user that is running Liferay:

```
lucene.dir=${resource.repositories.root}/lucene/
```

Change this to the folder of your choice. To make the change take effect, you will need to restart Liferay. You can point all of the nodes to this folder, and they will use the same index.

Like Jackrabbit, however, this is not the best way to share the search index, as it could result in file corruption if different nodes try reindexing at the same time. We do not recommend this for a production system. A better way is to share the index is via a database, where the database can enforce data integrity on the index. This is very easy to do; it is a simple change to your *portal-ext.properties* file.

There is a single property called *lucene.store.type*. By default this is set to go to the file system. You can change this so that the index is stored in the database by making it the following:

```
lucene.store.type=jdbc
```

The next time Liferay is started, new tables will be created in the Liferay database, and the index will be stored there. If all the Liferay nodes point to the same database tables, they will be able to share the index.

Alternatively, you leave the configuration alone, and each node will then have its own index. This ensures that there are no collisions when multiple nodes update the index, because they all will have separate indexes.

Hot Deploy

Plugins which are hot deployed will need to be deployed separately to all of the Liferay nodes. Each node should, therefore, have its own hot deploy folder. This folder needs to be writable by the user under which Liferay is running, because plugins are moved from this folder to a temporary folder when they are deployed. This is to prevent the system from entering an endless loop, because the presence of a plugin in the folder is what triggers the hot deploy process.

When you want to deploy a plugin, copy that plugin to the hot deploy folders of all of the Liferay nodes. Depending on the number of nodes, it may be best to create a script to do this. Once the plugin has been deployed to all of the nodes, you can then make use of it (by adding the portlet to a page or choosing the theme as the look and feel for a page or page hierarchy).

Some containers contain a facility which allows the end user to deploy an application to one node, after which it will get copied to all of the other nodes. If you have configured your application server to support this, you won't need to hot deploy a plugin to all of the nodes—your application server will handle it transparently. Make sure, however, that you use Liferay's hot deploy mechanism to deploy plugins, as in many cases Liferay slightly modifies plugin .war files when hot deploying them.

All of the above will get basic Liferay clustering working; however, the configuration can be further optimized. We will see how to do this next.

Distributed Caching

Liferay 4.3.1 and higher uses **Ehcache**, which has robust distributed caching support. This means that the cache can be distributed across multiple Liferay nodes running concurrently. Enabling this cache can increase performance dramatically. For example, say that two users are browsing the message boards. The first user clicks on a thread in order to read it. Liferay must look up that thread from the database and format it for display in the browser. With a distributed Ehcache running, this thread can be pulled from the database and stored in a cache for quick retrieval. Say then that the second user wants to read the same forum thread and clicks on it. This time, because the thread is in the local cache, no trip to the database is necessary, and so retrieving the data is much faster.

This could be done by simply having a cache running separately on each node, but the power of *distributed* caching allows for more functionality. The first user can post a message to the thread he or she was reading, and the cache will be updated across all of the nodes, making the new post available immediately from the local cache. Without that, the second user would need to wait until the cache was invalidated on the node he or she connected to before he or she could see the updated forum post.

Configuring distributed caching requires the modification of the *portal-ext.properties* file as well as one or more other files depending on what you want to cache. The first thing you will want to do is determine where on your server you will want to store your cache configuration files. This will have to be somewhere on Liferay's class path, so you will need to find where your application server has stored the deployed version of Liferay, and create a folder in Liferay's *WEB-INF/classes* folder to store the files. Because the original, default files are stored inside of a .jar file, you will need to extract them to this area and then tell Liferay (by use of the *portal-ext.properties* file) where they are.

For example, say you are running Liferay on Tomcat. Tomcat stores the deployed version of Liferay in *<Tomcat Home>/webapps/ROOT*. Inside of this folder is the folder structure *WEB-INF/classes*. You can create a new folder in here called *myehcache* to store the custom versions of the cache configuration files. Copy the files from the */ehcache* folder—which is inside the *portal-impl.jar file*—into the *myehcache* folder you just created. You then need to modify the properties in *portal-ext.properties* that point to these files. Copy / paste the **Hibernate** section of *portal.properties* into your *portal-ext.properties* file and then modify the *net.sf.ehcache.configurationResourceName* property to point to the clustered version of the configuration file that is now in your custom folder:

```
net.sf.ehcache.configurationResourceName=/myehcache/hibernate-clustered.xml
```

Now that Liferay is pointing to your custom file, you can modify the settings in this file to change the cache configuration for Hibernate.

Next, copy / paste the *Ehcache* section from the *portal.properties* file into your *portal-ext.properties* file. Modify the properties so that they point to the files that are in your custom folder. For example:

```
ehcache.multi.vm.config.location=/myehcache/liferay-multi-vm.xml
```

If you are going to enable distributed clustering, uncomment the following line and point it to your custom version of the file:

```
ehcache.multi.vm.config.location=/myehcache/liferay-multi-vm-clustered.xml
```

You can now take a look at the settings in these files and tune them to fit your environment and application.

Alternatively, if your Liferay project is using the extension environment to make customizations to Liferay, you can place your cache configuration in the extension environment. The settings there will override the default settings that ship with Liferay. If you wish to do this, you can create new versions of the files in *ext-impl/classes/ehcache*. The files should be postfixed with *-ext.xml*. For example, the custom version of *hibernate.xml* should be called *hibernate-ext.xml,* and the custom version of *liferay-multi-vm-clustered.xml* should be called *liferay-multi-vm-clustered-ext.xml.* You can then modify the files and tune them to fit your environment / application, and they will be deployed along with the rest of your extension environment.

Hibernate Cache Settings

By default, Hibernate (Liferay's database persistence layer) is configured to use Ehcache as its cache provider. This is the recommended setting. The default configuration, however, points to a file that does not have clustering enabled. To enable clustering, copy the *Hibernate* section from *portal.properties* into your *portal-ext.properties* file. To enable a clustered cache, comment out the default file (*hibernate.xml*) and uncomment the clustered version of the file, making sure that you change the path so that it points to your custom version of the file:

```
net.sf.ehcache.configurationResourceName=/myehcache/hibernate-clustered.xml
```

Next, open this file in a text editor. You will notice that the configuration is already set up to perform distributed caching through a multi-cast connection. It is likely, however, that the configuration is not set up optimally for your particular application. You will notice that by default, the only object cached in the Hibernate cache is the User object (*com.liferay.portal.model.impl.UserImpl*). This means that when a user logs in, his or her User object will go in the cache so that any portal operation that requires access to it (such as permission checking) can retrieve that object very quickly from the cache.

You may wish to add other objects to the cache. For example, a large part of your application may be document management using the Document Library portlet. In this case, you may want to cache Document Library objects, such as *DLFileEntryImpl* in order to improve performance as users access documents. To do that, add another block to the configuration file with the class you want to cache:

```
<cache
   name="com.liferay.portlet.documentlibrary.model.impl.DLFileEntryImpl"
   maxElementsInMemory="10000"
   eternal="false"
   timeToIdleSeconds="600"
   overflowToDisk="true"
>
   <cacheEventListenerFactory
         class="net.sf.ehcache.distribution.RMICacheReplicatorFactory"
         properties="replicatePuts=false,replicateUpdatesViaCopy=false"
                     propertySeparator=","
   />
   <bootstrapCacheLoaderFactory class="net.sf.ehcache.distribution.RMIBoot-
strapCacheLoaderFactory" />
</cache>
```

Your site may use the message boards portlet, and those message boards may get a lot of traffic. To cache the threads on the message boards, configure a block with the

MBMessageImpl class:

```
<cache
   name="com.liferay.portlet.messageboards.model.impl.MBMessageImpl"
   maxElementsInMemory="10000"
   eternal="false"
   timeToIdleSeconds="600"
   overflowToDisk="true"
>
   <cacheEventListenerFactory
         class="net.sf.ehcache.distribution.RMICacheReplicatorFactory"
         properties="replicatePuts=false,replicateUpdatesViaCopy=false"
         propertySeparator=","
   />
   <bootstrapCacheLoaderFactory class="net.sf.ehcache.distribution.RMIBoot-
strapCacheLoaderFactory" />
</cache>
```

Note that if your developers have overridden any of these classes, you will have to specify the overridden versions rather than the stock ones that come with Liferay Portal.

As you can see, it is easy to add specific data to be cached. Be careful, however, as too much caching can actually reduce performance if the JVM runs out of memory and starts garbage collecting too frequently. You will likely need to experiment with the memory settings on your JVM as well as the cache settings above. You can find the specifics about these settings in the documentation for Ehcache.

Clustering Jackrabbit

If you are using the Document Library, by default you are using the JSR-170 document repository, which is the Apache product *Jackrabbit*. You have already configured basic data sharing among nodes by moving its configuration into a database. The next thing you need to do is configure clustering for Jackrabbit, so that each node knows about data being entered into the repository by other nodes.

You can find the Jackrabbit configuration file in *<Liferay User Home>/liferay/jackrabbit*. The file is called *repository.xml*. You have likely already edited this file when you modified the configuration to move the data into the database.

At the bottom of this file is a cluster configuration that is commented out. If you are using a MySQL database, you can uncomment this section and use it as-is. You will need to change the cluster ID for each node so that they don't conflict with one another.

If you are using another database, the only changes necessary are the connection, credentials, and schema settings. Modify them according to your database of choice and then save the file. This is all it takes to set up clustering for Jackrabbit.

Workflow

The workflow portlet allows a user to define any number of simple to complex business processes/workflows, deploy them, and manage them through a portal interface. The power of this portlet is that it allows users to create forms-based data entry applications that are fully integrated with Liferay's permissions system. They have knowledge of users, groups, and roles without writing a single line of code—it only requires the creation of a single XML document.

The portlet relies on Apache ServiceMix or Mule to function as an Enterprise Service Bus (ESB) that acts as a broker between the portal and a workflow engine. Essentially, the portal provides a generic interface through which workflow services are requested via normal HTTP calls. The requests are routed through the ESB which in turn calls a workflow engine implementation that the user has defined in the ESB configuration. By default, Liferay provides an implementation of JBoss' jBPM workflow engine.

Installation and Test

Though the workflow portlet is installed in Liferay by default, it is nonfunctional without the jBPM and one of the ESB plugins. These are conveniently located on the *web* tab of the **Plugin Installer** portlet. You will need to have jBPM and *one* of the ESB plugins installed. At the time of this writing, we recommend the Mule ESB plugin, as the ServiceMix plugin is currently being reworked.

Once you install the plugins, follow these steps to get everything configured properly:

1. Make sure the following property in *portal-ext.properties* is set to the following:

```
jbi.workflow.url=http://localhost:8080/mule-web/workflow
```

2. Restart your application server if you needed to change the above property.
3. Login to the portal as the portal administrator. The default credentials are *test@liferay.com/test*.
4. Add the *Workflow* portlet to a page.
5. Click on the *Definitions* tab.
6. Click on the *Add* button.
7. Copy and paste the contents of *jbpm-web.war/WEB-INF/definitions/datatypes_definition.xml* into the text area and click the *Save New Version* button.
8. Click on the *Add Instance* icon.
9. From the *Instances* tab, click on the *Manage* icon next to *Enter data.*
10. Fill out the form and click the *Save* button; alternatively, you can test the various error checking capabilities by inputting incorrect values and clicking the *Save* button.
11. Eventually, enter correct values and click the *Save* button.
12. From the *Instances* tab, click on the *Manage* icon next to *View Data.*

13. Confirm that all the data was entered correctly and click the *Finished* button.
14. Confirm that the instance is now in the *End* state.

Using Different Databases

The default implementation of jBPM uses an HSQL database found in *jbpm-web.war/WEB-INF/sql/jbpm.**. To change the location of the HSQL database, change the value of the *hibernate.connection.url* property in *jbpm-web.war/WEB-INF/classes/hibernate.cfg.xml*. The location is relatively addressed from wherever the startup script for your server is located.

To use a database other than HSQL, first create the database schema using one of the SQL create scripts supplied in the *jbpm-web.war/WEB-INF/sql* directory. Then uncomment the corresponding hibernate connection properties block in *jbpm-web.war/WEB-INF/classes/hibernate.cfg.xml*.

Technical Explanations

Since the default implementation of the workflow portlet relies heavily on the capabilities of jBPM, this section gives a technical overview of jBPM and explains how it integrates into Liferay using jBPM Process Definition Language (JPDL) formatted XML files. It does not, however, give an in depth view of jBPM. For that, please refer to the jBPM user guide (http://docs.jboss.com/jbpm/v3/userguide).

Process Definitions

Before the workflow portlet can be used, business processes must be defined. Business processes in jBPM are defined by XML documents known as *process definitions* which are written in jBPM Process Definition Language (JPDL). This XML format specifies entities such as the process roles (known as *swimlanes*), the various states in the process (known as *nodes*), the tasks associated with each node, the roles associated with each task, the transitions from one node to the next, the variables associated with each task's form, the external actions executed on entry or exit of a node, and many others. For an in depth understanding of process definitions and JPDL, refer to JBoss' jBPM user guide at the link above.

There are three sample process definition XMLs that are packaged with the portlet. They can be found in *jbpm-web.war/WEB-INF/definitions*. We used one in the quick start section above to create a sample workflow. An explanation of each is included below.

Integrating with Users, Communities, and Roles

In JPDL, there is the notion of process roles called *swimlanes*. Swimlanes can be associated with Liferay users, communities, and roles via the IdentityAssignmentHandler class.

```
  <swimlane name="approver">
    <assignment class="com.liferay.jbpm.handler.IdentityAssignmentHandler"
config-type="field">
```

```
        <type>user</type>
        <companyId>10095</companyId>
        <id>10112</id>
    </assignment>
</swimlane>
```

In the XML above, the *approver* swimlane is associated with the Liferay user that has a User ID of *10112* and belongs to a Company ID of *10095*. You can also associate a Liferay user with a swimlane by email address as shown in the following XML snippet.

```
  <swimlane name="shipper">
    <assignment class="com.liferay.jbpm.handler.IdentityAssignmentHandler"
config-type="field">
        <type>user</type>
        <companyId>10095</companyId>
        <name>test.lax.2@liferay.com</name>
    </assignment>
  </swimlane>
```

In the XML above, the *shipper* swimlane is associated with the Liferay user that has an email address of "test.lax.2@liferay.com" and belongs to a Company ID of *10095*.

```
  <swimlane name="salesman">
    <assignment class="com.liferay.jbpm.handler.IdentityAssignmentHandler"
config-type="field">
        <type>community</type>
        <companyId>10095</companyId>
        <id>3</id>
    </assignment>
  </swimlane>
```

In the XML above, the *salesman* swimlane is associated with any Liferay user that belongs to a Community with the Group ID of 3 (which defaults to the *Support* community if you are using the embedded HSQL database that comes with the Liferay Portal bundles) and Company ID of *10095*. In other words, the salesman swimlane is assigned to the pool of *Support* users. If one of these users were to manage a salesman task, he/she would automatically be assigned to all other salesman tasks in the workflow.

```
  <swimlane name="accountant">
    <assignment class="com.liferay.jbpm.handler.IdentityAssignmentHandler"
config-type="field">
        <type>community</type>
        <companyId>10095</companyId>
        <name>Support</name>
    </assignment>
  </swimlane>
```

The XML above shows an alternative way to associate the *accountant* swimlane with the Support community using the actual community's name. Since community names must be unique per Company ID, this format accomplishes the same results as the previous XML.

```
  <swimlane name="user_admin">
    <assignment class="com.liferay.jbpm.handler.IdentityAssignmentHandler"
config-type="field">
      <type>role</type>
      <companyId>10095</companyId>
      <id>1001</id>
    </assignment>
  </swimlane>

  <swimlane name="user_interviewer">
    <assignment class="com.liferay.jbpm.handler.IdentityAssignmentHandler"
config-type="field">
      <type>role</type>
      <companyId>10095</companyId>
      <name>User Interviewer</name>
    </assignment>
  </swimlane>
```

The two XML snippets above are very similar to the Group XML snippets. Both associate their respective swimlanes with a role, but the first XML does so using the Role ID, and the second XML does so using the role's unique name.

Data Types and Error Checking

Currently, jBPM doesn't have support for variable data types. However, data types have been dealt with in the workflow portlet by incorporating them into the names of the controller variables. The table below shows the data types supported by the portlet as well as the syntax for the variable names:

Data Type	Syntax	Description
Check-box	checkbox:name:checked-Value	**name:** the caption next to the checkbox checkedValue = the value assigned to the variable if the checkbox is checked
Date	date:name	**name:** the caption next to the date selector object
Email	email:name	**name:** the caption next to the text input field
Number	number:name	**name:** the caption next to the text input field
Pass-word	password:name	**name:** the caption next to the text input field
Phone	phone:name	**name:** the caption next to the text input field
Radio Button	radio:name:option1,option2,... *	**name:** the caption next to the radio buttons **option1,option2,...* :** a comma-delimited list of options that represent the different radio button options
Select Box	select:name:option1,option2, ...*	**name:** the caption next to the select box **option1,option2,...* :** a comma-delimited list of options that represent the different options in the select drop-down
Text	text:name	**name:** the caption next to the text input field
Textarea	textarea:name	**name:** the caption next to the textarea input field

Note that for all name and option values, the values should be entered in the XML in lowercase with hyphens used between words:

```
radio:are-you-hungry:yes,no,a-little-bit
```

In addition, you should register the corresponding display values in the *Language.properties* file:

```
are-you-hungry=Are you hungry?
yes=Yes
no=No
a-little-bit=A little bit
```

This will ensure that the values are displayed correctly in the portlet to the user.

By default, all variables are readable and writable by the user. Therefore, they can be defined as follows:

```
<variable name="textarea:comments" />
```

However, if variables should only be readable or writable, or if variables are required, these must be specified in the variable definition:

```
<variable name="text:name" access="read,write,required" />
<variable name="date:birthday" access="read" />
```

Variables of data type Date, Number, Email, and Phone are validated in the service call. Also, required fields are validated to ensure a value of some kind was submitted. If invalid values are submitted, the user is returned to the original form and error messages are displayed next to the invalid input fields.

Refer to the sample definition *jbpm-web.war/WEB-INF/definitions/datatypes_definition.xml* for examples of all data types in use in a single form.

JBoss also provides a graphical JPDL editor which is implemented as an Eclipse plugin. This editor allows you to design workflows graphically, rather than using an XML editor. You can find this tool at http://www.jboss.org/tools.

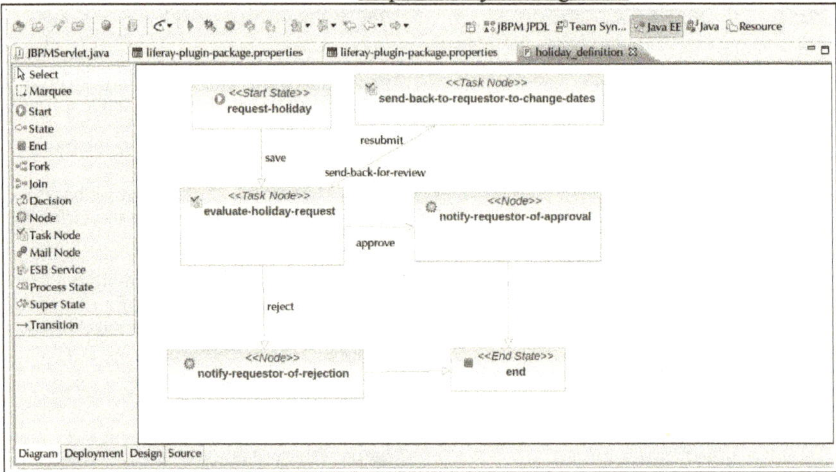

Illustration 79: The JPDL editor from JBoss

Sample Process Definitions

The best way to understand JPDL is to look over the 3 sample XML files included with the workflow portlet. They can be found in *jbpm-web.war/WEB-INF/definitions/*. Below is a quick summary of each:

datatypes_definition.xml – a good guide to follow to understand how to use each of the data types described in the section above

holiday_definition.xml – a simple workflow that allows an employee to make a holiday request with a start and end date, and then a manager can either approve, reject, or send the request back for review

websale_definition.xml – a more complex workflow that emulates an online auction site in which control of the workflow passes through various roles. It is the most complicated of the 3 workflows, but it demonstrates almost all of the BPM features offered by jBPM

Notes:

- The JPDL definition XMLs can be created through a graphical design tool offered by JBoss, but that is beyond the scope of this document (see http://docs.jboss.com/jbpm/v3/gpd for a detailed explanation) and is also beyond the scope of the portal.
- For nodes that have tasks associated with them, each of the variables in the controller will be converted to a form element that the user must update.
- For nodes that have tasks associated with them, each of the transitions out of the node is represented as a button in the task's form. The transition's *name* attribute should always be in lowercase with hyphens between words and registered in *Language.properties*. The display value is used as the button's name.
- Many of the action handler classes found in the *com.liferay.jbpm.handler* package are just place holders that output relevant text to the console. Conceivably, these classes could perform operations such as sending out emails, initiating batch processes, updating legacy systems, etc.
- The websale workflow demonstrates the following jBPM concepts, all of which are discussed in further detail in the jBPM user guide (http://docs.jboss.com/jbpm/v3/userguide):
    - Events
    - Beanshell scripting
    - Swimlanes
    - Tasks
        - Assigment(User/Pool)
        - Controllers
        - Variables
        - Timers
    - Node Types
        - State
        - Task
        - Fork
        - Join
        - Decision
    - Transitions
    - Actions

Warning Messages

If you have warning messages turned on for your server, in your console you may see some variant of the following message output several times when jBPM is called:

```
WARN  [org.hibernate.engine.StatefulPersistenceContext] Narrowing proxy to
class org.jbpm.graph.node.TaskNode - this operation breaks ==
```

According to the following post on the JBoss forums (from Koen Aers, one of the key contributors to the jBPM project), this is not an error and is not of significance. He explains the reason this warning is thrown here: http://www.jboss.com/?module=bb&op=viewtopic&t=73123. Basically, the issue boils down to Hibernate doing lazy loading of the class. After a query, a collection is returned which holds a collection of stubs of the class. When a particular instance is retrieved, Hibernate goes and gets it from the database and replaces the stub with an actual instance, thereby breaking the == operator.

Administration

Once you have defined your business processes by successfully writing process definitions for them, the next step is to deploy your business processes. Once they are deployed, users can manage the life of each process instance as control is passed from one role to the next. This section is meant for end users who will actually be executing predefined process definitions.

Deploying Workflows

Once the user logs in to the portal and adds the workflow portlet to her page, he or she will see something similar to the following:

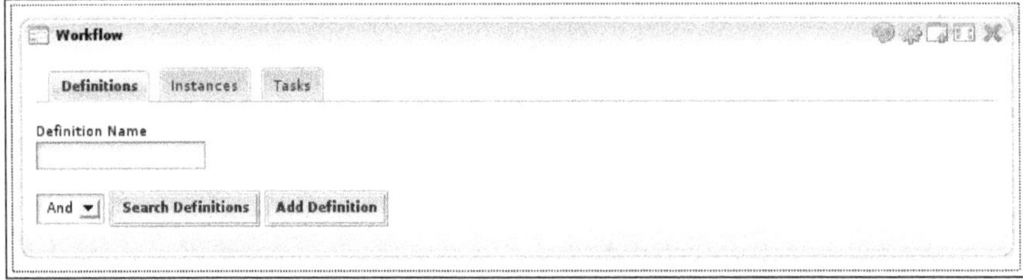

Illustration 80: Default view of the Workflow Portlet

If she clicks on the "Definitions" tab, he or she will see the following:

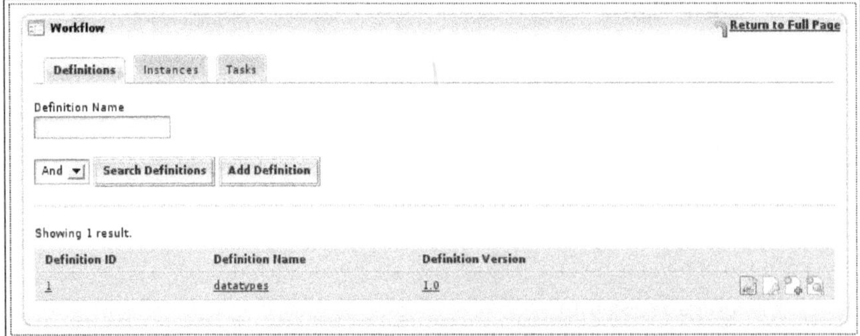

Illustration 81: Workflow Definitions

The *Definitions* tab displays all of the workflows that have been deployed in the system. To deploy a workflow, click on the *Add Definition* button. The user will see the following screen:

Illustration 82: Adding a Workflow Definition

At this point, the user can paste in the contents of a definition XML (see *jbpm-web.war/WEB-INF/definitions* for examples) and click the *Save New Version* button. If the XML is invalid, an error message will be displayed. If the XML is valid, it will be deployed, the user will be returned to the *Definitions* tab, and a success message will be displayed.

Because business processes may change over time, every version of the workflows is maintained. To edit an existing version, click on the *Edit* icon next to the definition name. Update the XML in the text area, and click the *Save New Version* button. The new version number will be incremented by 1 from the previous version. To start a new instance of a workflow definition, click on the *Add Instance* icon. A new instance will appear on the *Instances* tab. To view all the instances of a particular definition, click on the *View Instances* icon. Finally, the user can also search for a definition by name using the *Definition Name* input box.

Managing Instances

After a definition is deployed and an instance of that definition is started, it is up to the user to manage the life cycle of the instance. Instance management is controlled from the *Instances* tab. Below is an example of what the user might see:

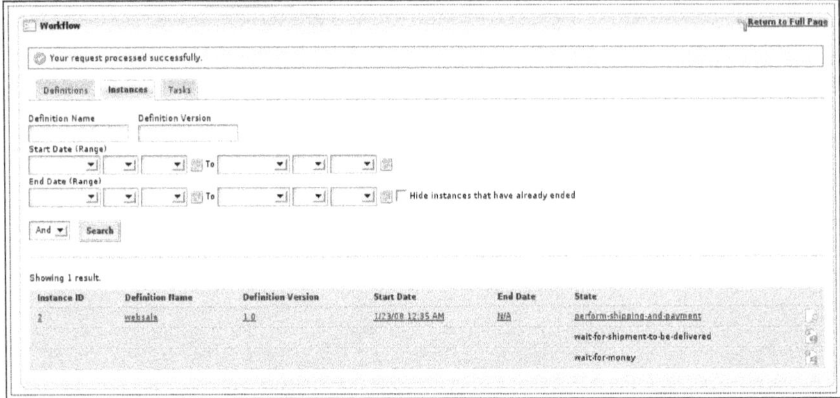

Illustration 83: Workflow Instances

The *Instances* tab displays every instance of every version of every workflow deployed in the system. They are listed alphabetically by **Definition Name** followed by **Start Date** in descending order. The search form at the top of the screen allows the user to find specific instances to manage. In particular, the *Hide instances that have already ended* check box allows the user to display only active, running instances. The date ranges also allow the user to search by *Start Date* and/or *End Date* (**NOTE:** Date ranges are inclusive of the day. For example, if the *Start Date* range was set to January 23, 2008 – January 23, 2008, then only instances that were started between January 28, 2008, 12:00am to January 28, 2008, 11:59pm would be displayed). The first row for each instance describes the state of the instance. Any subsequent rows in the instance define tasks associated with the current state. Often times, the current state and current task have the same name. In the example screen shot above, notice that web sale version 1.0 is currently in the "Perform shipping and payment" state, and it has two outstanding tasks associated with it – "Wait for shipment to be delivered" and "Wait for money."

The right-most column in the results table displays what actions the current user can perform on the given instance in its current state. The table below shows all of the possible actions and what each means:

Action	Explanation
Blank	3 possibilities: ● The user doesn't have the appropriate role / swimlane to perform an action on the instance in its current state ● The user doesn't have permissions to perform an action ● The instance has already ended
Manage icon ( )	The user directly has the appropriate role / swimlane to perform an action or the user belongs to a group which has the appropriate role / swimlane. If the user clicks on the "Manage" icon, she will be taken to a form which must be submitted to complete the task. See section 3.3 for more details
Signal icon ( )	The instance is currently in a wait state and must be "signalled" to continue. Typically, signals come from eternal processes (e.g., the arrival of a package, the successful update of a legacy system, etc.) and are not manually entered by a user. However, in the case that user intervention is required, the "Signal" icon is available.
Waiting on sibling tokens to complete	This only occurs when the process has forked into multiple subprocesses. In order for the main process to continue, all of the subprocesses must complete. As each of the subprocesses completes, they will go into this state. Once all subprocesses complete, the main process will continue like normal.

Managing Tasks

Task management is controlled from the "Tasks" tab. Below is an example of what the user might see:

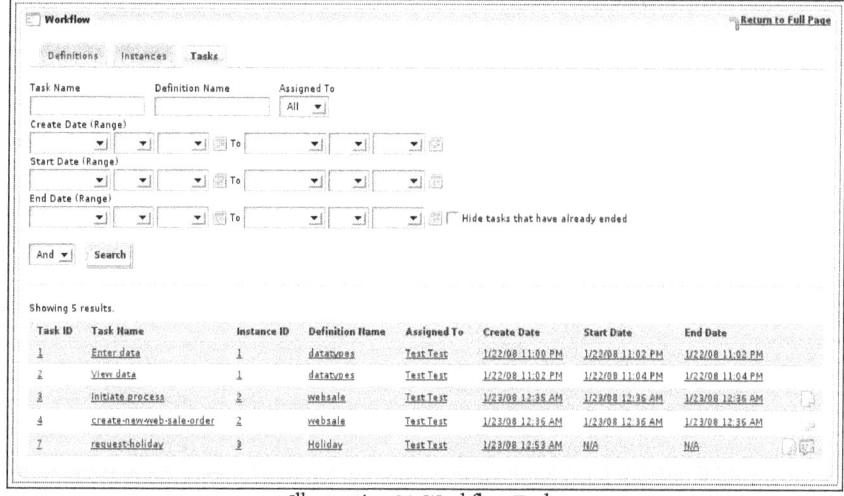

Illustration 84: Workflow Tasks

The *Tasks* tab displays every task that has either been assigned directly to the user or to the group/role pool that the user belongs to. They are listed by **Create Date** in ascending order, and the tasks assigned directly to the user are listed before the tasks assigned to the user's pool (if the **Assigned To** column is blank, that means the task is open to the pool). The search form at the top of the screen allows the user to find specific tasks to manage. In particular, the *Hide tasks that have already ended* check box allows the user to display only active tasks. The date ranges also allow the user to search by task *Create Date*, *Start Date*, and/or *End Date*. The user can also choose to only display tasks assigned directly to her, tasks assigned to her pool, or all tasks assigned to either by using the *Assigned To* drop-down.

The right-most column in the results table displays what actions the current user can perform on the given task. It will either be blank or the *Manage* icon. The logic to determine which of these will be displayed is exactly the same logic described in the table in the section above labeled **Data Types and Error Checking**.

If the user clicks the *Manage* icon, a form similar to the following will be displayed:

Illustration 85: Workflow Form

These task forms are generated from the control variables associated with the task and defined in the definition XML. Depending on the data type, the corresponding element is created in the form. Required fields are denoted by a red asterisk. If the user submits the form with invalid data, she will be returned to the form with error messages next to each of the invalid fields. If all data is valid and the user submits the form, she will be returned to the *Tasks* tab with a success message displayed.

Future Enhancements

Logging

Currently, the workflow portlet has no notion of logging other than the ability to review all of the tasks that a user has assigned to them or has completed. However, jBPM provides rather robust logging functionality so administrators/users can monitor every action that has ever been taken in a particular workflow.

The only reason logging functionality has not been built out in the current release is because the Liferay development team is not sure what the most effective logging metrics would be to the end user. If you or your organization has logging requirements, please submit them to the Liferay Forums, and we will review those requirements for possible inclusion in future versions of the Workflow portlet.

Customizable Front-End

Though the workflow portlet's strength is that it can provide a forms-based data entry application virtually on-the-fly, it is obvious that there is not much control over what the forms look like when they are rendered by the portlet. To address this concern, the Liferay development team plans to create style sheets and templates that can be applied to the vanilla forms. The functionality would be very similar to how XSL style sheets are currently applied to Journal Articles in the Liferay Journal Content Management System. This enhancement would give organizations flexibility in layout and UI design of their forms.

File Upload Data Type

There have already been several requests to add a file data type to provide a means for users to upload files that are associated with workflow tasks. This will definitely be a future enhancement.

Frequently Asked Questions

How do you write a new process definition?

The best way to learn how to write a new process definition is to use one of the sample definition XMLs (found in *jbpm-web.war/WEB-INF/definitions/*) as a starting point. In particular, *websale_definition.xml* demonstrates most of the BPM features offered by jBPM. For an exhaustive explanation of JPDL, visit JBoss' documentation at http://docs.jboss.com/jbpm/v3/userguide/jpdl.html. There is also a graphical JPDL designer available at http://labs.jboss.com/jbossjbpm/downloads.

Why are there "Duplicate File" exceptions when I change databases for jBPM?

Since we are using ServiceMix as the service broker for our workflow implementation (by default, we are using jBPM), we cannot rely on the workflow engine to maintain versions of our process definitions. Therefore, we maintain the process definition XMLs as system documents in our document library. The XMLs are named based on their definition IDs, and the definition IDs are maintained in the jBPM database. Therefore, if you were to switch databases to a new instance, the definition IDs would also be reset, and when the system tries to store the process definition XML, it will find a duplicate XML already exists. The only way to ensure that this exception does not occur is by clearing out the *<User Home>/liferay/jackrabbit* folder before switching databases. However, be warned that this will delete ALL the files that are stored in your Document Library. It is recommended that once you decide on a jBPM database that suits your needs, you should only use that database.

Deploying A Customized Liferay

As described in the *Installation* chapter of this book, Liferay allows for complete customization of the portal through the Extension Environment. Deploying the extension environment to a server requires one of two scenarios:

- The Liferay development tools (JDK, Ant, etc.) are installed on the server, the Liferay Portal source code is available on the server, and the extension environment is checked out to a directory on the server.

- On a client machine which contains the Liferay development tools, a drive can be mapped or a folder mounted which points to the installation directory on the server.

Once one of these two requirements have been met, deploying to the server becomes as easy as deploying locally to the developer's machine.

Deploying Directly on the Server

Deploying the extension environment directly on the server is the recommended method. To do this, you will have to create two new configuration files which define the settings for the deployment. In the extension environment, create a file called *app.server.<username>properties*, where *<username>* is the user name of the account under which the server executable runs. If, for example, you have a Glassfish server running under the user name of *glassfish*, your file would be called *app.server.glassfish.properties*. This file will override the default values which are found in *app.server.properties*. You will need to configure two properties in this file: the server type and the server path.

The server type should be one of the following:

```
app.server.type=geronimo-tomcat
app.server.type=glassfish
app.server.type=jboss-jetty
app.server.type=jboss-tomcat
app.server.type=jetty
app.server.type=jonas-jetty
app.server.type=jonas-tomcat
app.server.type=oc4j
app.server.type=resin
app.server.type=tomcat
```

The path property is similar to the server type. It should look like this:

```
app.server.<server name>.dir
```

Replace <server name> with the server type above. For example, if you are using Glassfish, your property would be:

```
app.server.glassfish.dir=/home/glassfish/glassfish-v2
```

The value of the property should be the fully qualified path to the server directory.

Next, create another file similar to the first one called *release.<username>.properties*. Again, substitute *<username>* with the user name the server runs under and under whose credentials you will be doing the deployment. This file will override the default values found in *release.properties*.

This file requires two properties:

```
lp.source.dir
lp.ext.dir
```

Set the value for the *lp.source.dir* property to be equal to the fully qualified directory name for where you have installed the Liferay Portal source. Set the value for the *lp.ext.dir* property to be equal to the fully qualified directory name for where you have installed the Extension Environment you have checked out from your source code repository. For example:

```
lp.source.dir=/home/glassfish/lportal/portal
lp.ext.dir=/home/glassfish/lportal/ext
```

Once you have set up these two properties files, run the following Ant task:

```
ant deploy
```

Your customized Liferay will be automatically compiled and deployed to your application server.

Deploying from a Client Machine

If you will be deploying a customized Liferay from a client machine, you will need to map a drive (on Windows) or a folder on your file system (Mac or Linux) to the server. Once you have done this, follow the same procedure outlined above, with the exception that the *<username>* should be the user name of the user logged in to the client, not the user name on the server. You will not need to change the *release.<username>.properties* file; only the *app.server.<username>.properties* file will need to be modified.

If you are using a developer's machine to do the deployment, these configuration files will already exist. Modify the *app.server.<username>.properties* file to match the application server type and location of the directory in which it is installed from your mapped drive or folder. Then run the above Ant task to deploy the extension environment.

Note that this second method is not a best practice, as it enables changes to be made locally on a developer's machine which can then be deployed directly to a server without source code management being done first. It is better to have developers check in all their code, version that code, and then pull that version from your source code management software to deploy it to a server.

Performance Tuning

Once you have your portal up and running, you may find a need to tune it for performance, especially if your site winds up generating more traffic than you'd anticipated. There are some definite steps you can take with regard to improving Liferay's performance.

Memory

Memory is one of the first things to look at when you want to optimize performance. If you have any disk swapping, that will have a serious impact on performance. Make sure that your server has an optimal amount of memory and that your JVM is tuned to use it.

There are three JVM command switches that control the amount of memory it will use.

```
-Xms
-Xmx
-XX:MaxPermSize
```

These three settings control the amount of memory available to the JVM initially, the maximum amount of memory into which the JVM can grow, and the separate area of the heap called Permanent Generation space.

The first two settings should be set to something reasonable. For example, by default, the Tomcat start script, called *catalina.sh* (or *catalina.bat*) sets the options to

```
-Xms128m -Xmx1024m -XX:MaxPermSize=128m
```

This is perfectly reasonable for a moderately sized machine or a developer machine. These settings allow the JVM to initially take 128MB of RAM, grow up to 1024MB of RAM, and have a PermGen space of 128MB. If, however, you have Liferay on a server with 4GB of RAM and you are having performance problems, the first thing you might want to look at is increasing the memory available to the JVM. You will be able to tell if memory is a problem by running a profiler (such as Jprobe or YourKit) on the server. If you see Garbage Collection (GC) running frequently, you will definitely want to increase the amount of memory available to the JVM.

Issues with PermGen space can also affect performance. PermGen space contains long-lived classes, anonymous classes and interned Strings. Hibernate, in particular—which Liferay uses extensively—has been known to make use of PermGen space. If you increase the amount of memory available to the JVM, you may want to increase the amount of PermGen space accordingly.

Properties File Changes

There are also some changes you can make to your *portal-ext.properties* file once you are in a production environment.

Set the following to false to disable checking the last modified date on server side CSS and JavaScript.

```
last.modified.check=false
```

Set this property to true to load the theme's merged CSS files for faster loading for production. By default it is set to false for easier debugging for development. You can also disable fast loading by setting the URL parameter *css_fast_load* to *0*.

```
theme.css.fast.load=true
```

Set this property to true to load the combined JavaScript files from the property *javascript.files* into one compacted file for faster loading for production. By default it is set to false for easier debugging for development. You can also disable fast loading by setting the URL parameter *js_fast_load* to *0*.

```
javascript.fast.load=true
```

Servlet Filters

Liferay comes by default with 15 servlet filters enabled and running. It is likely that for your installation, you don't need them all. Two filters that you can disable without any impact are the *Compression Filter* and the *Strip Filter*. These filters are responsible for shrinking the size of the response (to save bandwidth). The Strip Filter removes whitespace from the response object, and the Compression Filter compresses it. This obviously requires some processing, and so disabling these two filters can enhance performance.

To disable a servlet filter, simply comment it out of your *web.xml* file.

If there is a feature supported by a servlet filter that you know you are not using, you can comment it out as well to achieve some performance gains. For example, if you are not using CAS for single sign-on, comment out the CAS Filter. If you are not using NTLM for single sign-ons, comment out the Ntlm Filter. If you are not using the Virtual Hosting for Communities feature, comment out the Virtual Host Filter. The fewer servlet filters you are running, the less processing power is needed for each request.

Portlets

Liferay comes pre-bundled with many portlets which contain a lot of functionality, but not every web site that is running on Liferay needs to use them all. In *portlet.xml* and *liferay-portlet.xml*, comment out the ones you are not using. While having a loan calculator, analog clock, or game of hangman available for your users to add to pages is nice, those portlets may be taking up resources that are needed by custom portlets you have written for your site. If you are having performance problems, commenting out some of the unused portlets may give you the performance boost you need.

6. Maintaining A Liferay Portal

Maintaining a running implementation of Liferay Portal is not much different from maintaining the application server environment upon which it is running. There are, however, several factors which administrators should be aware of when they are responsible for a running instance of Liferay. This chapter will cover these issues, outlining for system administrators some specifics about keeping a running Liferay instance stable and secure.

This chapter will cover the following topics:

- Liferay Monitoring using Google Analytics
- Backing Up a Liferay Installation
- Changing Logging Levels
- Upgrading Liferay

The discussion on back up will cover what parts of Liferay should be backed up. We will not cover specific backup software or procedures; generally, most organizations have standards for doing backups of their systems, and Liferay as a Java EE application fits well into these standards.

Liferay Monitoring Using Google Analytics

Liferay includes built-in support for Google Analytics, allowing administrators to make use of Google's tool set for analyzing site traffic data. When you sign up for Google Analytics, a snippet of code is provided which needs to be added to your web pages in order to allow Google's system to register the page hit. It can be a tedious process to add this code to every page on a site, especially if it is a large site and there is a lot of user-generated content.

This problem can be solved in Liferay by putting Google's code into a custom theme written especially for the site on which the portal is running. Doing this, however, requires that a theme developer make specific changes to the theme, and it prevents users from using the many freely available themes that are available for Liferay "out of the box."

Because of this, support for Google Analytics has been built into Liferay, and can be turned on through a simple user interface. This allows Liferay Administrators to make use of Google Analytics on a community by community basis and turn it on and off when needed.

To enable Google Analytics support, go to the Manage Pages screen for the community for which you want to enable support. You can do this through the Communities portlet or by clicking the *Manage Pages* link in the Dock while you are on a page in the community. Click the top level link on the left side to go to the settings for all pages of the community.

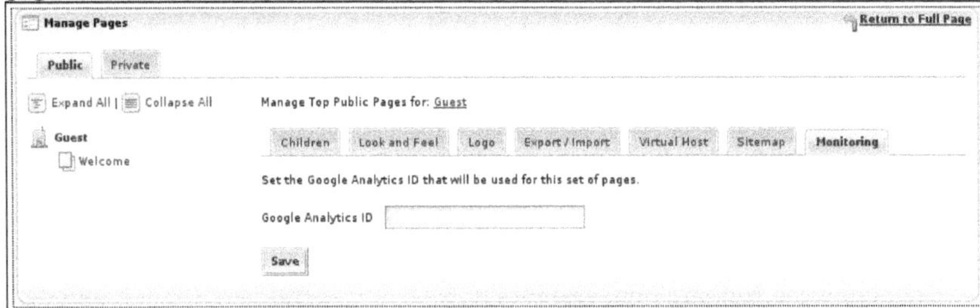

Illustration 86: Setting Up Google Analytics

Click the **Monitoring** Tab. Put your Google Analytics ID (which should have been provided to you when you signed up for the service) in the field and click *Save*. All of the pages in the community you selected will now have the Google Analytics code in them and will be tracked.

Backing Up A Liferay Installation

Once you have an installation of Liferay Portal running, you will want to have proper backup procedures in place in case of a catastrophic failure of some kind. Liferay is not very different from any other application that may be running in your application server, but there are some specific components that need to be backed up in addition to your regular backup procedures for your application server.

Source Code

If you have extended Liferay or have written portlet or theme plugins, they should be stored in a source code repository such as Subversion, CVS, or Git. This repository should be backed up on a regular basis to preserve your ongoing work.

If you are extending Liferay with the Extension Environment, you will want to make sure that you also store the version of the Liferay source on which your extension environment is based. This allows your developers convenient access to all of the tools they need to build your extension and deploy it to a server.

Liferay's File System

Liferay's configuration file, *portal-ext.properties*, gets stored in the *WEB-INF/classes* folder in the location to which your application server deployed Liferay. At a minimum, this file should be backed up, but it is generally best to back up your whole application server.

Liferay also stores configuration files, search indexes, cache information, and the default Jackrabbit document repository in a folder called *liferay*. This folder resides in the home directory of the user ID under which Liferay is running. On Unix-based systems, this folder will likely be in */home/<user id>*. This folder should be backed up also.

Database

Liferay's database is the central repository for all of the Portal's information and is the most important component which needs to be backed up. You can do this by either backing up the database live (if your database allows this) or by exporting the database and then backing up the exported file. For example, MySQL ships with a *mysqldump* utility which allows you to export the entire database and data into a large SQL file. This file can then be backed up. In case of a database failure, it can be used to recreate the state of the database at the time the dump was created.

If you are using Liferay's Document Library extensively, it is likely that you have configured Jackrabbit to store documents in a database rather than the file system. In this case, the Jackrabbit database should be backed up also.

Liferay's Logging System

Liferay uses Log4j extensively to implement logging for nearly every class in the portal. If you need to debug something specific while a system is running, you can use the **Admin** portlet to set logging levels by class dynamically.

The Admin portlet appears in the Admin section of the *Add Content* menu. Add this portlet to an administrative page somewhere in your portal.

To view the log levels, select the *Server* tab, then the *Log Levels* tab.

You will then see a paginated list of logging categories. These categories correspond to Liferay classes that have log messages in them. By default, all categories are set to display messages only if there is an error that occurs in the class. This is why you see ERROR displayed in all of the drop down list boxes on the right side of the portlet.

Each category is filtered by its place in the class hierarchy. For example, if you wanted to see logging for a specific class that is registered in the Admin portlet, you would browse to that specific class and change its log level to something that is more descriptive, such as DEBUG. Once you click the *Save* button at the bottom of the list, you will start seeing DEBUG messages from that class in your application server's log file.

If you are not sure which class you want to see log messages for, you can find a place higher up in the hierarchy and select the package name instead of an individual class name. If you do this, messages for every class lower in the hierarchy will be displayed in your application server's log file.

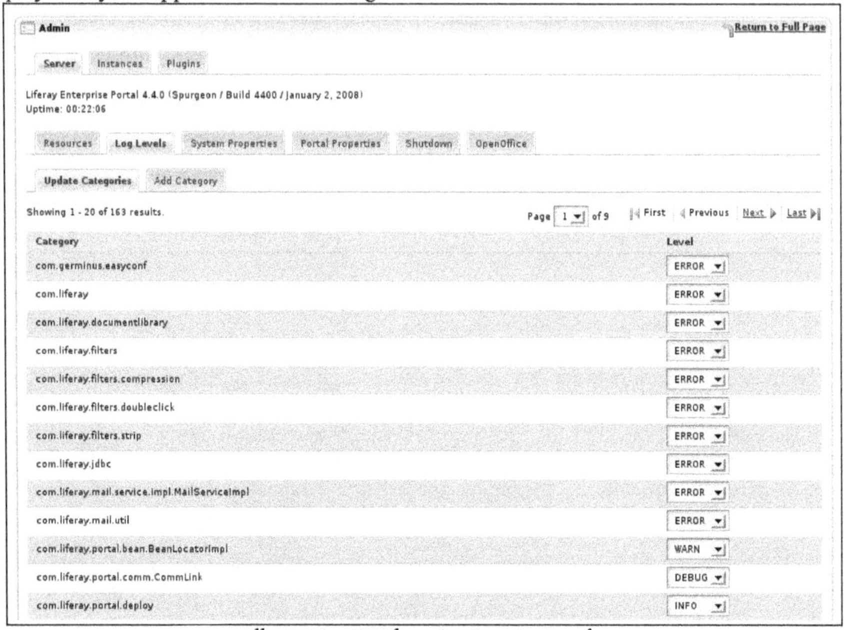

Illustration 87: Changing Logging Levels

Be careful when you do this. If you set the log level to DEBUG somewhere near the top of the hierarchy (such as *com.liferay*, for example), you may wind up with a lot of messages in your log file. This could make it difficult to find the one you were looking for, and causes the server to do more work writing messages to its log file.

If you are working in the extension environment or have created a plugin and want to set the log level for one of your own classes, you can register that class (so long as it uses Log4J to do its logging) with the Admin portlet so that you can control the log levels more easily.

You will first need to implement Log4J logging in your class, with a statement such as the following (taken from Liferay's JCRHook class):

```
private static Log _log = LogFactory.getLog(JCRHook.class);
```

You would then use this *_log* variable to create log messages in your code for the various logging levels:

```
_log.error("Reindexing " + node.getName(), e1);
```

To enable your logging messages to appear in your server's log file via the Admin portlet, click the *Add Category* tab on the same *Log Levels* page.

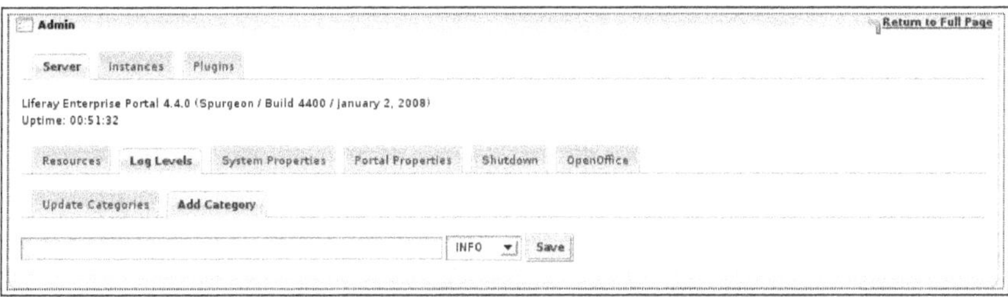

Illustration 88: Adding a Logging Category

You will see that you can add a logging category to the Admin portlet. Simply put in the fully qualified name of your class or of the package that contains the classes whose log messages you want to view, choose a log level, and then click the *Save* button. You will now start to see log messages from your own class or classes in the server's log file.

Upgrading Liferay

Liferay upgrades are fairly straightforward. A consistent set of steps is all you need to follow to upgrade a standard Liferay installation. Things do get more complicated if your organization has used the extension environment to customize Liferay, as it is possible that API changes in the new version will break your existing code. This, however, is usually fairly straightforward for your developers to fix. Portlet plugins are generally backwards compatible, as they are written to the Java standard. This includes Portlet 1.0 (JSR-168) portlets, as the Portlet 2.0 (JSR-286) standard has also been designed to be backwards-compatible. Theme plugins may require some modifications in order to take advantage of new features. Much effort has been made to make upgrades as painless as possible; however, this is not a guarantee that everything will work without modification. Extension environment changes are the most complicating factor in an upgrade, so it is important to test as much as possible.

As a general rule, you can upgrade from one major release to the next major release. For example, you can upgrade directly from Liferay 4.3.x to 4.4.x, but not from 4.3.x to 5.0.x. If you need to upgrade over several major releases, you will need to run the upgrade procedure for each major release until you reach the release you want. This doesn't mean you need to run the procedure for every point release (i.e., 4.3.5 to 4.3.6 to 4.4.0 to 4.4.1, etc.); you only need to run the procedure for the major releases. A good practice is to use the latest version of each major release to upgrade your system. So if you wanted to upgrade from Liferay 4.3.5 to Liferay 5.1.1, you would first run the upgrade procedure for 4.4.2, then 5.0.1, and then 5.1.1.

Liferay Upgrade Procedure

Liferay 4.3.0 and higher can auto-detect whether the database requires an upgrade the first time the new version is started. When Liferay does this, it will automatically upgrade the database to the format required by the new version. In order to do this, Liferay *must* be accessing the database with an ID that can create, drop, and modify tables. Make sure that you have granted these permissions to the ID before you attempt to upgrade Liferay. It is also a good idea to backup your database before attempting an upgrade in case something goes wrong during the process.

Tip: Liferay versions prior to 4.3.0 require that you manually run SQL scripts on your database to perform an upgrade. If you need to upgrade from Liferay 4.1.x to 4.2.x, you can find these SQL scripts in the source code archive for the version of Liferay you are running. They will be in the *SQL* folder of the archive.

Upgrade Steps

It takes only four steps to upgrade a standard Liferay installation:

1. Copy your customized *portal-ext.properties* file to a safe place, and then undeploy the old version of Liferay and shut down your application server.
2. Copy the new versions of the dependency .jars to a location on your server's class path, overwriting the ones you already have for the old version of Liferay.
3. Deploy the new Liferay .war file to your application server. Follow the deployment instructions in Chapter 1 or in Chapter 5 (if you have customized Liferay).
4. Start (or restart) your application server. Watch the console as Liferay starts: it should upgrade the database automatically. Review the *portal.properties* changes and re-configure your previous customizations as necessary, restarting when customizations are complete.

That's all there is to it. Everything else is handled by Liferay's upgrade procedure. Note that as stated above, if you have to upgrade over several Liferay versions, you will need to repeat these steps for each major release.

What follows are instructions for upgrading for specific versions.

Upgrading Liferay 4.3 to Liferay 4.4

Prerequisite

In order to upgrade to 4.4.x, you must start at 4.3.0 or above. If you are using version 4.2.2 or below, please see the upgrade instructions on Liferay's wiki at http://wiki.liferay.com.

Follow the generic upgrade steps above. Make sure your Liferay .war and dependency .jars are all the same version.

If Your Developers Have Customized Liferay

If you are deploying Liferay from an extension environment, ensure that your developers have:

1. Run Service Builder for each custom service.
2. Edited their custom {Model}LocalServiceImpl classes and make them extend

from {Model}LocalServiceBaseImpl.

3. Run Service Builder again for each of the custom services after the previous change.

Many of the DTD references in the various *-ext.xml* files have changed (*liferay-portlet-ext.xml* in particular). Be sure to compare your *<!DOCTYPE* references with the main file to insure they reference the same DTD.

Example:

Liferay 4.3.x:

```
<!DOCTYPE liferay-portlet-app PUBLIC "-LiferayDTD Portlet Application
4.3.0EN" "http://www.liferay.com/dtd/liferay-portlet-app_4_3_0.dtd">
```

Liferay 4.4.x:

```
<!DOCTYPE liferay-portlet-app PUBLIC "-LiferayDTD Portlet Application
4.4.0EN" "http://www.liferay.com/dtd/liferay-portlet-app_4_4_0.dtd">
```

Upgrading Liferay 4.4 to Liferay 5.0

Prerequisite

In order to upgrade to 5.0.x, you must start at 4.4.0 or above.

Follow the generic upgrade steps above. Make sure your Liferay .war and dependency .jars are all the same version.

If Your Developers Have Customized Liferay

If you are deploying Liferay from an extension environment, ensure that your developers have upgraded their Service Builder .xml files to the new DTDs.

The generated code is slightly different, and custom written finders and *LocalServiceImpl* methods need to be adopted. The *system-ext.properties* and *portal-ext.properties* files have moved from *ext-impl/classes* to *ext-impl/src.*

Converting wiki pages (optional)

If you were using the wiki portlet, you will be happy to find many new features and improvements in 5.0—and everything is backwards compatible.

You may wish to convert your existing pages from the old Classic Wiki syntax to the new Creole (http://www.wikicreole.org) syntax because it's more powerful and easier to learn and use. It may also be more familiar to your users if they have experience with other popular wikis like MediaWiki or Confluence. To that end, Liferay 5.0 includes an automatic translator that will convert all of the pages in the database to Creole. To run it, edit *portal-ext.properties* and set:

```
verify.processes=com.liferay.portal.verify.VerifyWikiCreole
verify.frequency=-1
```

Start the server and let the process do the whole translation for you automatically. Remember to change those properties back to their original state before the next startup; otherwise the process will run every time you start Liferay.

Upgrade Troubleshooting

- The parameter *p_p_action* is now called *p_p_lifecycle.* This has to be adapted for example in the FriendlyURLMappers if you want them to trigger a *processAction().*
- You need to copy *parent-build.xml* in *ext-impl* from our Subversion repository; otherwise, some files will be missing when deploying.
- Upload in Struts portlets is broken. See http://support.liferay.com/browse/LEP-6412 and http://support.liferay.com/browse/LEP-6479.

Upgrading Liferay 5.0 to Liferay 5.1

Changes in configuration properties

Because of changes in the default configuration, Liferay now comes with several configuration files containing the defaults for previous versions. If the portal is not operating the way you are used to, it is likely that this is because a default value has been changed. You can revert to the previous behavior by following the process below.

How to keep the old values

The default values of some properties has been changed. In order to keep the previous values you have to pass the following system property when running Liferay:

```
java ... -Dexternal-properties=portal-legacy-5.0.properties
```

Each application server has different methods to add this system property. In Tomcat, you would modify *catalina.sh/catalina.bat* or *catalina.conf* (depending on the exact version you are using).

What has been changed?

Here is a description of the most significant changes. Check the file *portal-legacy-5.0.properties* for a full list of changed properties.

- **layout.user.private.layouts.power.user.required:** It's no longer required to be Power User to have a personal community. This new property allows falling back to the old behavior.
- **permissions.user.check.algorithm:** the default value is now a new algorithm that is much faster.

If Your Developers Have Customized Liferay

Following is a list of API changes. If your developers used the extension environment to develop custom code review the following items and adapt your code accordingly:

- Several classes have been moved from portal-impl to portal-kernel to make them available to plugins. If you were using any of those classes you will have to change the import package.
- The JSPPortlet class has been moved to util-bridges so that it can be used from plugins. In order to adapt to this change do the following:
  - Any references to *com.liferay.portlet.JSPPortlet* need to be changed to *com.liferay.util.bridges.jsp.JSPPortlet*
  - Check that the paths to your JSP files in *portlet.xml* are absolute paths (from the docroot). For example, if your view.jsp lives in *docroot/html/*, set your view-jsp to */html/view.jsp*.
- Error handling has been changed in order to provide a better end-user experience. The following construct:

```
catch (Exception e) {
    req.setAttribute(PageContext.EXCEPTION, e);
    return mapping.findForward(ActionConstants.COMMON_ERROR);
}
```

  should be replaced with

```
catch (Exception e) {
   PortalUtil.sendError(e, request, response);
   return null;
}
```

  Note that you can also optionally include an *HttpServletResponse* code in the *sendError* method.

Upgrading Themes

There were a few changes between the Classic theme in 5.0 and the Classic theme in 5.1. However, these changes were predominantly CSS only changes, but if you built your theme from the plugins directory, and used the _diffs directory and placed your CSS changes in custom.css, you may need to make a few adjustments to your CSS.

New CSS file

There is a new file which your developers will need to include a file called *application.css*. The list of these files is located in */css/main.css*. At the top, right after *base.css*, you would add this line:

```
@import url(application.css);
```

This file includes all of the styling that is used for application elements, such as dialogs, inline popups, tabs, tags, and other elements.

Some rules were added (that may need to be overwritten for your theme) and some rules were removed (and may need to be re-added). If however, your theme is already built, and you edited the files directly, for the most part, you won't be affected. Overall, most changes are minor, but there are a couple that could cause confusion. These are covered below.

The Parent Element of the Dock May Change Positioning When Upgrading

In 5.1 a change was made to the Dock JavaScript which is a fix, but older themes may rely on the "buggy" behavior. Essentially, the CSS positioning of the Dock's parent was always set to *relative;* however, there are often times when a theme requires that it use a different positioning mechanism. The script now looks to see what the theme developer has specified and uses that. There is, however, one caveat. Sometimes, you absolutely must not have a positioned parent at all. The script, however, needs a positioned parent in most cases, and will apply one whenever the CSS position is set to *position: static*, since that is what the browser will return if no positioning is applied. So the problem in that situation is that if you must have *position: static,* the script will always overwrite it. In order to account for this, checking has been added so that if your CSS selector has these two rules:

```
position: static;
top: 0;
```

then it will use static positioning. The thinking is that because setting *top: 0* on a statically positioned item has no effect visually, we use it as a trigger to say that you *really* want to use static positioning. However, it now will allow you to define other positioning (absolute, relative, or fixed) without worrying about your defined styling being overwritten.

The Class Names for Different UI Components Have Changed

One of the only changes that will have a real impact is that the style *.popup* for the inline popups has been changed to *.ui-dialog*. Other class name changes have been made, but have been left on the elements for now so that breakages will be kept to a minimum. However, default styling for those class names have been removed from the Classic theme.

The class names that have been changed are as follows:

- .portlet-section-header is now .results-header
- .portlet-section-body is now .results-row
- .portlet-section-body-hover is now .results-row.hover
- .portlet-section-alternate is now .results-row.alt
- .portlet-section-alternate-hover is now .results-row.alt.hover
- .popup is now .ui-dialog
- .tabs is now .ui-tabs
- .tag is now .ui-tag
- .autocomplete-box is now .ui-autocomplete-results
- .drag-indicator is now .ui-proxy

Change in Theme CSS Fast Load

In 5.0.1, the default setting for *theme.css.fast.load* was *false* which means that when developers edited the deployed CSS files, the changes would take effect immediately on the next page load. Now, for the sake of better *out of the box* performance, the default in 5.1 has been changed to *true*. Of course this means that when developers edit the deployed CSS files directly, they will *not* see the changes take effect immediately on the next page load. Instead, developers should make the change in the pre-deployed theme and run the deploy process on the theme for the changes to be bundled and packed into the *everything_packed.css* file.

This of course might make it harder for theme developers to do real-time testing. So, the solution to get the old behavior is simply to revert *theme.css.fast.load* to *false* and restart the portal.

Change in Javascript Fast Load

For the same reasons as described above, a change was made to *javascript.-fast.load* from *false* to *true*.

Developers may want to revert it to *false* for the same reason.

Upgrading PHP Portlets

Some changes were made to the handling of PHP portlets, including the addition of new init-param values (see: http://support.liferay.com/browse/LEP-6465). Also, major changes to *util-java* classes (such as the elimination of StringMaker, for example) requires that some of the JARs in WEB-INF/lib be updated.

To upgrade an old PHP portlet, developers should first make a back-up of the existing portlet. Then the PHP portions (including HTML, images, CSS, javascript), should be zipped and re-deployed through the Plug-In Installer. Liferay, as usual, will inject the needed files, including everything in the WEB-INF directory, the Quercus libraries, and so forth.

If your developers are uneasy about this approach, you can also deploy an empty index.php file in a ZIP through the Plug-In Installer and then use the result to do a "DIFF" of your existing portlet with the injected portions of the new portlet. Then the parts that need to be changed can be manually updated in the existing portlet. This might useful, for example if you want to make sure the ID of your portlet does not change (especially if you have many instances scattered throughout your site), or if you've been using the *liferay-plugin-package.xml* file to keep track of versions and compatibility.

Javascript changes

The Javascript in Liferay has undergone a refactoring to use the jQuery UI engine, upgrading jQuery to the latest version (version 1.2.6 in Liferay 5.1), and removing the Interface library. We've also removed and changed many of our methods that were polluting the global name space and/or were not being used anymore.

Changed methods

addPortlet, addPortletHTML: These have now been changed to Liferay.Portlet.add() and Liferay.Portlet.addHTML(), respectively.

ShowLayoutTemplates: This is now Liferay.Layout.showTemplates().

StarRating, ThumbnailRating, Tooltip, Tabs: These are now Liferay.Portal.StarRating(), Liferay.Portal.ThumbnailRating(), Liferay.Portal.Tooltip, and Liferay.Portal.Tabs respectively.

Element.disable: Please use Liferay.Util.disableElements().

Element.remove: Please use jQuery(selector).remove().

Viewport.frame, Viewport.scroll, Viewport.page: These are now Liferay.Util.viewport.frame(), Liferay.Util.viewport.scroll(), and Liferay.Util.viewport.page(), respectively.

Removed Javascript methods

AjaxUtil, AjaxRequest, and loadPage: Please use jQuery.ajax or any of the other jQuery AJAX methods.

LinkedList, NavFlyout, DragLink, PhotoSlider, PortletHeaderBar: No longer needed.

Coordinates, Coordinate, MousePos: No longer needed. If you need mouse coordinates during an event (such as *onMousemove*, *onMouseover*), or if you're attaching events with jQuery, you can reliably use the *event.pageX* and *event.pageY* properties, like so:

```
jQuery(window).mousemove( function(event){ var x = event.pageX; var y =
event.pageY; } );
```

Liferay.Util.toJSONString, Liferay.Util.toJSONObject: No longer needed. You can use jQuery.parseJSON(str) and jQuery.toJSON(obj) respectively.

Liferay.Util.getSelectedIndex: No longer needed, as it was being used to select the "checked" item in a group of radio buttons. To do the same thing, you would do something like:

```
jQuery(Element|Selector).filter(':checked');
```

If you absolutely must have the actual numerical index of the selected item, you could do:

```
var radioGroup = jQuery(Element|Selector);
var index = radioGroup.index(radioGroup.filter(':checked')[0]);
```

7. Appendix: Documentation License

The text of this book is copyrighted by Liferay, Inc., and is released under the *Creative Commons Attribution-Sharealike 3.0 Unported* license.

Creative Commons License

CREATIVE COMMONS CORPORATION IS NOT A LAW FIRM AND DOES NOT PROVIDE LEGAL SERVICES. DISTRIBUTION OF THIS LICENSE DOES NOT CREATE AN ATTORNEY-CLIENT RELATIONSHIP. CREATIVE COMMONS PROVIDES THIS INFORMATION ON AN "AS-IS" BASIS. CREATIVE COMMONS MAKES NO WARRANTIES REGARDING THE INFORMATION PROVIDED, AND DISCLAIMS LIABILITY FOR DAMAGES RESULTING FROM ITS USE.

License

THE WORK (AS DEFINED BELOW) IS PROVIDED UNDER THE TERMS OF THIS CREATIVE COMMONS PUBLIC LICENSE ("CCPL" OR "LICENSE"). THE WORK IS PROTECTED BY COPYRIGHT AND/OR OTHER APPLICABLE LAW. ANY USE OF THE WORK OTHER THAN AS AUTHORIZED UNDER THIS LICENSE OR COPYRIGHT LAW IS PROHIBITED.

BY EXERCISING ANY RIGHTS TO THE WORK PROVIDED HERE, YOU ACCEPT AND AGREE TO BE BOUND BY THE TERMS OF THIS LICENSE. TO THE EXTENT THIS LICENSE MAY BE CONSIDERED TO BE A CONTRACT, THE LICENSOR GRANTS YOU THE RIGHTS CONTAINED HERE IN CONSIDERATION OF YOUR ACCEPTANCE OF SUCH TERMS AND CONDITIONS.

1. Definitions

a. **"Adaptation"** means a work based upon the Work, or upon the Work and other pre-existing works, such as a translation, adaptation, derivative work, arrangement of music or other alterations of a literary or artistic work, or phonogram or performance and includes cinematographic adaptations or any other form in which the Work may be recast, transformed, or adapted including in any form recognizably derived from the original, except that a work that constitutes a Collection will not be considered an Adaptation for the purpose of this License. For the avoidance of doubt, where the Work is a musical work, performance or phonogram, the synchronization of the Work in timed-relation with a moving image ("synching") will be considered an Adaptation for the purpose of this License.
b. **"Collection"** means a collection of literary or artistic works, such as encyclopedias and anthologies, or performances, phonograms or broadcasts, or other works or subject matter other than works listed in Section 1(f) below, which, by reason of the selection and arrangement of their contents, constitute intellectual creations, in which the Work is included in its entirety in unmodified form along with one or more other contributions, each constituting separate and independent works in themselves, which together are assembled into a collective whole. A work that constitutes a Collection will not be considered an Adaptation (as defined below) for the purposes of this License.
c. **"Creative Commons Compatible License"** means a license that is listed at http://creativecommons.org/compatiblelicenses that has been approved by Creative Commons as being essentially equivalent to this License, including, at a minimum, because that license: (i) contains terms that have the same purpose, meaning and effect as the License Elements of this License; and, (ii) explicitly permits the relicensing of adaptations of works made available under that license under this License or a Creative Commons jurisdiction license with the same License Elements as this License.
d. **"Distribute"** means to make available to the public the original and copies of the Work or Adaptation, as appropriate, through sale or other transfer of ownership.
e. **"License Elements"** means the following high-level license attributes as selected by Licensor and indicated in the title of this License: Attribution, ShareAlike.
f. **"Licensor"** means the individual, individuals, entity or entities that offer(s) the Work under the terms of this License.
g. **"Original Author"** means, in the case of a literary or artistic work, the individual, individuals, entity or entities who created the Work or if no individual or entity can be identified, the publisher; and in addition (i) in the case of a performance the actors, singers, musicians, dancers, and other persons who act, sing, deliver, declaim, play in, interpret or otherwise perform literary or artistic works or expressions of folklore; (ii) in the case of a phonogram the producer being the person or legal entity who first fixes the sounds of a performance or other sounds; and, (iii) in the case of broadcasts, the organization that transmits the broadcast.
h. **"Work"** means the literary and/or artistic work offered under the terms of this License including without limitation any production in the literary, scientific and artistic domain, whatever may be the mode or form of its expression including digital form, such as a book, pamphlet and other writing; a

lecture, address, sermon or other work of the same nature; a dramatic or dramatico-musical work; a choreographic work or entertainment in dumb show; a musical composition with or without words; a cinematographic work to which are assimilated works expressed by a process analogous to cinematography; a work of drawing, painting, architecture, sculpture, engraving or lithography; a photographic work to which are assimilated works expressed by a process analogous to photography; a work of applied art; an illustration, map, plan, sketch or three-dimensional work relative to geography, topography, architecture or science; a performance; a broadcast; a phonogram; a compilation of data to the extent it is protected as a copyrightable work; or a work performed by a variety or circus performer to the extent it is not otherwise considered a literary or artistic work.

i. **"You"** means an individual or entity exercising rights under this License who has not previously violated the terms of this License with respect to the Work, or who has received express permission from the Licensor to exercise rights under this License despite a previous violation.
j. **"Publicly Perform"** means to perform public recitations of the Work and to communicate to the public those public recitations, by any means or process, including by wire or wireless means or public digital performances; to make available to the public Works in such a way that members of the public may access these Works from a place and at a place individually chosen by them; to perform the Work to the public by any means or process and the communication to the public of the performances of the Work, including by public digital performance; to broadcast and rebroadcast the Work by any means including signs, sounds or images.
k. **"Reproduce"** means to make copies of the Work by any means including without limitation by sound or visual recordings and the right of fixation and reproducing fixations of the Work, including storage of a protected performance or phonogram in digital form or other electronic medium.

2. Fair Dealing Rights. Nothing in this License is intended to reduce, limit, or restrict any uses free from copyright or rights arising from limitations or exceptions that are provided for in connection with the copyright protection under copyright law or other applicable laws.

3. License Grant. Subject to the terms and conditions of this License, Licensor hereby grants You a worldwide, royalty-free, non-exclusive, perpetual (for the duration of the applicable copyright) license to exercise the rights in the Work as stated below:

a. to Reproduce the Work, to incorporate the Work into one or more Collections, and to Reproduce the Work as incorporated in the Collections;
b. to create and Reproduce Adaptations provided that any such Adaptation, including any translation in any medium, takes reasonable steps to clearly label, demarcate or otherwise identify that changes were made to the original Work. For example, a translation could be marked "The original work was translated from English to Spanish," or a modification could indicate "The original work has been modified.";
c. to Distribute and Publicly Perform the Work including as incorporated in Collections; and,
d. to Distribute and Publicly Perform Adaptations.

e. For the avoidance of doubt:

    i. **Non-waivable Compulsory License Schemes.** In those jurisdictions in which the right to collect royalties through any statutory or compulsory licensing scheme cannot be waived, the Licensor reserves the exclusive right to collect such royalties for any exercise by You of the rights granted under this License;
    ii. **Waivable Compulsory License Schemes.** In those jurisdictions in which the right to collect royalties through any statutory or compulsory licensing scheme can be waived, the Licensor waives the exclusive right to collect such royalties for any exercise by You of the rights granted under this License; and,
    iii. **Voluntary License Schemes.** The Licensor waives the right to collect royalties, whether individually or, in the event that the Licensor is a member of a collecting society that administers voluntary licensing schemes, via that society, from any exercise by You of the rights granted under this License.

The above rights may be exercised in all media and formats whether now known or hereafter devised. The above rights include the right to make such modifications as are technically necessary to exercise the rights in other media and formats. Subject to Section 8(f), all rights not expressly granted by Licensor are hereby reserved.

4. Restrictions. The license granted in Section 3 above is expressly made subject to and limited by the following restrictions:

a. You may Distribute or Publicly Perform the Work only under the terms of this License. You must include a copy of, or the Uniform Resource Identifier (URI) for, this License with every copy of the Work You Distribute or Publicly Perform. You may not offer or impose any terms on the Work that restrict the terms of this License or the ability of the recipient of the Work to exercise the rights granted to that recipient under the terms of the License. You may not sublicense the Work. You must keep intact all notices that refer to this License and to the disclaimer of warranties with every copy of the Work You Distribute or Publicly Perform. When You Distribute or Publicly Perform the Work, You may not impose any effective technological measures on the Work that restrict the ability of a recipient of the Work from You to exercise the rights granted to that recipient under the terms of the License. This Section 4(a) applies to the Work as incorporated in a Collection, but this does not require the Collection apart from the Work itself to be made subject to the terms of this License. If You create a Collection, upon notice from any Licensor You must, to the extent practicable, remove from the Collection any credit as required by Section 4(c), as requested. If You create an Adaptation, upon notice from any Licensor You must, to the extent practicable, remove from the Adaptation any credit as required by Section 4(c), as requested.
b. You may Distribute or Publicly Perform an Adaptation only under the terms of: (i) this License; (ii) a later version of this License with the same License Elements as this License; (iii) a Creative Commons jurisdiction license (either this or a later license version) that contains the same License Elements as this License (e.g., Attribution-ShareAlike 3.0 US)); (iv) a Creative Com-

mons Compatible License. If you license the Adaptation under one of the licenses mentioned in (iv), you must comply with the terms of that license. If you license the Adaptation under the terms of any of the licenses mentioned in (i), (ii) or (iii) (the "Applicable License"), you must comply with the terms of the Applicable License generally and the following provisions: (I) You must include a copy of, or the URI for, the Applicable License with every copy of each Adaptation You Distribute or Publicly Perform; (II) You may not offer or impose any terms on the Adaptation that restrict the terms of the Applicable License or the ability of the recipient of the Adaptation to exercise the rights granted to that recipient under the terms of the Applicable License; (III) You must keep intact all notices that refer to the Applicable License and to the disclaimer of warranties with every copy of the Work as included in the Adaptation You Distribute or Publicly Perform; (IV) when You Distribute or Publicly Perform the Adaptation, You may not impose any effective technological measures on the Adaptation that restrict the ability of a recipient of the Adaptation from You to exercise the rights granted to that recipient under the terms of the Applicable License. This Section 4(b) applies to the Adaptation as incorporated in a Collection, but this does not require the Collection apart from the Adaptation itself to be made subject to the terms of the Applicable License.

c. If You Distribute, or Publicly Perform the Work or any Adaptations or Collections, You must, unless a request has been made pursuant to Section 4(a), keep intact all copyright notices for the Work and provide, reasonable to the medium or means You are utilizing: (i) the name of the Original Author (or pseudonym, if applicable) if supplied, and/or if the Original Author and/or Licensor designate another party or parties (e.g., a sponsor institute, publishing entity, journal) for attribution ("Attribution Parties") in Licensor's copyright notice, terms of service or by other reasonable means, the name of such party or parties; (ii) the title of the Work if supplied; (iii) to the extent reasonably practicable, the URI, if any, that Licensor specifies to be associated with the Work, unless such URI does not refer to the copyright notice or licensing information for the Work; and (iv) , consistent with Ssection 3(b), in the case of an Adaptation, a credit identifying the use of the Work in the Adaptation (e.g., "French translation of the Work by Original Author," or "Screenplay based on original Work by Original Author"). The credit required by this Section 4(c) may be implemented in any reasonable manner; provided, however, that in the case of a Adaptation or Collection, at a minimum such credit will appear, if a credit for all contributing authors of the Adaptation or Collection appears, then as part of these credits and in a manner at least as prominent as the credits for the other contributing authors. For the avoidance of doubt, You may only use the credit required by this Section for the purpose of attribution in the manner set out above and, by exercising Your rights under this License, You may not implicitly or explicitly assert or imply any connection with, sponsorship or endorsement by the Original Author, Licensor and/or Attribution Parties, as appropriate, of You or Your use of the Work, without the separate, express prior written permission of the Original Author, Licensor and/or Attribution Parties.
d. Except as otherwise agreed in writing by the Licensor or as may be otherwise permitted by applicable law, if You Reproduce, Distribute or Publicly Perform the Work either by itself or as part of any Adaptations or Collec-

tions, You must not distort, mutilate, modify or take other derogatory action in relation to the Work which would be prejudicial to the Original Author's honor or reputation. Licensor agrees that in those jurisdictions (e.g. Japan), in which any exercise of the right granted in Section 3(b) of this License (the right to make Adaptations) would be deemed to be a distortion, mutilation, modification or other derogatory action prejudicial to the Original Author's honor and reputation, the Licensor will waive or not assert, as appropriate, this Section, to the fullest extent permitted by the applicable national law, to enable You to reasonably exercise Your right under Section 3(b) of this License (right to make Adaptations) but not otherwise.

5. Representations, Warranties and Disclaimer

UNLESS OTHERWISE MUTUALLY AGREED TO BY THE PARTIES IN WRITING, LICENSOR OFFERS THE WORK AS-IS AND MAKES NO REPRESENTATIONS OR WARRANTIES OF ANY KIND CONCERNING THE WORK, EXPRESS, IMPLIED, STATUTORY OR OTHERWISE, INCLUDING, WITHOUT LIMITATION, WARRANTIES OF TITLE, MERCHANTIBILITY, FITNESS FOR A PARTICULAR PURPOSE, NONINFRINGEMENT, OR THE ABSENCE OF LATENT OR OTHER DEFECTS, ACCURACY, OR THE PRESENCE OF ABSENCE OF ERRORS, WHETHER OR NOT DISCOVERABLE. SOME JURISDICTIONS DO NOT ALLOW THE EXCLUSION OF IMPLIED WARRANTIES, SO SUCH EXCLUSION MAY NOT APPLY TO YOU.

6. Limitation on Liability. EXCEPT TO THE EXTENT REQUIRED BY APPLICABLE LAW, IN NO EVENT WILL LICENSOR BE LIABLE TO YOU ON ANY LEGAL THEORY FOR ANY SPECIAL, INCIDENTAL, CONSEQUENTIAL, PUNITIVE OR EXEMPLARY DAMAGES ARISING OUT OF THIS LICENSE OR THE USE OF THE WORK, EVEN IF LICENSOR HAS BEEN ADVISED OF THE POSSIBILITY OF SUCH DAMAGES.

7. Termination

a. This License and the rights granted hereunder will terminate automatically upon any breach by You of the terms of this License. Individuals or entities who have received Adaptations or Collections from You under this License, however, will not have their licenses terminated provided such individuals or entities remain in full compliance with those licenses. Sections 1, 2, 5, 6, 7, and 8 will survive any termination of this License.
b. Subject to the above terms and conditions, the license granted here is perpetual (for the duration of the applicable copyright in the Work). Notwithstanding the above, Licensor reserves the right to release the Work under different license terms or to stop distributing the Work at any time; provided, however that any such election will not serve to withdraw this License (or any other license that has been, or is required to be, granted under the terms of this License), and this License will continue in full force and effect unless terminated as stated above.

8. Miscellaneous

a. Each time You Distribute or Publicly Perform the Work or a Collection, the Licensor offers to the recipient a license to the Work on the same terms and conditions as the license granted to You under this License.
b. Each time You Distribute or Publicly Perform an Adaptation, Licensor offers to the recipient a license to the original Work on the same terms and condi-

tions as the license granted to You under this License.

c. If any provision of this License is invalid or unenforceable under applicable law, it shall not affect the validity or enforceability of the remainder of the terms of this License, and without further action by the parties to this agreement, such provision shall be reformed to the minimum extent necessary to make such provision valid and enforceable.
d. No term or provision of this License shall be deemed waived and no breach consented to unless such waiver or consent shall be in writing and signed by the party to be charged with such waiver or consent.
e. This License constitutes the entire agreement between the parties with respect to the Work licensed here. There are no understandings, agreements or representations with respect to the Work not specified here. Licensor shall not be bound by any additional provisions that may appear in any communication from You. This License may not be modified without the mutual written agreement of the Licensor and You.
f. The rights granted under, and the subject matter referenced, in this License were drafted utilizing the terminology of the Berne Convention for the Protection of Literary and Artistic Works (as amended on September 28, 1979), the Rome Convention of 1961, the WIPO Copyright Treaty of 1996, the WIPO Performances and Phonograms Treaty of 1996 and the Universal Copyright Convention (as revised on July 24, 1971). These rights and subject matter take effect in the relevant jurisdiction in which the License terms are sought to be enforced according to the corresponding provisions of the implementation of those treaty provisions in the applicable national law. If the standard suite of rights granted under applicable copyright law includes additional rights not granted under this License, such additional rights are deemed to be included in the License; this License is not intended to restrict the license of any rights under applicable law.

Creative Commons Notice

Creative Commons is not a party to this License, and makes no warranty whatsoever in connection with the Work. Creative Commons will not be liable to You or any party on any legal theory for any damages whatsoever, including without limitation any general, special, incidental or consequential damages arising in connection to this license. Notwithstanding the foregoing two (2) sentences, if Creative Commons has expressly identified itself as the Licensor hereunder, it shall have all rights and obligations of Licensor.

Except for the limited purpose of indicating to the public that the Work is licensed under the CCPL, Creative Commons does not authorize the use by either party of the trademark "Creative Commons" or any related trademark or logo of Creative Commons without the prior written consent of Creative Commons. Any permitted use will be in compliance with Creative Commons' then-current trademark usage guidelines, as may be published on its website or otherwise made available upon request from time to time. For the avoidance of doubt, this trademark restriction does not form part of the License.

Creative Commons may be contacted at http://creativecommons.org/.

8. Colophon

The text and layout were accomplished using OpenOffice.org 2.4 running on Kubuntu Linux. The file is one large document, rather than a multi-linked master document. It's just easier to manage that way. The PDF was exported directly from OpenOffice.org. Some content written for this book was also exported to the Liferay wiki at http://wiki.liferay.com. It is the intent of the author to continue doing this for every edition of this book that is published. We also expect that some more community documentation will make it into the official documentation.

All of the fonts used in the creation of this book are open source fonts that are freely available. The body text font is Gentium Book Basic, created by SIL International. It can be found here: http://scripts.sil.org/cms/scripts/page.php?site_id=nrsi&item_id=Gentium.

The font for the titles is MgOpen Cosmetica. The text on the cover of the book is the same. This change was made from the First Edition for more uniformity and consistency. The text used in tables is MgOpen Moderna. These fonts were originally created by Magenta Ltd. and then released under an open source license. They can be found here: http://www.ellak.gr/fonts/mgopen/index.en.html.

The font used for source code is Liberation Mono, created by Red Hat, Inc. The Liberation fonts can be found here: https://www.redhat.com/promo/fonts.

Screen shots that were taken by the author were taken using Ksnapshot, an excellent screen shot program that is part of the KDE desktop. Some were even taken using the KDE 4.1 version of Ksnapshot. Other screen shots were taken by the contributors using unknown software. Drawings inside the book (such as the Unbreakable Liferay diagram) were created in OpenOffice.org draw, using some stencils from Dia (http://www.gnome.org/projects/dia). Some drawings and screen shots were touched up using the GIMP.

The cover of the book was done in a combination of programs. The picture was touched up using the GIMP (http://www.gimp.org). The Liferay logo was converted from a PDF into a Scalable Vector Graphics file by pdf2svg (http://www.cityinthesky.-co.uk/pdf2svg.html). This was then touched up in Karbon14 (http://www.koffice.org/karbon) and then imported into InkScape (http://www.inkscape.org), which was used to design the front cover. You may be wondering why it had to be done this way: it happened for the first edition and even I don't remember why. The background for the front cover was created entirely using the GIMP. The front cover was exported to PDF format using InkScape's exporter.

The picture on the front cover is a picture of Crepuscular Rays. These are rays of sunlight which appear to spring from a hidden source—usually from behind a cloud, but can also appear diffused through trees. The rays are actually parallel, and it is perspective that makes them appear to converge at the Sun. Also known as God's rays, crepuscular rays can be spectacular and certainly seemed appropriate for the cover of a book about a product called *Liferay* Portal. This great shot was taken by none other than Liferay's CEO, Bryan Cheung, in Langen, Germany, near the offices of Liferay's European headquarters.

Rich Sezov, August 2008

INDEX

A

Admin......1, 2, 4, 6, 8, 11, 12, 23, 26, 28, 34, 37-39, 41, 49, 60, 64, 65, 77, 79, 84, 87, 91-96, 98-116, 118, 120, 122-127, 133, 136, 141-144, 148, 149, 153, 163, 164, 169, 182, 183, 188-190, 193, 196, 198, 200, 201, 203, 204, 206, 207, 213-215, 222, 227, 230, 234, 238, 245-249, 260

Administrators...37, 93, 95, 96, 103, 104, 109, 110, 133, 136, 142-144, 148, 149, 200, 213, 238, 245, 246

AJAX....................................17, 179, 256

Ant.3, 6, 11-13, 15, 17, 20, 22, 23, 27-36, 61, 64, 78, 87, 88, 91, 93-104, 107, 109, 110, 113-118, 120-125, 127, 128, 130, 131, 135, 137, 145-147, 149, 152, 153, 157, 158, 160, 161, 166, 170, 171, 178, 180, 188, 192, 196, 197, 199, 200, 203, 204, 206, 209, 210, 214-216, 219, 220, 223-225, 229, 233, 234, 239, 241, 242, 246-249, 252-255, 257-263

App.server.properties.............31-33, 240

Authentication pipeline...........5, 152, 153

Auto deploy.......5, 55, 130-132, 203, 204

Auto login.......................................5, 155

B

Back up.........................94, 205, 245, 247

Blogs......6, 104, 122, 154, 169, 177, 183, 184, 186

Bundle...3, 11, 15, 19-24, 29, 32-37, 195, 201, 202, 219, 229, 243, 255

C

Caching..........7, 135, 174, 178, 180, 217, 223-226

Calendar...6, 17, 105-107, 122, 153, 169, 184

Captcha..................................5, 158, 159

Cas.....4, 5, 20, 23, 28, 58, 101, 104, 114, 115, 119-121, 128, 136, 151, 153, 155, 175, 194, 203, 205, 210, 213, 216, 221, 223, 225, 231, 233, 237, 243, 246, 247,

249, 254, 258, 259, 261

Chat...184

Clustering........7, 11, 171, 175, 181, 217, 218, 223-226

Communities......4, 6, 7, 95-98, 102, 103, 109, 110, 113, 121, 122, 126, 184, 206, 228, 243, 246

Community.....7, 15, 16, 92-98, 103, 109, 110, 127, 133, 142, 143, 154, 166, 167, 185, 191, 193, 194, 198, 206, 207, 211, 214, 215, 229, 246, 252, 265

Company.....71, 115, 128, 141, 142, 144, 145, 147, 167, 169, 170, 209, 229, 230

Company ID......................................229

Context. 52, 54, 55, 57-59, 63, 72, 85, 88, 89, 128, 131, 134, 187, 200, 234, 253

CSS....7, 8, 133, 148, 174, 178, 180, 185, 191, 192, 242, 253-255

D

Database.....3, 7, 8, 15, 17, 21-25, 27, 28, 33-40, 42, 44, 47-51, 56-58, 60, 61, 63-65, 67, 69, 71, 79, 81, 82, 113-115, 118, 123, 125, 127, 129, 130, 136, 148, 153, 156, 158, 171, 172, 175, 211, 213, 215, 218-220, 222-226, 228, 229, 234, 239, 247, 249-251

Developers.....3, 8, 16, 21-23, 26, 28, 29, 31, 32, 91, 92, 136, 168, 196, 210, 226, 241, 246, 249-255

Document Library....6, 16, 103, 124, 176, 184, 185, 214, 225, 226, 239, 247

E

Ehcache...5, 17, 135, 137, 175, 180, 217, 223-226

Email. 4, 12, 91-93, 98, 99, 102, 113, 114, 116, 122, 123, 125, 126, 141, 142, 149, 150, 152, 153, 156, 164, 176, 183, 184, 186-190, 192, 195, 229, 231-233

Enterprise...11, 12, 15, 16, 34-36, 41, 55, 65, 77, 88, 95, 98, 100-102, 104, 109-112, 114, 116, 118, 120, 122, 125, 142, 169, 196, 197, 204, 205, 217-221, 227

Enterprise Admin......12, 95, 98, 100-102, 104, 109, 111, 112, 114, 116, 118, 120, 122, 125

Extension environment. .3, 22, 26, 27, 29, 31-34, 119, 224, 225, 239-241, 246, 248-252

Extension environment—..................119

G

Geronimo.............3, 36, 38, 39, 131, 240

Glassfish...3, 23, 33, 36, 39-41, 131, 202, 203, 240, 241

Group.............4, 5, 13, 17, 38, 91, 95-98, 101-109, 112, 113, 117-119, 121, 122, 126, 133, 137, 142, 143, 146, 150, 151, 153, 158, 161, 167, 175, 182, 189, 209, 211, 215, 227, 229, 230, 237, 256

Groups........4, 5, 17, 91, 95-98, 101-104, 106-109, 112, 113, 117-119, 122, 126, 137, 142, 143, 150, 151, 158, 167, 175, 227

H

Hibernate....5, 7, 17, 45, 48, 55, 134-136, 175, 224, 225, 228, 234, 242

Hot deploy...5, 7, 55, 129, 130, 132, 133, 197, 201-205, 219, 222, 223

HSQL........24, 33, 36, 172, 219, 228, 229

Html...136, 137, 144, 167, 169, 170, 178, 185, 189, 190, 194, 195, 239, 253, 255, 265, 266

I

Image Gallery.................................6, 186

Invitation................................6, 169, 186

J

JAAS.....5, 43, 45, 47, 58, 59, 65, 70, 148, 149

Jackrabbit........7, 176, 218-220, 222, 226, 239, 247

Jackrabbit—.......................................219

Jar....20, 21, 24, 29, 38, 39, 42-45, 47-49, 55-58, 60, 63, 65, 78-80, 120, 128, 132,

171, 219, 224

Jar file.....24, 29, 55, 58, 63, 79, 120, 128, 219, 224

Javascript......5, 8, 17, 137, 139-141, 148, 174, 179, 213, 242, 254-256

Jboss. 3, 23, 33, 36, 43-48, 130, 131, 203, 227, 228, 232-234, 239, 240

JCR..6, 129, 134, 176, 184, 185, 219, 248

Jetty........................3, 36, 41-43, 131, 240

Jonas....................................36, 131, 240

Journal.....6, 35, 121, 154, 169, 170, 174, 175, 178, 181, 186-188, 239, 261

Journal Articles........................6, 188, 239

Jsp.......133, 137, 160, 164-166, 169, 170, 177, 194, 195, 253

JSR-286.....................15, 17, 92, 196, 249

L

Language........3, 5, 18, 92, 108, 113, 140, 144, 145, 164, 183, 184, 186, 193, 196, 216, 228, 231, 233

Language.properties...164, 183, 184, 186, 231, 233

LDAP...............4, 5, 91, 98, 113-120, 126, 149-151, 153, 157

Liferay........1-4, 6-8, 11-13, 15-52, 54-67, 69-72, 77-79, 81, 83, 85, 87-89, 91-102, 104, 105, 113-138, 140-142, 146-153, 155-170, 172, 174-190, 192-230, 233, 238-243, 245-253, 255-257, 265, 266

Liferay (4.2.x and below).....................215

Liferay Portal. 8, 11, 12, 15-17, 20, 21, 26, 32, 36-38, 41, 57, 65, 77, 78, 88, 89, 91, 115, 116, 118, 121, 124-126, 152, 168, 195, 197, 198, 200, 213, 217, 220, 226, 229, 239, 241, 245, 246, 266

Liferay-portlet.xml.......146, 147, 177, 243

Location......22-24, 29, 33, 36, 50, 52, 80, 97, 102, 110, 118, 128, 134, 137, 169, 189, 203, 204, 219, 221, 222, 224, 228, 241, 247, 250

Locations...169

Logging......8, 43, 92, 141, 147, 149, 160, 161, 178, 215, 238, 245, 247-249

Logs.......6, 20, 25, 34, 93, 104, 114, 118, 122, 147, 154, 160, 169, 177, 178, 183, 184, 186, 225, 234, 253

Look and feel.......3, 5, 16, 146, 191, 197, 200, 201, 223

Lucene....6, 7, 17, 171-173, 218, 220-223

M

Mail.....4, 6, 12, 37, 41-44, 47, 56-58, 64, 69, 83, 86, 91-93, 98, 99, 102, 113, 114, 116, 122, 123, 125, 126, 134, 135, 141, 142, 149, 150, 152, 153, 156, 164, 170, 176, 183, 184, 186-190, 192, 195, 229, 231-233

Memory...8, 43, 126, 137, 148, 160, 173, 180, 225, 226, 241, 242

Message boards......7, 110, 190, 223, 225

My Places............................7, 93, 94, 191

Mysql....22-25, 27-29, 33, 34, 37, 38, 40, 42, 44, 47, 50, 55, 56, 58, 60, 61, 65, 66, 71, 79, 136, 172, 220, 226, 247

N

Navigation.......................7, 113, 140, 191

Ntlm....4, 5, 121, 151, 152, 155, 179, 243

O

OpenId........................4, 5, 121, 152, 155

OpenSSO....................4, 5, 122, 152, 155

Organization.........3-5, 16, 23, 26, 28, 35, 91-93, 95-99, 101-103, 109, 110, 113, 115, 119, 126, 141, 143, 144, 150, 158, 166, 167, 170, 191, 196, 197, 199, 208, 209, 211, 215, 238, 239, 245, 249, 258

Organizations.............4, 5, 16, 91, 95-98, 101-103, 109, 126, 144, 158, 197, 215, 239, 245

P

Passwords......5, 112, 149, 152, 156, 157, 215

Performance Tuning........................8, 241

Permissions....4, 5, 15, 16, 35, 37, 96, 97, 101-104, 109, 110, 112, 157, 158, 167, 209, 214, 227, 237, 249, 252

Plugin....3-5, 7, 17, 26, 29, 31, 32, 55, 92, 125-127, 132, 133, 195-209, 211-213, 219-223, 227, 232, 246, 248, 249, 253, 255

Portal...........11, 12, 15-17, 20, 21, 24-26, 28-48, 52, 54-60, 63, 65, 69-72, 77, 78, 82, 85, 88, 89, 91-101, 103, 104, 109-116, 118, 120, 121, 123-132, 134-136, 138, 140-144, 147-170, 172, 174, 175, 177-182, 185-188, 192, 195-204, 207, 213-215, 217, 219-227, 229, 233, 234, 239, 241, 242, 245-247, 251-253, 255, 256, 266

Portal-ext.properties......4, 54, 55, 88, 89, 114, 118, 127, 128, 201, 203, 204, 214, 215, 219, 222-225, 227, 242, 247, 250, 251

Portal.properties. .55, 104, 118, 128, 213, 219, 222, 224, 225, 250

Portlet........4-8, 12, 15-17, 26, 34, 60, 79, 91-95, 97-102, 104-112, 114, 116, 118, 120, 122-125, 127, 129-134, 138, 140, 146-149, 153, 154, 158, 159, 161-170, 174-177, 179, 181-188, 190-215, 221-223, 225-228, 230-232, 234, 238, 239, 243, 246-249, 251-256

Portlet.xml. 131, 146, 147, 168, 177, 243, 253

Pramati..21, 36

Properties...4, 5, 8, 12, 31-33, 40, 44, 47, 54, 55, 57, 67-69, 81, 82, 88, 89, 104, 114, 118-120, 124, 126-128, 135-137, 140, 142, 144, 149, 152, 153, 156, 161-164, 166, 175, 177, 179, 182-184, 186, 187, 189, 194, 201, 203, 204, 213-215, 219, 222-228, 231, 233, 240-242, 247, 250-252, 256

R

Release.properties........................31, 240

Request...5, 6, 65, 98, 123, 142, 145-147, 155, 159, 160, 167-169, 180, 184-189, 192, 196, 220, 222, 227, 232, 239, 243, 253, 256, 260, 261, 263

RequestImpl..142

Resin.....................4, 36, 56, 57, 132, 240

Role............4, 5, 7, 45, 48, 59, 91, 95-98, 100-104, 109, 110, 112, 113, 122, 126, 142-144, 158, 174, 182, 193, 227, 228, 230, 232, 234, 237

Roles..4, 5, 7, 45, 48, 91, 95-98, 100-104, 109, 110, 112, 113, 122, 126, 142-144, 158, 174, 193, 227, 228, 232

S

Schema...................5, 129, 222, 226, 228

Service Builder....................213, 250, 251

Services Oriented Architecture.......7, 213

Servlet......6, 8, 15, 22, 36, 37, 46, 47, 62, 63, 92, 128, 130, 142, 147, 148, 151, 156, 159, 160, 167, 178-182, 185-187, 192, 196, 201, 214, 243, 253

Session...5, 41-44, 47, 56, 58, 64, 69, 83, 86, 134, 135, 140, 141, 146-148, 155, 156, 158, 160, 168, 176, 178-180

Shopping.........................7, 155, 170, 192

Single sign-on...4, 98, 113, 115, 119-122, 126, 197, 243

Smtp.......43, 44, 47, 56, 58, 99, 176, 190

Social Bookmarks............................6, 177

Software catalog.............7, 192, 205-209, 211-213

Solr..220-222

Spring....5, 6, 17, 55, 134, 135, 182, 196, 214, 221, 266

SQL......3, 5, 22-25, 27-29, 33-38, 40, 42, 44, 47, 50, 51, 55, 56, 58, 60, 61, 65, 66, 71, 79, 135-137, 141, 172, 219, 220, 226, 228, 229, 247

SSO with MAC...............................5, 156

Swimlane.....................228-230, 233, 237

T

Tags. 7, 24, 30, 33, 45, 48, 140, 155, 167, 193, 196, 208, 212, 253

Theme..5, 7, 8, 16, 26, 92, 113, 125, 127, 130, 132-134, 137, 146, 161-163, 178,

185, 195, 197, 199-201, 204, 205, 208, 223, 242, 246, 249, 253-255

Time zone........................5, 113, 144, 145

Tomcat......3, 4, 20, 22-26, 29, 32-34, 36, 38, 39, 46, 57-59, 120, 130-132, 147, 159, 201, 202, 204, 205, 216, 221, 224, 240, 242, 252

U

Upgrade.....5, 8, 11, 12, 26, 35, 129, 205, 207, 210, 222, 249-252, 255

User......3-5, 7, 12, 15, 16, 23, 25, 27, 28, 31-33, 35-40, 42-45, 47-49, 51, 56-61, 63, 69-71, 78, 82, 91-126, 129, 137, 140-156, 158-164, 166-171, 174, 176, 179, 180, 182, 183, 185, 188-191, 193, 196, 201, 203-210, 212-216, 220-241, 243, 246, 247, 251-253

Users...4, 5, 7, 12, 15, 16, 36, 45, 48, 57, 91, 93-98, 100-104, 106, 107, 109-126, 137, 140-151, 153-155, 158-164, 167, 168, 170, 171, 174, 179, 180, 185, 188, 190, 196, 204-210, 212, 213, 215, 223, 225, 227-229, 234, 238, 239, 243, 246, 251

V

Velocity.............6, 17, 178, 180, 187, 188

Virtual Host........6, 72, 87, 113, 125, 178, 180, 243

W

War file......20, 26, 41, 48, 51, 52, 62, 64, 65, 78, 79, 89, 195, 200, 202, 204, 208, 212, 222, 223, 250

Web Form.......................................7, 193

WEB-INF....43, 54, 55, 57, 120, 127, 128, 201, 203, 221, 222, 224, 227, 228, 232, 235, 239, 247, 255

Web.xml......46, 131, 134, 146, 151, 167, 201, 243

WebDAV...........6, 17, 181, 182, 185, 214

WebLogic.4, 20, 60, 62-64, 131, 136, 203

WebSphere........4, 20, 65, 70, 78, 79, 88, 131, 204

Wiki.......7, 8, 13, 79, 155, 156, 170, 175, 193-195, 250, 251, 265

Workflow.3, 7, 8, 16, 134, 176, 197, 217, 218, 226-230, 232-236, 238, 239

WSDL.....................................7, 215, 216

X

Xml........24, 33, 42-49, 52, 53, 55-60, 63, 131, 133-137, 146, 147, 151, 155, 167-169, 176, 177, 180, 185, 187, 201, 205, 206, 211-213, 219, 221, 222, 224-233, 235, 238, 239, 243, 251-253, 255

Z

ZIP..21, 27-30, 32, 33, 35, 36, 38, 41, 44, 45, 47, 48, 57, 63, 179, 185, 255

www.ingramcontent.com/pod-product-compliance
Lightning Source LLC
Chambersburg PA
CBHW051227050326
40689CB00007B/826

9780615247335